D0662116

Educating Zion

Educating Zion

Edited by

John W. Welch
Don E. Norton

BYU Studies
Brigham Young University
Provo, Utah

BYU Studies Monographs

The Truth, The Way, The Life:
An Elementary Treatise on Theology

The Journals of William E. McLellin, 1831–1836

Hearts Turned to the Fathers:
A History of the Genealogical Society of Utah, 1894–1994

"We Rejoice in Christ": A Bibliography of
LDS Writings on Jesus Christ and the New Testament

Mormon Americana:
A Guide to Sources and Collections in the United States

Second Crop

Behind the Iron Curtain:
Recollections of Latter-day Saints in East Germany, 1945–1989

Life in Utah: Centennial Selections from BYU Studies

© 1996 BYU Studies. All rights reserved.

No part of this book may be reproduced in any form or by any means without permission in writing from the publisher. For information about subscribing to *BYU Studies,* a quarterly multidisciplinary LDS journal, write to: BYU Studies, 403 CB, PO Box 24098, Provo, Utah 84602-4098.

Library of Congress Cataloging-in-Publication Data

Educating Zion / edited by John W. Welch, Don E. Norton.
    p.   cm. — (BYU Studies monographs)
    Includes index.
    ISBN 0-8425-2340-5
    1. Brigham Young University—History.   I. Welch, John W. (John Woodland).   II. Norton, Don E.   III. Series.
LD571.B672E38 1996
378.792'24—dc21   96-51292
                                                      CIP

Printed in the United States of America
10 9 8 7 6 5 4

CONTENTS

Foreword

From its inception over a century ago, the goal of Brigham Young University has been to offer "a new kind of education" for Zion, one based on precepts "revealed by the Lord," as Karl G. Maeser once remarked. Today, BYU is widely recognized for its deep commitments to inspired religious values and rigorous intellectual learning.

An environment that nurtures both spiritual and academic experience does not emerge accidentally. This effort to educate Zion has been guided and shaped by wise leaders who have spoken about learning not only with the mind, but also with the spirit. This volume gathers several of those key speeches delivered at BYU by Church and university authorities.

The most famous foundational instruction was given by Brigham Young to Karl G. Maeser not to teach even the multiplication tables without the Holy Ghost. This counsel has offered guidance to BYU educators in many ways. For example, the Holy Ghost softens hearts so that teaching can occur in an atmosphere of human kindness and the love of Christ, with deep respect for the divine potential in all human beings, along with frequent affirmations of the truth and goodness of the restored gospel of Jesus Christ. The Holy Ghost also guides teachers in discerning between truth and error, in choosing between good and evil, and in deciding what they should teach or when and how they should say things. Moreover, revelations provide axioms from which reason can derive useful and insightful implications. Teaching with the Holy Ghost thus involves identifying those propositions, examining them coherently, and determining their potential or inevitable consequences. Overriding all of these intellectual activities is the witness of the Holy Ghost that all religious and scholarly truths are to be woven together into an integrated whole. Ultimately, BYU and Church leaders desire the Holy Ghost to be felt in education in order to engender ethical behavior and moral service that will improve conditions in society as a whole and will bring praise to God and eternal life to all his children.

For Latter-day Saints, the gospel of Jesus Christ offers the means to infuse secular institutions with the Spirit of the Lord and thus to shape and use worldly experience to achieve righteous purposes.

To these ends, the priorities established by the Church for higher education in Zion come through loud and clear in these speeches. First and foremost is the goal of providing an education for eternity. Second is the spirit of faith and confidence to pursue excellence and attract the best and most moral minds of our age, both as scholars and as students. Third, steady tendencies toward secularization, trendy extremes, academic vogues, and religious dogmatism are to be avoided. Fourth, membership in the BYU community assumes a sacred trust. These and many other fundamental characteristics of education in Zion are consistently taught and reinforced in these selected speeches.

We hope this collection will keep these basic principles accessible to new and old members of this house of learning and will help to instill those values in the lives of all who might pass this way. Several of these speeches are published here for the first time. These talks have been gathered from among many in *BYU Studies,* BYU Special Collections and Manuscripts, *Brigham Young Magazine,* the annual University Conference addresses, *BYU Speeches of the Year,* and other similar sources at BYU. We are grateful to Jennifer Hurlbut, Doris Dant, Nancy Lund, and others on the BYU Studies staff who have labored to bring this publication to light. Except for minor formatting, editing, and occasional ellipses, these speeches are reproduced here in the form in which they were originally delivered.

John W. Welch
Don E. Norton

History of the Academy

Karl G. Maeser

When, at the April conference 1876, President Brigham Young appointed me as principal of the educational institution that has been established at Provo and bears the name of its illustrious founder, it was with no comprehension of the magnitude of the work that the appointee laid out the plans for his new mission.

Adding another experimental term to one conducted by his predecessor, he found premises inadequate, facilities limited, students few in number and poorly prepared, and financial conditions exceedingly discouraging. To make matters still worse, there were many even among the influential men in the community who not only had no confidence in the stability of the new venture, but openly opposed it by using their influence against it. Yet there were not wanting some signs prophetic of a more prosperous future, in the growing enthusiasm of the students, in the spreading influence outside the schoolroom, in the unqualified support of President Abraham O. Smoot, and in the approval of the Presidency of the Church. This was the condition of affairs when in August of the same year the first term of the first academic year was commenced.

The two experimental terms had demonstrated the fact that the strength of the Brigham Young Academy was not in her financial condition, nor could her aims be to enter, for the present, into competition with institutions of higher education in our country, nor was her distinguishing characteristic to be sought in the professional efficiency of her teachers alone, for all of these advantages have been claimed and enjoyed by schools of learning before, and yet the necessity for the establishment of a new kind of educational institution for Zion had been revealed by the Lord to the Prophet Brigham Young. The lack of what element created that necessity? It has been said the Saints will be saviors upon Mount Zion, that they are destined to redeem the world. Redeem the world from what? From the thralldom of sin, ignorance, and degradation! In order to do this, Zion will have to take the lead in everything and consequently also in education. But there is much education already, much science, much art, much skill, and much so-called civilization—in fact, so much that this generation is fast getting into the notion that they can get along without a god, like the Titans of old that wanted to storm the heavens by piling one mountain on top of another.

A glance over the conditions of mankind in this our day with its misery, discontent, and corruption, and disintegration of the social, religious, and philosophic fabrics, shows that this generation has been put into the balance and has been found wanting. A following, therefore, in the old grooves, would simply lead to the same results, and that is what the Lord has designed shall be avoided in Zion. President Brigham Young felt it in his heart that an educational system ought to be inaugurated in Zion in which, as he put it in his terse way of saying things, neither the alphabet nor the multiplication table should be taught without the Spirit of God.

Thus was started this nucleus of a new system. When, years after, a certain person could find no other fault with it than that it should have started some twenty years before, I thanked God that it hadn't; for if it had been thus started without teachers to comprehend its aims, without boards to enter into its spirit, and without students to feel its necessity, unavoidable failure would have postponed a successful commencement for a generation or more.

All the above-mentioned adversities of the infant institution were blessings in disguise. Without means, by relying upon the liberality of her patrons, the Academy engendered a growing interest among the people in its aims. Without teachers

BYU President Karl G. Maeser in his office, 1884. Courtesy BYU Archives.

sufficiently devoted to its sacred cause to labor for a mere nominal salary, the Academy was forced to create a Normal department composed of volunteers, to raise her own teachers; without a board of members experienced in educational affairs, they went through an empirical training in having their attentions turned gradually from the primitive conditions of the beginning to the more complex organization of the school's further advancement.

If amidst all these changing scenes clouds of discouragement did occasionally darken the horizon of our vision, they were always dispelled by the voice of the spirit whispering: "O ye of little faith."

Amid the ever-changing scenes of development which Brigham Young Academy has passed through, whether holding forth in one single room under makeshift arrangements or enjoying the benefits of more suitable facilities: whether in rented premises, fitted up for the time being, or in her own palatial habitation; whether laboring according to the humble programme of the primary and intermediate grades or aspiring to academic or collegiate honors; there must go through it all, like a golden thread, one thing constant: the spirit of the latter-day work. As long as this principle shall be the mainspring of all her labors, whether in teaching the alphabet or the multiplication tables, or unfolding the advanced truths of science and art, the future of Brigham Young Academy will surpass in glory the fondest hopes of her most ardent admirers.

This address was delivered on October 16, 1891, at Brigham Young Academy's first Founder's Day exercises. Karl G. Maeser served as president of Brigham Young University from 1876 to 1892. Printed in Reinhard Maeser, *Karl G. Maeser* (Provo, Utah: Brigham Young University, 1928), 128–32.

Inaugural Address

Franklin S. Harris

We are happy indeed to be connected with an institution that is engaged in the great cause of education, for we realize that on education more than on any other factor depends the welfare of mankind. Redemption from the ills of the world is dependent on our ability to understand the laws of the universe and to live in conformity therewith. Intelligence is the great emancipator, and ignorance is the chief agency of destruction. Sin, inefficiency, and disease are merely manifestations of ignorance. The overcoming of these is the triumph of education and the vindication of the power of intelligence.

By its very name, a university stands for universal knowledge. It cannot concede that any particular body of fact is worthy of attention while some other type of learning should be excluded. And yet many so-called universities attempt to discriminate against many of the most fundamental truths in God's great universe. Many there are who would eliminate any study of God or of spiritual laws, and yet those who have made a study of these things find them just as tangible and worthy of study and analysis as are the physical forces of the world.

Fortunately, when Brigham Young University was founded, there were no limitations placed upon it, and none have since been imposed. It stands with open arms to receive truth from whatever source it may come, and it does not dictate to the Giver of all as to the way in which He shall reveal his truth. It is willing with Cowper to say, "God is His own interpreter and

Franklin S. Harris in Logan in 1920, the year before he was inaugu-rated as president of BYU. Courtesy BYU Archives.

He will make it plain." We have here an institution which acknowledges no limitations but goes out boldly with the statement that "if there is anything virtuous, lovely, or of good report or praiseworthy, we seek after these things" (A of F 1:13).

Nor would we limit those who shall receive the benefits of education. We have no patience with the theory that some are born to be saved and others to be damned. Likewise, there seems to be no foundation for the belief held by some that only the select few should receive the benefits of education while the great majority of humanity must be sentenced to eternal ignorance. Education should be universal in its benefits, and all the world should be made better by its teachings.

In this as in everything else, however, there will be various degrees of advancement. All do not have the same opportunities or the same capabilities. The talents of persons vary not only in degree, but also in quality. Some are gifted in music or language, while others who find these subjects difficult have ability in mathematics and engineering. Thus education must be sufficiently broad to fit in with various temperaments, and it should be so arranged that the natural talents of the individual may be used to the best advantage.

Since it will probably be a long while before a college education can be available to all people, we have a particular responsibility to fit those who come to us for leadership.

The colleges of the land must recognize that they are training most of the future leaders of the country. This fact should impress them with the grave responsibility of their task. The leaders will determine the nature of the civilization of the future, and the colleges will largely determine the nature of the leaders.

It is with the full recognition of this responsibility that Brigham Young University is laying its plans for future development. It is conscious of the fact that unless it trains men and women for leadership in the various activities in which they engage, it has no excuse for existence. It is our purpose therefore not only to train our students in the useful arts and sciences of the day, but also to fit them to lead in various civic, religious, and industrial problems that arise out of the complex conditions of modern life.

In preparing students to measure up to these exacting requirements, the university must establish rigorous academic standards. College is no place to idle away time. There is serious business in hand, and those who are not on a learning bent should be eliminated and their places taken by others who will make better use of their opportunities.

Brigham Young University aims to maintain standards equal to those of any college in the land. It is not so much interested in building a big institution as in building a good one. Its faculty, its equipment, and its requirements must be maintained at the highest possible standard.

The institution cannot attempt to compete with every institution in the land. Schools, like business houses, must specialize. While we take all truth for our province, there are certain types of work to which we must direct our chief energies; there are certain fundamental aims that must direct our building for the immediate future.

There has grown out of the history of the institution a particular mandate that must be respected—a certain fire that must be kept burning. This has been peculiar to the institution ever since President Young sent Doctor Maeser here to open its doors. It is difficult to define just what that something is, but it has to do with the lives of students apart from their regular school work. It establishes in their minds wholesome ideals and gives them a respect for proper living. It helps them to form good habits and to throw off bad ones. It teaches them to enjoy uplifting amusements rather than to seek corrupt diversions. It teaches them the sacredness of the family as a unit in society, and it imparts to them a particular responsibility as a citizen. It has nothing to do with long-faced sanctimoniousness but is rather that quality of high spirituality that teaches wisdom and moderation in all of the activities of life.

The first task of the future is to preserve at the institution this spirit that comes to us from the past—the true spirit of the Brigham Young University. This spirit places character above learning, and indelibly burns into the consciousness of the student the fact that the most enduring joy is dependent on spiritual growth which looks toward eternal progression.

We must be satisfied with nothing short of the highest standards in our courses. We must have on our faculty none but those who possess unquestioned integrity and scholarship; we must have a library adequate to our needs; and we must have the best equipment that can be procured. Only by maintaining these standards can we hope to be worthy of the leadership that has been assigned to us.

One cannot look toward the future of Brigham Young University without becoming enthusiastic. The very fact that it is engaged in the work of helping to banish from the world ignorance—that great archenemy—and that it is devoting its energies to the teaching of truth to a large group of young people who are to assume leadership in building up the world makes one grow humble in feeling and reverent in attitude.

It now remains for us who are charged with the responsibility of conducting the institution to live up to our possibilities. May God grant us wisdom and strength to play well our part.

This address was given by Franklin S. Harris in 1921, when he was inaugurated as president of Brigham Young University. President Harris served from 1921 to 1945. The address is presented in edited form for a general audience; President Harris's administrative comments about specific department goals are omitted.

The Church University

David O. McKay

Brigham Young University is primarily a religious institution. It was established for the sole purpose of associating with the facts of science, art, literature, and philosophy the truths of the gospel of Jesus Christ. Even more specifically, its purpose is to teach the gospel as it has been revealed in this age to the Prophet Joseph Smith and other leaders who have succeeded him. The ideal that should impregnate all university instruction was tersely designated by President Brigham Young when he said to Brother Karl G. Maeser, "Brother Maeser, I want you to remember that you ought not to teach even the alphabet or the multiplication tables without the Spirit of God. That is all. God bless you. Good-bye."

Emphasis on the need of religious education was again given in the year 1888, when the Church added to the parent institution the present system of Church education in order, as was stated, "that we should have schools wherein the Bible, the Book of Mormon, and the Book of Doctrine and Covenants can be used as textbooks, and where the principles of our religion may form a part of the teachings of the schools."

In making religion its paramount objective, the university touches the very heart of all true progress. By so doing, it declares with Ruskin that "anything which makes religion a second object makes it no object—He who offers to God a second place offers Him no place." It believes that "by living according

President David O. McKay, center, and Sister Emma McKay at the ribbon-cutting ceremony of the David O. McKay Building on the BYU campus, November 30, 1954. BYU President Ernest L. Wilkinson stands at far left, and Presidents Stephen L. Richards and J. Reuben Clark Jr. stand at right. Courtesy BYU Archives.

to the rules of religion, a man becomes the wisest, the best, and the happiest creature that he is capable of being."

I emphasize *religion* because the Church university offers more than mere theological instruction. Theology as a science "treats of the existence, character, and attributes of God," and theological training may consist merely of intellectual study. Religion is subjective and denotes the influences and motives of human conduct and duty which are found in the character and will of God. One may study theology without being religious; one may be religious without being moral; one may be moral without being religious. It is evident, then, that true religious training must include instruction in relation to God and to his laws and government and also in relation to man's duty to man.

Such teaching is given effectively not necessarily in a formal theology class, but in literature, art, geology, biology, and other classes. Teachers in the Church university are free to associate with scientific truths the revealed word of God. Thus all facts may be viewed by the students not through the green glass of prejudice or doubt, but in the clear sunlight of truth.

It is the aim of this university to make students *feel* that life is never more noble and beautiful than when it conforms to the principles of the gospel of Jesus Christ.

This address was given at Brigham Young University around 1937, when David O. McKay was a member of the Quorum of the Twelve Apostles.

The Charted Course
of the Church in Education

J. Reuben Clark Jr.

As a schoolboy, I was thrilled with the great debate between those two giants Webster and Hayne. The beauty of their oratory, the sublimity of Webster's lofty expression of patriotism, the forecast of the civil struggle to come for the mastery of freedom over slavery—all stirred me to the very depths. The debate began over the Foot Resolution concerning the public lands. It developed into a consideration of great fundamental problems of constitutional law. I have never forgotten the opening paragraph of Webster's reply, by which he brought back to its place of beginning this debate that had drifted so far from its course. That paragraph reads:

> Mr. President: When the mariner has been tossed for many days in thick weather, and on an unknown sea, he naturally avails himself of the first pause in the storm, the earliest glance of the sun, to take his latitude, and ascertain how far the elements have driven him from his true course. Let us imitate this prudence, and, before we float farther on the waves of this debate, refer to the point from which we departed, that we may at least be able to conjecture where we now are. I ask for the reading of the resolution.

Now I hasten to express the hope that you will not think that I think this is a Webster-Hayne occasion or that I think I am a Daniel Webster. If you were to think those things—or either of them—you would make a grievous mistake. I admit I am old, but I am not that old. But Webster seemed to invoke so sensible a procedure for occasions where, after a wandering on the high seas or in the wilderness, effort is to be made to get back to the place of starting, that I thought you would excuse me if I invoked and in a way used this same procedure to restate some of the more outstanding and essential fundamentals underlying our Church school education.

The following are to me those fundamentals: The Church is the organized priesthood of God; the priesthood can exist without the Church, but the Church cannot exist without the priesthood. The mission of the Church is first, to teach, encourage, assist, and protect individual members in their striving to live the perfect life, temporally and spiritually, as laid down in the gospel—"Be ye therefore perfect, even as your Father which is in Heaven is perfect," said the Master (Matt. 5:48); second, the Church is to maintain, teach, encourage, and protect, temporally and spiritually, the membership as a group in living the gospel; third, the Church is militantly to proclaim the truth, calling upon all men to repent and to live in obedience to the gospel, "for every knee shall bow, and every tongue confess" (Mosiah 27:31).

In all this, there are for the Church and for its members two prime things that may not be overlooked, forgotten, shaded, or discarded.

First, that Jesus Christ is the Son of God, the Only Begotten of the Father in the flesh, the Creator of the world, the Lamb of God, the Sacrifice for the sins of the world, the Atoner for Adam's transgression; that he was crucified; that his spirit left his body; that he died; that he was laid away in the tomb; that on the third day his spirit was reunited with his body, which again became a living being; that he was raised from the tomb a resurrected being, a perfect being, the Firstfruits of the Resurrection; that he later ascended to the Father; and that because of his death and by and through his resurrection every man born into the world since the beginning will be likewise literally resurrected. This doctrine is as old as the world. Job declared: "And though after my skin worms destroy this body, yet in my flesh shall I see God: Whom I shall see for myself, and mine eyes shall behold, and not another" (Job 19:26–27). The

President J. Reuben Clark Jr., at podium, introduces Ernest L. Wilkinson, right, as the new president of BYU, October 16, 1950. At far left are Elders Richard L. Evans and Henry D. Moyle; at far right is President George Albert Smith. Courtesy BYU Archives.

resurrected body is a body of flesh and bones and spirit, and Job uttered a great and everlasting truth. These positive facts, and all other facts necessarily implied therein, must all be honestly believed, in full faith, by every member of the Church.

The second of the two things to which we must all give full faith is that the Father and the Son actually and in truth and very deed appeared to the Prophet Joseph in a vision in the woods; that other heavenly visions followed to Joseph and to others; that the gospel and the Holy Priesthood after the Order of the Son of God were in truth and fact restored to the earth, from which they had been lost by the apostasy of the primitive Church; that the Lord again set up his Church, through Joseph Smith; that the Book of Mormon is just what it professes to be; that to the Prophet came numerous revelations for the guidance, upbuilding, organization, and encouragement of the Church and its members; that the Prophet's successors, likewise called of God, have received revelations as the needs of the Church have required, and that they will continue to receive revelations as the Church and its members, living the truth they already have, shall stand in need of more; that this is in truth The Church of Jesus Christ of Latter-day Saints; and that its foundation beliefs are the laws and principles laid down in the Articles of Faith. These facts also, and each of them, together with all things necessarily implied therein or flowing therefrom, must stand, unchanged, unmodified, without dilution, excuse, apology, or avoidance; they may not be explained away or submerged. Without these two great beliefs, the Church would cease to be the Church.

Any individual who does not accept the fullness of these doctrines as to Jesus of Nazareth or as to the restoration of the gospel and holy priesthood is not a Latter-day Saint; the hundreds of thousands of faithful, God-fearing men and women who compose the great body of the Church membership do believe these things fully and completely; and they support the Church and its institutions because of this belief.

I have set out these matters because they are the latitude and longitude of the actual location and position of the Church, both in this world and in eternity. Knowing our true position, we can change our bearings if they need changing: we can lay down anew our true course. And here we may wisely recall that Paul said, "But though we, or an angel from heaven, preach any other gospel unto you than that which we have preached unto you, let him be accursed" (Gal. 1:8).

As I have already said, I am to say something about the religious education of the youth of the Church. I shall bring together what I have to say under two general headings—the student and the teacher. I shall speak very frankly, for we have passed the place where we may wisely talk in ambiguous words and veiled phrases. We must say plainly what we mean, because the future of our youth, both here on earth and in the hereafter, as well as the welfare of the whole Church is at stake.

The youth of the Church, your students, are in great majority sound in thought and in spirit. The problem primarily is to keep them sound, not to convert them.

The youth of the Church are hungry for things of the Spirit; they are eager to learn the gospel, and they want it straight, undiluted.

They want to know about the fundamentals I have just set out—about our beliefs; they want to gain testimonies of their truth; they are not now doubters, but inquirers, seekers after truth. Doubt must not be planted in their hearts. Great is the burden and the condemnation of any teacher who sows doubt in a trusting soul.

These students crave the faith their fathers and mothers have; they want it in its simplicity and purity. There are few indeed who have not seen the manifestations of its divine power; they not only wish to be the beneficiaries of this faith, but they want to be themselves able to call it forth to work.

They want to believe in the ordinances of the gospel; they wish to understand them so far as they may.

They are prepared to understand the truth which is as old as the gospel and which was expressed thus by Paul (a master of logic and metaphysics unapproached by the modern critics who decry all religion):

> For what man knoweth the things of a man, save the spirit of man which is in him? even so the things of God knoweth no man, but the Spirit of God. Now we have received, not the spirit of the world, but the spirit which is

of God; that we might know the things that are freely given to us of God. (1 Cor. 2:11–12)

For they that are after the flesh do mind the things of the flesh; but they that are after the Spirit the things of the Spirit. (Rom. 8:5)

This I say then, Walk in the Spirit, and ye shall not fulfil the lust of the flesh. For the flesh lusteth against the Spirit, and the Spirit against the flesh: and these are contrary the one to the other: so that ye cannot do the things that ye would. But if ye be led of the Spirit, ye are not under the law. (Gal. 5:16–18)

Our youth understand, too, the principle declared in modern revelation:

Ye cannot behold with your natural eyes, for the present time, the design of your God concerning those things which shall come hereafter, and the glory which shall follow after much tribulation. (D&C 58:3)

By the power of the Spirit our eyes were opened and our understandings were enlightened, so as to see and understand the things of God— . . . And while we meditated upon these things, the Lord touched the eyes of our understandings and they were opened, and the glory of the Lord shone round about. And we beheld the glory of the Son, on the right hand of the Father, and received of his fulness; And saw the holy angels, and them who are sanctified before his throne, worshiping God, and the Lamb, who worship him forever and ever. And now, after the many testimonies which have been given of him, this is the testimony, last of all, which we give of him: That he lives! For we saw him, even on the right hand of God; and we heard the voice bearing record that he is the Only Begotten of the Father—That by him, and through him, and of him, the worlds are and were created, and the inhabitants thereof are begotten sons and daughters unto God. And while we were yet in the Spirit, the Lord commanded us that we should write the vision. (D&C 76:12, 19–24, 28)

These students are prepared, too, to understand what Moses meant when he declared:

> But now mine own eyes have beheld God; but not my nat-
> ural, but my spiritual eyes, for my natural eyes could not
> have beheld; for I should have withered and died in his
> presence; but his glory was upon me; and I beheld his face,
> for I was transfigured before him. (Moses 1:11)

These students are prepared to believe and understand
that all these things are matters of faith, not to be explained or
understood by any process of human reason and probably not
by any experiment of known physical science.

These students (to put the matter shortly) are prepared to
understand and to believe that there is a natural world and
there is a spiritual world; that the things of the natural world
will not explain the things of the spiritual world; that the things
of the spiritual world cannot be understood or comprehended
by the things of the natural world; that you cannot rationalize
the things of the Spirit, because first, the things of the Spirit are
not sufficiently known and comprehended, and secondly, because finite mind and reason cannot comprehend nor explain
infinite wisdom and ultimate truth.

These students already know that they must be "honest,
true, chaste, benevolent, virtuous, and [do] good to all men"
and that "if there is anything virtuous, lovely, or of good report
or praiseworthy, we seek after these things" (A of F 1:13)—these
things they have been taught from very birth. They should be
encouraged in all proper ways to do these things which they
know to be true, but they do not need to have a year's course of
instruction to make them believe and know them.

These students fully sense the hollowness of teachings that
would make the gospel plan a mere system of ethics. They know
that Christ's teachings are in the highest degree ethical, but they
also know they are more than this. They will see that ethics
relate primarily to the doings of this life and that to make of the
gospel a mere system of ethics is to confess a lack of faith, if not
a disbelief, in the hereafter. They know that the gospel teachings not only touch this life, but the life that is to come, with its
salvation and exaltation as the final goal.

These students hunger and thirst, as did their fathers
before them, for a testimony of the things of the Spirit and of

the hereafter; and knowing that you cannot rationalize eternity, they seek faith, and the knowledge which follows faith. They sense by the Spirit they have that the testimony they seek is engendered and nurtured by the testimony of others and that to gain this testimony which they seek for—one living, burning, honest testimony of a righteous God-fearing person that Jesus is the Christ and that Joseph was God's prophet—is worth a thousand books and lectures aimed at debasing the gospel to a system of ethics or seeking to rationalize infinity.

Two thousand years ago, the Master said, "Or what man is there of you, whom if his son ask bread, will he give him a stone? Or if he ask a fish, will he give him a serpent?" (Matt. 7:9–10).

These students, born under the covenant, can understand that age and maturity and intellectual training are not in any way or to any degree necessary to communion with the Lord and his Spirit. They know the story of the youth Samuel in the temple, of Jesus at twelve years confounding the doctors in the temple, of Joseph at fourteen seeing God the Father and the Son in one of the most glorious visions ever beheld by man. They are not as were the Corinthians, of whom Paul said, "I have fed you with milk, and not with meat: for hitherto ye were not able to bear it, neither yet now are ye able" (1 Cor. 3:2).

They are rather as was Paul himself when he declared to the same Corinthians, "When I was a child, I spake as a child, I understood as a child, I thought as a child: but when I became a man, I put away childish things" (1 Cor. 13:11).

These students as they come to you are spiritually working toward a maturity which they will early reach if you but feed them the right food. They come to you possessing spiritual knowledge and experience the world does not know.

So much for your students and what they are and what they expect and what they are capable of. I am telling you the things that some of you teachers have told me and that many of your youth have told me.

May I not say now a few words to you teachers?

In the first place, there is neither reason nor is there excuse for our Church religious teaching and training facilities and institutions unless the youth are to be taught and trained in the principles of the gospel, embracing therein the two great elements that Jesus is the Christ and that Joseph was God's prophet. The teaching of a system of ethics to the students is not a sufficient reason for running our seminaries and institutes. The great public school system teaches ethics. The students of seminaries and institutes should of course be taught the ordinary canons of good and righteous living, for these are part, and an essential part, of the gospel. But there are the great principles involved in eternal life, the priesthood, the Resurrection, and many other like things, that go beyond these canons of good living. These great fundamental principles also must be taught to the youth; they are the things the youth wish first to know about.

The first requisite of a teacher for teaching these principles is a personal testimony of their truth. No amount of learning, no amount of study, and no number of scholastic degrees can take the place of this testimony, which is the *sine qua non* of the teacher in our Church school system. No Latter-day Saint teacher who does not have a real testimony of the truth of the gospel as revealed to and believed by the Latter-day Saints, and a testimony of the Sonship and Messiahship of Jesus and of the divine mission of Joseph Smith—including in all its reality the First Vision—has any place in the Church seminary and institute system. If there be any such, and I hope and pray there are none, he should at once resign; if the Commissioner knows of any such and he does not resign, the Commissioner should request his resignation. The First Presidency expects this pruning to be made.

This does not mean that we would cast out such teachers from the Church—not at all. We shall take up with them a labor of love, in all patience and long-suffering, to win them to the knowledge to which as God-fearing men and women they are entitled. But this does mean that our Church schools cannot be staffed by unconverted, untestimonied teachers.

But for you teachers, the mere possession of a testimony is not enough. You must have, besides this, one of the rarest and most precious of all the many elements of human character: moral courage. For in the absence of moral courage to declare your testimony, it will reach the students only after such dilution as will make it difficult, if not impossible, for them to detect it; and the spiritual and psychological effect of a weak and vacillating testimony may well be actually harmful instead of helpful.

The successful seminary or institute teacher must also possess another of the rare and valuable elements of character—a twin of moral courage and often mistaken for it. I mean intellectual courage—the courage to affirm principles, beliefs, and faith that may not always be considered as harmonizing with such knowledge—scientific or otherwise—as teachers or their educational colleagues may believe they possess.

Not unknown are cases where those of presumed faith, holding responsible positions, have felt that, since by affirming their full faith they might call down upon themselves the ridicule of their unbelieving colleagues, they must either modify or explain away their faith, destructively dilute it, or even pretend to cast it away. Such are hypocrites to their colleagues and to their coreligionists.

An object of pity (not of scorn, as some would have it) is that man or woman who, having the truth and knowing it, finds it necessary either to repudiate the truth or to compromise with error in order to live with or among unbelievers without inducing their supposed disfavor or derision. Tragic indeed is this situation, for in reality all such discardings and shadings in the end bring the very punishments that the weak-willed one sought to avoid. For there is nothing the world so values and reveres as the person who, having righteous convictions, stands for them in any and all circumstances; there is nothing toward which the world turns more contempt than the person who, having righteous convictions, either slips away from them, abandons them, or repudiates them. For Latter-day Saint psychologists, chemists, physicists, geologists, archeologists, or any other scientists to explain away, misinterpret, evade or elude, or—most of all— repudiate or deny the great fundamental doctrines of the Church in which they profess to believe is to lie to their intellect, to lose their self-respect, to bring sorrow to their friends, to break the hearts of and bring shame to their parents, to besmirch the Church and its members, and to forfeit the respect and honor of those whom they have sought, by their course, to win as friends and helpers.

I prayerfully hope there may not be any such among the teachers of the Church school system, but if there are any such, high or low, they must travel the same route as the teacher without the testimony. Sham and pretext and evasion and hypocrisy have, and can have, no place in the Church school system or in the character building and spiritual growth of our youth.

Another thing which must be watched in our Church institutions is this: It must not be possible for people to keep positions of spiritual trust who, not being converted themselves, being really unbelievers, seek to turn aside the beliefs, education, and activities of our youth, and our aged also, from the ways they should follow, into other paths of education, beliefs, and activities that (though leading where the unbeliever would go) do not bring us to the places where the gospel would take us. That this works as a conscience-balm to the unbeliever who directs it is of no importance. This is the grossest betrayal of trust; and there is too much reason to think it has happened.

I wish to mention another thing that has happened in other lines, as a caution against the same thing happening in the Church educational system. On more than one occasion, our Church members have gone to other places for special training in particular lines; they have had the training which was supposedly the last word, the most modern view; then they have brought it back and dosed it upon us without any thought as to whether we needed it or not. I refrain from mentioning well-known and, I believe, well-recognized instances of this sort of thing. I do not wish to wound any feelings.

But before trying on the newest-fangled ideas in any line of thought, education, activity, or what not, experts should just stop and consider that however backward they think we are, and however backward we may actually be in some things, in other things we are far out in the lead, and therefore these new methods may be old, if not worn out, with us.

In whatever relates to community life and activity in general; to clean group social amusement and entertainment; to closely knit and carefully directed religious worship and activity; to a positive, clear-cut, faith-promoting spirituality; to a real, everyday, practical religion; to a firm-fixed desire and acutely sensed need for faith in God, we are far in the vanguard of on-marching humanity. Before effort is made to inoculate us with new ideas, experts should kindly consider whether the methods, used to spur community spirit or build religious activities among groups that are decadent and maybe dead to these things, are quite applicable to us, and whether their effort to impose these upon us is not a rather crude, even gross anachronism. For example, to apply to our spiritually minded and religiously alert youth a plan evolved to teach religion to youth having no interest or concern in matters of the Spirit would not only fail in meeting our actual religious needs, but would tend to destroy the best qualities which our youth now possess.

I have already indicated that our youth are not children spiritually; they are well on toward the normal spiritual maturity of the world. To treat them as children spiritually, as the world might treat the same age group, is therefore and likewise an anachronism. I say once more there is scarcely a youth that comes through your seminary or institute door who has not been the conscious beneficiary of spiritual blessings, or who has not seen the efficacy of prayer, or who has not witnessed the power of faith to heal the sick, or who has not beheld spiritual outpourings of which the world at large is today ignorant. You do not have to sneak up behind these spiritually experienced youth and whisper religion in their ears; you can come right out, face to face, and talk with them. You do not need to disguise religious truths with a cloak of worldly things; you can bring these truths to them openly, in their natural guise. Youth may prove to be not more fearful of them than you are. There is no need for gradual approaches, for "bedtime" stories, for coddling, for patronizing, or for any of the other childish devices used in efforts to reach those spiritually inexperienced and all but spiritually dead.

You teachers have a great mission. As teachers you stand upon the highest peak in education, for what teaching can compare in priceless value and in far-reaching effect with that which deals with humans as they were in the eternity of yesterday, as they are in the mortality of today, and as they will be in the forever of tomorrow. Not only time, but eternity is your field. Salvation not only of yourself, but also of those who come within the purlieus of your temple is the blessing you seek and which, by doing your duty, you will gain. How brilliant will be your crown of glory, with each soul saved an encrusted jewel thereon.

But to get this blessing and to be so crowned, you must, I say once more, you must teach the gospel. You have no other function and no other reason for your presence in a Church school system.

You do have an interest in matters purely cultural and in matters of purely secular knowledge; but I repeat again for emphasis, your chief interest, your essential and all but sole duty, is to teach the gospel of the Lord Jesus Christ as it has been revealed in these latter days. You are to teach this gospel using as your sources and authorities the standard works of the Church and the words of those whom God has called to lead his people in these last days. You are not, whether high or low, to intrude into your work your own peculiar philosophy, no matter what its source or how pleasing or rational it seems to you to be. To do so would be to have as many different churches as we have seminaries—and that is chaos.

You are not, whether high or low, to change the doctrines of the Church or to modify them, as they are declared by and in the standard works of the Church and by those whose authority it is to declare the mind and will of the Lord to the Church. The Lord has declared he is "the same yesterday, today, and forever" (2 Ne. 27:23).

I urge you not to fall into that childish error, so common now, of believing that merely because we have gone so far in harnessing the forces of nature and turning them to our own use, therefore the truths of the Spirit have been changed or transformed. It is a vital and significant fact that our conquest of the things of the Spirit has not marched side by side with our conquest of things material. The opposite sometimes seems to be true. Our power to reason has not matched our power to figure. Remember always and cherish the great truth of the Intercessory Prayer: "And this is life eternal, that they might know thee the only true God, and Jesus Christ, whom thou hast sent" (John 17:3). This is an ultimate truth; so are all spiritual truths. They are not changed by the discovery of a new element, a new ethereal wave, nor by clipping off a few seconds, minutes, or hours of a speed record.

You are not to teach the philosophies of the world, ancient or modern, pagan or Christian, for this is the field of the public schools. Your sole field is the gospel, and that is boundless in its own sphere.

We pay taxes to support those state institutions whose function and work it is to teach the arts, the sciences, literature, history, the languages, and so on through the whole secular curriculum. These institutions are to do this work. But we use the tithes of the Church to carry on the Church school system, and these are impressed with a holy trust. The Church seminaries and institutes are to teach the gospel.

In thus stating this function time and time again, and with such continued insistence as I have done, it is fully appreciated that carrying out the function may involve the matter of "released time" for our seminaries and institutes. But our course is clear. If we cannot teach the gospel, the doctrines of the Church, and the standard works of the Church, all of them, on "released time" in our seminaries and institutes, then we must face giving up "released time" and try to work out some other plan of carrying on the gospel work in those institutions. If to work out some other plan be impossible, we shall face the abandonment of the seminaries and institutes and the return to Church colleges and academies. We are not now sure, in the light of developments, that these should ever have been given up. We are clear upon this point, namely, that we shall not feel justified in appropriating one further tithing dollar to the upkeep of our seminaries and institutes unless they can be used to teach the gospel in the manner prescribed. The tithing represents too much toil, too much self-denial, too much sacrifice, too much faith, to be used for the colorless instruction of the youth of the Church in elementary ethics. This decision and situation must be faced when the next budget is considered. In saying this, I am speaking for the First Presidency.

All that has been said regarding the character of religious teaching and the results which in the very nature of things must follow a failure properly to teach the gospel, applies with full and equal force to seminaries, to institutes, and to any and every other educational institution belonging to the Church school system.

The First Presidency earnestly solicits the wholehearted help and cooperation of all you men and women who, from your work on the firing line, know so well the greatness of the problem which faces us and which so vitally and intimately affects the spiritual health and the salvation of our youth, as well as the future welfare of the whole Church. We need you, the Church needs you, the Lord needs you. Restrain not yourselves, nor withhold your helping hand.

In closing, I wish to pay a humble, but sincere, tribute to teachers. I pay my tribute to your industry, your loyalty, your sacrifice, your willing eagerness for service in the cause of truth, your faith in God and in his work, and your earnest desire to do the things that our ordained leader and prophet would have you do. And I entreat you not to make the mistake of thrusting aside your leader's counsel, or of failing to carry out his wish, or of refusing to follow his direction.

May God bless you always in all your righteous endeavors; may he quicken your understanding, increase your wisdom, enlighten you by experience, bestow upon you patience and charity and, as among your most precious gifts, endow you with the discernment of spirits that you may certainly know the spirit of righteousness and its opposite as they come to you; may he give you entrance to the hearts of those you teach and then make you know that as you enter there you stand in holy places, which must be neither polluted nor defiled, either by false or corrupting doctrine or by sinful misdeed; may he enrich your knowledge with the skill and power to teach righteousness; may your faith and your testimonies increase, and your ability to encourage and foster them in others grow greater every day— all that the youth of Zion may be taught, built up, encouraged, heartened, that they may not fall by the wayside, but go on to eternal life, that as these blessings come to them, you through them may be blessed also.

This address was given to Church seminary and institute leaders on August 8, 1938, at the BYU Summer School in Aspen Grove, when J. Reuben Clark Jr. was First Counselor in the First Presidency.

The Calling of BYU

Ernest L. Wilkinson

The Challenge in a Changing World Environment

As school begins this year, we see signs on every hand that
we are living in a universe, not just a world, of change and ferment. Our modern vocabulary is filled with terms unknown a
few years ago, but now on the lips of every literate person. This
is truly a scientific and complex environment—one fraught with
great potentials for good but beset with grave dangers as well.

We humans have left evidence of our existence in the im-
plements we used, the cities we built, our burial places, memo-
rials, public structures, roads, and irrigation canals; yes, in the
civilizations we built—some of which we destroyed from without and others that disintegrated from within. Our mode of
travel and transport has been extended from foot to flight and
from muscle-bound back to mighty and versatile machine. The
fantastic means of communication today are miraculous compared with the primitive grimace, gesture, and grunt.

Our material and physical state has been advanced from an
animal existence to the luxury of thermostatically controlled,
air-conditioned, soap-scented, fluorescent-lighted, push-button
comfort. We are clothed in synthetic fabrics of rainbow hues;
amply nourished, replete with vitamins; irradiated, inoculated,
and chlorinated.

Today's concerns, in America at least, are more likely to be
those of obesity and geriatrics than starvation and pediatrics.

BYU President Ernest L. Wilkinson at his desk, May 1959. Courtesy BYU Archives.

In short, to "live like a king" has lost its appeal. Regal luxury has become commonplace—and free from a king's responsibility!

The prophetic novels of Jules Verne or Edward Bellamy seemed fantastic to their early readers. Today so many scientific marvels have become reality that the speed of sound is a unit of aircraft velocity, and the speed of light a term in the equation of space travel. The electron and the atom are hard at work in our service, and the fourth dimension is no longer a science-fiction nightmare.

The sky is no longer the limit. The real limit, today, is only the boundary of our vision and ability, and both are a measure of our training for the future. It was recently observed that of all the scientists who have ever walked the earth 90 percent are living today! Furthermore, it is estimated that during the past decade more learned data has been accumulated than during all the preceding period of recorded history! Undoubtedly, we are living in a stunning era of accelerated knowledge. In reality, we are in danger of being "submerged" by data—of all kinds, in all fields of leadership. But this staggering challenge, instead of discouraging our pursuit of knowledge, must inspire us to greater intellectual mastery.

The True Books of Education

American education is but a mirror for our culture. We cannot expect our educational system to be pluperfect when we ourselves tolerate a growing contempt for work, barbarous music and art, a sensual and sensational press, tawdry drama, and corrupted media of communication. We might fight constantly against the rising obscenity and growing vulgarity of our society. BYU should be in the vanguard of those who would fight for the highest standards in life—including those of the intellectual order. What, then, can be done at this institution?

I would submit that we should persistently struggle for greater academic attainment. We need a toughened attitude toward our curriculum, on the part of both teachers and students. We also know that greater application of reasoning power is obtained where the challenge is most severe and exciting. There is no doubt in my mind that we should do everything possible on this campus to stimulate the latent intellectual talent of our students.

We should sponsor an enthusiastic revival of stern, conscientious study habits. Brigham Young's definition that "education is the power to think clearly, to act well in the world's work, and the power to appreciate life"[1] must never be forgotten at this institution. Students should be taught how to think, encouraged to actually do some thinking, and inspired to take action on the results of their thinking, and then taught a reverence for and appreciation of life in all its component parts. Above all, we must remember that quality, not quantity, is the true yardstick of education. American schools, on all levels, must continue to stress training for citizenship and character because these are the qualities essential to freedom.

But a delicate balance is required. We minimize the stern and exacting disciplines at our own peril in an age fraught with unimaginable danger. However, if in the process of emphasizing these disciplines we lose sight of the more subtle qualities absolutely necessary to human freedom, we may reap the bitter harvest of trading shadow for substance. Our citizenship and character training can never become so nebulous as to lose significant meaning, nor can it be discarded as a mere "frill." We need both specialized and generalized outlooks on life and its challenges. We should not be forced to choose between but should strive for quality in both approaches to education.

Above all else, we must remember that the youth we teach here will be the future leaders of the Church, the nation, and the world. We must not fail them! Let us provide them with the intellectual tools they will need to meet the test of their times.

The Emphasis on Spiritual Truth

This age-old dilemma of knowledge, which can elevate and at the same time submerge us, confronts us on many fronts. Uppermost, of course, in our minds is the urgent crisis of civilization itself that is inherent in the existence of nuclear research. But if the others are less serious, they are by no means simple. As medicine and nutritional science progress, the general population and proportion of older people rise. Shifts to new automated technology bring temporary unemployment and make certain skills obsolete. Increasing leisure, accompanied by lack of inspiration for its intelligent use, nourishes frustration and dilutes spiritual values. The horrible prospect of a future society resembling George Orwell's *1984* cannot be ignored or taken lightly.

But growth of knowledge, no matter how rapid and how spectacular, even though sometimes misapplied, can never become a threat to true education if accompanied by constant critical vigilance and by a never-ending process of sifting which will separate the universal principle from the practical application and the firm truth from the wild guess. However, this sober task is becoming increasingly difficult. Society demands vast numbers of people trained in a vast variety of skills. In response to this sharp demand, universities tend to multiply their course offerings, to sponsor specialized projects, and are inexorably forced to train rather than educate the students.

We are tempted to tell our students that the field they want to study has grown so enormously and has become so complex and so intricate that they must specialize as soon as possible. We suggest, further, that once embarked upon the process of specialization, they will have little or no time for anything else, and it will take all their time to keep up with the developments in their own specialty. After some years of this brainwashing process, decorated perhaps with the "Order of the Ph.D.," young scholars will go out to attempt to contribute to the growth of knowledge in their specialties, while at the same time forgetting the other values of life. I submit that this type of counsel should never be given on this campus! As I see it, the true purpose of education in the Latter-day Saint environment is not to awe or frighten with vastness and complexity, but rather to impress with the simplicity that comes from real insight—not to depress and discourage students by the bewildering array of data, but to bring order out of the chaos of information and inspire them with the great spiritual principles which bring harmony, order, joy, and happiness in human life.

We must therefore teach our students about the divine nature of man. Each human being has a tremendous potential for good or evil. But we should recognize that evil does not automatically disappear because we have higher standards of living or better housing or that it will disappear with socialized medicine. On the contrary, the evil in the world could very well increase! All around us, in today's public drama, we see vigorous activity apparently geared to the premise (which I consider false) that the best policy is that which is directed solely toward the pursuit of a higher standard of living. Is this the way life should be? I think not! "For what is a man profited, if he shall gain the whole world, and lose his own soul? or what shall a man give in exchange for his soul?" (Matt. 16:26).

In considering the awesome importance of the BYU teacher in this learning process affecting our students, I sincerely believe that these scriptures are also very relevant here: "And they shall also teach their children to pray, and to walk uprightly before the Lord" (D&C 68:28). "Let him that is ignorant learn wisdom by humbling himself and calling upon the Lord his God, that his eyes may be opened that he may see, and his ears opened that he may hear" (D&C 136:32).

> O that cunning plan of the evil one! O the vainness, and the frailties, and the foolishness of men! When they are learned they think they are wise, and they hearken not unto the counsel of God, for they set it aside, supposing they know of themselves, wherefore, their wisdom is foolishness and it profiteth them not. And they shall perish.
>
> But to be learned is good if they hearken unto the counsels of God. (2 Ne. 9:28–29)

At BYU we have a twofold responsibility—a grave responsibility which demands a great deal of our faculty and staff:

1. Proper academic development—to meet the tests and challenges of the world.
2. Proper spiritual development—to meet the basic inner needs of the students and help them understand their relationship to others and to God, the Heavenly Father.

Five Steps to Insure an Optimum Environment

It is especially important that faculty and staff remember this responsibility always. Each classroom, each office, and each workshop should be affected strongly, in its own way, by the gospel of Jesus Christ. This attitude of basic reverence for eternal principles should be the hallmark of BYU.

Basically, our university, in attempting to teach students that each of us, as a son or daughter of God, is a free agent with unlimited possibilities for eternal development and in constantly emphasizing a never-ending search for truth and a proper understanding of that truth, should be keenly interested in supporting certain steps, taken to insure the optimum environment.

The first step is that of strong encouragement for the proper development of a deep-seated interest in LDS spiritual values. Superficiality should not be tolerated. Thorough understanding of one's religious perspective is essential.

On this subject, I get from time to time reports that a student's testimony has been impaired or actually destroyed by some thoughtless or irreverent teacher. On investigation I occasionally find the accusation to be true. In those rare and unusual cases where I have found such a deed to have been done purposely and premeditated by the teacher, we have had to terminate his or her services. Obviously, the teacher had no testimony of the divinity of our restored gospel and therefore either came to our faculty under false pretenses or apostatized after arriving. Sometimes, however, a teacher will carelessly affect the life of a young student by destroying the bridge which supports the student's testimony without at the same time providing a stronger and more enduring bridge in its place. Admitting that the testimonies of some students are immature and indeed sometimes not solidly based, we must never be guilty of impairing their faith in an all-wise creator and in the divinity of the restored gospel. It is our duty to improve and enlarge, not impair or crush, the testimonies of our students. I urge all of you to give serious consideration to this duty that none of us by flippant comment, sarcastic innuendo, or irreverent attitude, or otherwise, be guilty of depriving students of the motivating spiritual power which their parents probably sent them here to obtain and retain. Such irresponsible conduct in this institution is tantamount to blasphemy.

In the meetings of the board of trustees, President David O. McKay has often suggested that the greatest opportunity for a teacher at this institution is to teach some principle of the gospel in a class in chemistry or geology or sociology. In that respect, we have more freedom of speech in this university than we would have in a public institution, for there we would be forbidden to teach Mormon doctrines.

The second step is that of a constant emphasis upon the basic religious nature of all knowledge. To accept the common authorship of God for all spheres of learning is the cornerstone of LDS education.

The acceptance of this truism comes to us direct from the Doctrine and Covenants:

> And I give unto you a commandment that you shall teach one another the doctrine of the kingdom. Teach ye diligently and my grace shall attend you, that you may be instructed more perfectly in theory, in principle, in doctrine, in the law of the gospel, in all things that pertain unto the kingdom of God, that are expedient for you to understand; Of things both in heaven and in the earth, and under the earth; things which have been, things which are, things which must shortly come to pass; things which are at home, things which are abroad; the wars and the perplexities of the nations, and the judgments which are on the land; and a knowledge also of countries and of kingdoms. (D&C 88:77–79)

The founder of this institution preached the same doctrine: "Every accomplishment, every polished grace, every useful attainment in mathematics, music, and in all science and art belong to the Saints, and they should avail themselves as expeditiously as possible of the wealth of knowledge the sciences offer to every diligent and persevering scholar."[2] Again: "There is nothing I would like better than to learn chemistry, botany, geology, and mineralogy, so that I could tell what I walk on, the properties of the air I breathe, [and] what I drink."[3] Again: "Let them also learn all the truth pertaining to the arts and sciences, and how to apply the same to their temporal wants. Let them study things that are upon the earth, that are in the earth, and that are in the heavens."[4] And finally:

> We should be a people of profound learning pertaining to the things of the world. We should be familiar with the various languages, for we wish to send [our people] to the different nations and to the islands of the sea. We wish Missionaries who may go to France to be able to

speak the French language fluently, and those who may go
to Germany, Italy, Spain, and so on to all nations, to be
familiar with the languages of those nations.

We also wish them to understand the geography, habits, customs, and laws of nations and kingdoms, whether
they be barbarians or civilized.[5]

The third step is a determination to place LDS religious
values in all of the activities of the institution—not merely in
the academic field, but also in the nonacademic areas. Are we
truly living up to the gospel of Jesus Christ in all of our various
facets of university life? It is essential that all of us, faculty and
staff, recognize this responsibility.

The fourth step is a definite program to combat effectively
those aspects of university life on all levels which tend to create
a secular environment. No LDS institution can possibly give aid
and comfort to those persons or forces which are obviously
inimical to the highest ideals of the Church.

The fifth step is a recognition that the university has an obligation to produce students who are fully appreciative of the
principles of the Latter-day Saint faith and of their roles in
the universe as sacred and independent individuals. Brother
Maeser gave utterance to this thought when he said, "There is a
Mt. Sinai for every child of God, if only he can be inspired to
climb it." All students should therefore be encouraged to recognize the great inherent power which they possess as human beings
and as children of God. But this is not the only result. Individuals who go forward from BYU should also realize that individual strengths are not to be used for themselves alone. Through
the spiritual influence of the campus community, they should
have acquired the vision and the inspiration to be concerned
about others, to be truly interested in rendering service wherever it is needed.

The Faculty as Examples of Spiritual Strength

In practical effect, this means that each of us at BYU
should be a living and walking example of the gospel of Jesus
Christ. We should strive as mightily as we can to live up to the
principles of the Church every day of the week and not just on

the Sabbath. For good or for ill, we stand as examples before our students. Any member of the faculty or staff who may scoff at and deride spiritual values is impairing his or her usefulness at this university. Though he or she clothes skepticism in brilliant and fascinating verbiage, he or she will ultimately be an un-happy person in this particular campus community. Further, what can a student's evaluation be when he or she observes that some of us pay only nominal attention to the spiritual principles that the institution publicly espouses? I strongly declare that once we become associated with this institution we also carry upon our shoulders the responsibility of exemplary living. This may not be easy, but it is certainly a realistic factor in our lives. If we treat this obligation lightly, we could unwittingly, as well as deliberately, offend or disillusion a student to the point that he or she finds it very difficult to gain or retain a testimony of the faith.

I confess to you that as I prepared this address and wrote these words I was almost afraid to utter them, for I know I do not fully measure up to this test. But I hereby pledge myself to make a more strenuous effort to approach the proper standard, and I hope that others of you will do so, also. Although I have now been here for nearly twelve years, never have I felt so keenly the responsibilities of my office and the need for spiri-tual guidance. I therefore pray humbly for that strength and for your spiritual support.

Students cannot truly succeed in this modern world—by the gauge of the whole being—without the firm support of reli-gious devotion. Their physical achievements of the future, no matter how impressive from the secular viewpoint, are but a mockery if they fail to recognize their deep obligation to God the Father. If students do not become deeply aware of the great personal need for spiritual motivation and do not work actively to obtain it, then our world is truly lost! Thus the obligation upon us, who deal so intimately with the youth of today, is indeed sacred and of preeminent importance.

The Faculty as Counselors

We should give loving attention to each student in our charge. I implore all of you as you are engaged in counseling students to take this responsibility to heart. These young men and women need guidance and counsel every step of the way. I'm not advocating pampering, but I feel that we should do everything in our power to avoid the pitiless and coldly impersonal attitude so prevalent on the campuses of many large universities. Each student is significant not only as a human being, but particularly as a brother or sister and as a child of God. With our spiritual background, we should not only be concerned about the students assigned to us, but also feel a personal responsibility for the success or failure of each student so assigned. And this concern must be expressed in kindness and understanding. The late John C. Swensen often told of his becoming so discouraged as a young student that he decided to return home. On his way to the railway station, he met Karl G. Maeser. Sensing the worried expression on the boy's face, Brother Maeser put his arm around him, spoke a word of encouragement, and John C. turned around and came back to the campus. In his lifetime, Brother Swensen in turn gave encouragement to hundreds of his students. I hope you will do likewise.

I recognize, of course, that time is often short and that students sometimes do their best to avoid faculty counseling. But this is an important and valuable work—not only from the viewpoint of the university, but also from that of the Church itself. Please strive constantly to draw close to your students; give them spiritual food along with academic advice. They will remember you, for good or otherwise, throughout their lives. It is a serious undertaking. Without faculty counseling, we cannot possibly succeed. With it, we can save hundreds of students each year.

One of the most thrilling examples of the type of student produced at the "Y," through our secular and spiritual environment, is that of a young English immigrant who first enrolled at Brigham Young Academy in 1876. Two years later, at the age of sixteen, he graduated and immediately joined the faculty as an instructor in elementary science, Latin, and English.

With the friendly encouragement of Dr. Karl G. Maeser and President John Taylor, the young Englishman journeyed back East and engaged in further study at Lehigh University and

John Hopkins University. Thus, he was among the very first LDS students to obtain advanced training at eastern universities. Returning to the "Y," the young scholar was appointed as professor of geology and chemistry. Later he became assistant to Brother Maeser. While serving in this capacity, he was appointed to the school's board of trustees. Having tremendous civic vigor, he also served as Provo City councilman, alderman, and justice of the peace.

Later, this English scholar was called to the position of president of the Latter-day Saints College in Salt Lake City. And five years later, he became president and professor of geology at the University of Utah. In 1911 he was called to the Council of the Twelve, and Dr. James E. Talmage served in this office with great ability and inspiration until his death in 1933, at the early age of seventy-one. One of the treasured memories of my life is that he officiated at the marriage ceremony of Sister Wilkinson and myself.

I am convinced that Elder Talmage's life and his outstanding accomplishments were influenced to a marked degree by his experiences at the "Y" and by the counsel and encouragement he received from Dr. Karl G. Maeser. In this respect, I sincerely exhort each of you to remember that there may be many other "James Talmages" in our student body. I am sure none of you realized that an Iranian student who attended here a relatively few years ago would in a few years become the largest producer of insurance for Metropolitan Life Insurance in the country. That happened last year. Remember always the great contributions which these young people may make both to the world and to the Church in years yet to come. We cannot, in all conscience, ignore the remarkable potential of our students. An effective advisement program, which can succeed only with your wholehearted cooperation, is a big step in the direction of developing this latent power of our youth.

In this connection, one of the more grievous problems related to student advisement is that dealing with dropout rate. Although there is no reasonable doubt about the value of a college education, many students do not remain in college for the standard four years. Obviously, some of these young people drop out because they cannot do the work. But there are often other, somewhat intangible explanations. Nevertheless, regardless of cause, we must be concerned about the dropout problem and the resulting economic loss both to the student and to society as a whole.

The BYU Stakes

I am very happy to note the continuing success and wonderful influence of the stakes of the Church on our campus. These three stakes, with their various wards, have given all of our students opportunity to participate in meaningful religious activity. In this particular era of history, filled as it is with confusion and uncertainty, the Church needs to be close to its young people. Our various campus stakes and wards certainly provide a chance for each individual student to contribute his or her share in building up the kingdom.

We must strive to enhance the work of the BYU stakes. Every faculty and staff member should be willing to cooperate cheerfully with the program of the Church on our campus. In this regard, I honestly believe that a remarkably high degree of cooperation already has been attained. But we need to work at it and keep the overall level continually high.

Gratitude and Appreciation

In conclusion, permit me to express my personal affection and gratitude to each of you. Brigham Young University is certainly a large university with an attractive campus and modern buildings. But all these advantages, while extremely significant, mean virtually nothing unless they are bolstered by the devoted, dedicated efforts of our faculty and staff. I know you have given freely of your devotion and dedication—often at considerable personal sacrifice—to the "Y". What progress we have achieved here is due largely to the outstanding contributions you have made—individually and as a group—to the improvement of our academic standards and the personal interest you have shown in guiding our students into proper, wholesome channels.

I heartily urge you to continue the fine record which you have already made. We need your help to fulfill the great and stimulating destiny of BYU.

This address was given at the annual faculty workshop at Brigham Young University on September 18, 1962. Ernest L. Wilkinson served as president of Brigham Young University from 1949 to 1971.

NOTES

[1]LeGrand Richards, *A Marvelous Work and a Wonder* (Salt Lake City: Deseret Book, 1958), 384.

[2]Brigham Young, in *Journal of Discourses*, 26 vols. (Liverpool: F. D. Richards, 1855–86), 10:224, April and May 1863 (hereafter cited as *JD*).

[3]Young, in *JD*, 16:170, August 31, 1873.

[4]Young, in *JD*, 8:9, March 4, 1860.

[5]Young, in *JD*, 8:40, April 8, 1860.

President Spencer W. Kimball at the BYU Centennial Convocation, October 10, 1975. Courtesy Mark A. Philbrick/BYU.

Climbing the Hills Just Ahead: Three Addresses

Spencer W. Kimball

I. Education for Eternity

I am constantly impressed with this beautiful campus. I am awed by the power of the administration and faculty, and as I see the thousands of students, I want to sing, "Behold! A Royal Army."

In all the world, the Brigham Young University is the greatest institution of learning. This statement I have made numerous times. I believe it sincerely. There are many criteria by which a university can be judged and appraised and evaluated. The special qualities of Brigham Young University lie not in its bigness; there are a number of much larger universities. It should not be judged by its affluence and the amount of money available for buildings, research, and other facilities. It should not be judged by prestige, for there are higher institutions as the world measures status.

The uniqueness of Brigham Young University lies in its special role—education for eternity—which it must carry in addition to the usual tasks of a university. This means concern—curricular and behavioral—not only for the "whole man," but also for the "eternal man." Where all universities seek to preserve the heritage of knowledge that history has washed to their feet, this faculty has a double heritage—the preserving of knowledge of men and the revealed truths sent from heaven.

While all universities seek to push back the frontiers of knowledge further and further, this faculty must do that and also keep new knowledge in perspective, so that the avalanche of facts does not carry away saving, exalting truths from the value systems of our youth.

In addition, this faculty must aid the youth of the kingdom in establishing yet another educational expectation—that there are yet "many great and important things" (A of F 1:9) to be revealed which require an intellectual and spiritual posture of readiness and openness. Where other institutions of higher education aim, in part, at educating and training students for various careers, this faculty must do that vital job and do it superbly well, but it must do far more. It must train a cadre of committed, educated youth who can serve effectively, not only in the world of work, but in the growing kingdom of God, in which skilled leadership is such a vital commodity.

This time of intellectual testing must also be a time of equivalent testing and flexing in things spiritual too. "The Spirit giveth light" (D&C 84:46). This revealed wisdom is so true in so many ways. When there is an inner emptiness in the life of man, his surroundings, however affluent, cannot compensate. When there is a crisis of purpose, nothing will really seem worthwhile or meaningful. When man's relationship with God has been breached, we will be, as Isaiah said, "like the troubled sea, when it cannot rest" (Isa. 57:20).

A university or an individual can have all the surface signs of security and yet still be empty inside. You must fill the classrooms and halls of this campus with facts, but fill them also with the Spirit of the Master Teacher, who said to the Nephites of the things he had done, "Even so shall ye do unto the world" (3 Ne. 18:25).

"Education for eternity" is not the kind of phrase one would expect to have carved in the stone of a new secular university; it is not the kind of commitment that would be widely shared in the retreat from real religion we see around us in the world. Yet it is a task for which we do not apologize. Those who do not share this purpose, however, will respect this faculty for its genuine achievements in the world of secular scholarship. The extra missions noted previously do not excuse you from reasonable achievement in your chosen field. You can, in fact, often be more effective in the service you render students if students see you as individuals who have blended successfully things secular and things spiritual in a way that has brought to you earned respect in both realms.

As I see you leaders here, knowing you personally and recognizing the depth of your knowledge, your outstanding accomplishments in your chosen fields, I honor you and appreciate you greatly. And then I realize also that in the breast of every one, there is a deep, spiritual feeling with the Master. We know there are good men and women elsewhere, but here, here we have a choice group.

When measured with the true measuring rod, the Brigham Young University stands preeminent. Certainly, the true measure of an institution of learning would be the impact it makes on the total lives of its students. On high levels in business, industry, professional and other fields, great men and women of prominence in many areas are BYU alumni. Orison S. Marden wrote:

> It is a sad sight to see thousands of students graduated every year from our grand institutions whose object is to make stalwart, independent, self-supporting men turned out into the world saplings instead of stalwart oaks, "memory glands" instead of brainy men, helpless instead of self-supporting, sickly instead of robust, weak instead of strong, leaning instead of erect.

You tell me that these nearly seven thousand returned missionaries render a stabilizing influence with their deep religious convictions and their serious application. You tell me that a high percentage of the twenty thousand students actually hold positions of leadership in Church organizations and that nearly all of them attend sacrament meetings and that the large majority who have income pay their tithing. These students voluntarily assemble weekly to hear religious messages from the leaders of the Church. What a great institution, where professors, staff members, and students work together in glorious harmony in stake presidencies, bishoprics, and quorum and auxiliary leadership.

It is notable that numerous students change their lives on this campus. Many who had never seriously planned missions for themselves now eagerly look forward to that day. Many who had given little thought to a temple marriage are here inspired to chart their course in that direction.

How the world needs a light in the dark, even a refuge—a vault for keeping the jewels and treasures of life, a big waste-basket into which could be dumped the trash and filth and destructive ideologies and eccentric activities. While great universities and colleges seem to have abandoned all attempts to influence the moral lives of their students, this university must "hold the line." Apparently such an attitude seems to be growing on the campuses of our nation, and what can we expect of the graduates tomorrow?

There are holes in the fabric of our political system; our social world continues to show corruption. A climate is coming into being which seems not to only permit crimes against society, but to actually encourage them indirectly. "Do We Have a Sick Society?" the *U.S. News and World Report* asks in a recent issue.

In the current issue of the *Instructor,* President David O. McKay, after speaking of our carelessness in keeping our bodies fit and calling attention to the physical decay, reminds us that spiritual decay is more serious:

> But great as is the peril of physical decay, greater is the peril of spiritual decay. The peril of this century is spiritual apathy. As the body requires sunlight, good food, proper exercise and rest, so the spirit of man requires the sunlight of the Holy Spirit, proper exercise of the spiritual functions, the avoiding of evils that affect spiritual health that are more ravaging in their effects than the dire diseases that attack the body. . . .
>
> Never before have the forces of evil been arrayed in such deadly formation as they are now. . . . Satan and his forces are attacking the high ideals and sacred standards which protect our spirituality. One cannot help but be alarmed by the ever-increasing crime wave.[1]

In our sick society, children are not required to work; time hangs heavily on their hands. Their crimes run into theft and beatings, and even murders fill more of their time. Haight-Ashbury in San Francisco, Dupont Circle in Washington, D.C., East Village in New York City may be net results of some of the laxities and looseness in morals with increases in illegitimacy. And numerous evils of our times may look to the deteriorating ethical standards proposed often by professors in what are termed great universities. God's ways and eternal standards are laughed at; "situational ethics," making each person his or her own moral judge and authority, seem to be responsible for the sickness of our society. How can it survive?

When these numerous other things are weighed and considered, we come to realize that our responsibility at BYU becomes greater and greater. We must carry the torch and light the way, and this faculty and staff must stand like a concrete wall to prevent these strange, worldly ideologies and concepts from invading this, one of the last bastions of resisting strength.

We should be knowledgeable. When we talk of godhood and creatorship and eternal increase, we have already soared far out beyond the comprehension of most men. To attain those great accomplishments, one would need to know all about astronomy, biology, physiology, psychology, and all of the arts and sciences. The obtaining of all this knowledge will come largely after our earth life. The questions are often asked, "Why a doctrine-teaching, a character-building university? Why not let people do, think, and move as they please?"

Robert Millikan said, "Science has gone ahead so fast, man can spend fifty to a hundred years just learning how to use wisely what he already knows." It is stated further that the western world has, in the past hundred years, seen more changes in the external conditions under which the average man lives, and also in his fundamental conceptions, than occurred during all the preceding four thousand years.

Our Brigham Young insisted, "Learn everything that the children of men know, and be prepared for the most refined society upon the face of the earth, then improve on this until we are prepared and permitted to enter the society of the blessed— the holy angels that dwell in the presence of God."[2]

The Lord seems never to have placed a premium on ignorance, and yet he has, in many cases, found his better-trained people unresponsive to the spiritual and has had to use spiritual giants with less training to carry on his work. Peter was said to be ignorant and unlearned, while Nicodemus was, as the Savior said, a master, a trained one, an educated man. And while Nicodemus would in his aging process gradually lose his prestige, his strength, and go to the grave a man of letters without eternal knowledge, Peter would go to his reputed crucifixion the greatest man in all the world, perhaps still lacking considerably in secular knowledge (which he would later acquire) but being preeminent in the greater, more important knowledge of the eternities and God and his creations and their destinies. And Paul gives us the key: "It is sown a natural body; it is raised a spiritual body. There is a natural body, and there is a spiritual body" (1 Cor. 15:44). "For what man knoweth the things of a man, save the spirit of man which is in him? even so the things of God knoweth no man, but the Spirit of God" (1 Cor. 2:11).

It is interesting to note that most of us have a tendency to want to ape the ways of our neighbor, in styles or curricula or universities. If New York or Paris speaks, the dresses are lengthened or shortened; if San Francisco's Haight-Ashbury speaks, men's hair grows longer, beards appear, and baths are less frequent. If the Joneses have a Cadillac, all want Cadillacs. If a nation has a king, all want a king. We seem reluctant to establish our own standards, make our own styles, follow our own patterns, which are based on dignity, comfort, and propriety.

Israel did want a king. "Now make us a king," they cried to Samuel, "to judge us like all the nations." And when Samuel prayed, the Lord said, "They have not rejected thee, but they have rejected me, that I should not reign over them" (1 Sam. 8:5–7). And then with the inspiration of the Lord, Samuel pointed out to them the hazards of having a king. The king would recruit their sons in battle. Their daughters would serve in confectioneries and kitchens and bakeries. Their sons would have to work his ground and reap his harvests and make his spears and swords and rebuild his chariots and train his horses. He would appropriate their vineyards and olive yards to feed his servants, and he would tax them heavily.

In spite of all these dire predictions, the people still said, "Nay; but we will have a king over us . . . like all the nations" (1 Sam. 8:19–20).

Though our world reels and trembles, we must stand firm and see that behavior troubles do not invade our campus like other campuses and that we are not like other universities.

We have been speaking of mind and spirit and body, of the immortal man and the mortal man. We have been speaking of earthly things and spiritual things, of time and eternity. Of the two, the spiritual development is the greater, for it is permanent, lasting, and it incorporates all other proper secular development.

The Lord inspired Nephi to correlate the secular and the spiritual, when he said, "To be learned is good if they hearken unto the counsels of God" (2 Ne. 9:29).

Someone has said, "If the world needs a bomb to destroy the cities and its peoples and the world, the laboratory of the American university can supply it." And we say, "If the world needs messengers of peace and teachers of righteousness and builders of character and inspirers of faith in God, here is the university that can do all this—here at the Brigham Young University."

Even here we give to the first cause our lesser attention, and though we are far in front of other institutions, still we give less time, less thought, less effort to the actual teaching of the spiritual as contrasted with the secular. But perhaps this imbalance of time and energy and effort is considerably compensated for, if all of you instructors in all classes teach the gospel, especially by example. Most of you teach eloquently in this manner. Most of you will frequently attend the temple and will serve in the stakes and wards, priesthood and auxiliary organizations. Some of you will be leaders in general Church positions. All of you will be living all the commandments of the Lord—paying a full tithing, observing the Word of Wisdom, not because it is expected, but because it is right.

In your homes will be an absence of friction and conflict, not because forty thousand eyes are upon you, but because you love the Lord, your family, and the program. You will observe the Sabbath day and keep it holy as you live all other commandments—not because the multitudes might see you, but because of the Lord who gave them. Your home evenings will be regular and inspirational, and your family prayers, both morning and night, will be constant—not because you are under command, but because you love your family and our BYU family of twenty thousand who will feel the spirituality emanating from you. You will always keep solvent, be honest to the nth degree and always full of integrity, not because you are required to do so to keep your position, but because you believe fully that God gives no commandments which are not for our own good. Your example is better than even your precept, for to teach one thing and to do another is like sounding brass and tinkling cymbals.

This university is not the place for mercenaries. The Revolutionary War was lost by the British, partly because they employed mercenaries to fight for them. But the winning colonists had a real cause. If your salary, which we hope is adequate, should be incidental and your grand and magnificent obsession would be the youth and their growth, their vision, their development, I would hope that each of you in joy and peace and satisfaction would continue to lift the souls and carry forward the character-building program.

It would be my hope that twenty thousand students might feel the normalcy and beauty of your lives. I hope you will each qualify for the students' admiration and affection. It is my hope that these youth will have abundant lives, beautiful family patterns, after the ideal of an eternal family, with you for their example.

This would lead me to expect from you honor, integrity, cleanliness, and faith; I would expect you to appear before these young people well-dressed, well-groomed, and positive—happy people from homes where peace and love have left their warm, vibrant influence as your day begins. I would want them to have the feeling that you, their instructor, that very morning had come from a loving home where peace reigns and love is enthroned and to know instinctively by your spirit that you were that morning on your knees with your family and that there were soft words of pleading to your Heavenly Father for guidance, not only for your little family kneeling with you, but for your larger family also at that moment scurrying about their apartments to get ready for your class. Brigham Young said, "Let our teachers ask the Father, in the name of Jesus, to bestow upon them and upon their scholars the Spirit of wisdom and intelligence from heaven; ask for skill to control and ability to teach on the part of the teacher, and willingness to be controlled and adaptability to be taught on the part of the scholars."[3]

I would like these youth to see their instructors in community life as dignified, happy cooperators; in Church life as devout, dependable, efficient leaders; and in personal life honorable, full of integrity; and as President John Taylor said, "Let us live so . . . that angels can minister to us and the Holy Ghost dwell with us."

Here there should be loyalty at its ultimate best. Loyalty is the stuff of which great souls are made. I would expect that no member of faculty or staff would continue in the employ of this institution if he or she did not have deep assurance of the divinity of the gospel of Christ, the truth of the Church, the correctness of the doctrines, and the destiny of the school.

The BYU is dedicated to the building of character and faith, for character is higher than intellect, and its teachers must in all propriety so dedicate themselves. That goal is the same as that of our Eternal Father: "To bring to pass the immortality and eternal life of man" (Moses 1:39). Every instructor knows before coming to this campus what the aims are and is committed to the furthering of those objectives.

If one cannot conscientiously accept the policies and program of the institution, there is no wrong in his moving to an environment that is compatible and friendly to his concepts. But for a Ford employee to downgrade his company or its products, for a General Electric man to be unappreciative of his company, for an employee of a bank to discredit that institution would be hypocrisy and disloyalty. There are ways to right wrongs, to improve services, to bring about proper changes. To set about to counter the established policies or approved interpretations of the doctrines of the Church would be disloyal and unbecoming of anyone.

No one could justifiably accept salary or favors from an institution whose policies he or she could not in principle accept and defend.

This is an institution peculiar and different from all others. Other schools have been organized by states, countries, churches, groups, and individuals. This great university was organized by the Lord God.

President J. Reuben Clark Jr. expresses clearly our concepts:

> Science and worldly knowledge must question every demonstration, every experiment, every conclusion, every phenomenon that seems a fact, for only by this method may the truths of the natural law become known to us, save by specific revelations.

> But we shall also expect you to know that in matters pertaining to our spiritual lives, God's revealed Will, His laws, His commandments declared not only directly by Himself, but by and through His servants must be taken unquestioned, because they are ultimate truths that shape and control our destinies.
>
> Now brethren and sisters, it is your privilege to teach the revealed word of God. You are not expected to advance new theories, give private interpretations nor to clarify the mysteries. You do not need to, nor can you nor anyone else answer all the questions that the youth can ask. You need not be embarrassed to tell them that you cannot fully answer certain questions, and that the Lord has not seen fit to reveal all His mysteries. Perhaps many would like to know the age of the earth, the exact method of its organization, the method of spirit procreation.[4]

The doctrines of the Church will be revealed through the prophet, and he will interpret them as is needed. To one such member who presumed to dictate to the prophet concerning a matter which has been settled long years, I wrote:

> I cannot believe you would presume to command your God to make demand on the prophet of God! No situation or condition could possibly justify you in any such monumental presumption. To any such, I must quote the Lord: "And thou shalt not command him who is at thy head, and at the head of the church" (D&C 28:6).

When the Lord has set a policy and his leaders have established it, certainly it would be bad taste and improper for people to keep sniping at it.[5]

I knew a man who received his bank salary yet secretly robbed his bank of its money. I knew a woman who was supported by a business, but she constantly revealed its inner weaknesses to her associates. I knew a man who received the confidences of persons in trouble and revealed them to his associates. I knew a man who belonged to the Church and enjoyed its blessings but secretly was constantly downgrading it .

This institution and its leaders should be like the Twelve as they were left in a very difficult world by the Savior: "The world hath hated them, because they are not of the world, even as I am not of the world. I pray not that thou shouldest take them out of the world, but that thou shouldest keep them from the evil. They are not of the world, even as I am not of the world" (John 17:14–16).

I liked President Ernest L. Wilkinson's statement in an address:

> If most institutions of higher learning aspire to be only communities of scholars, we are privileged to be also a congregation of disciples. . . . Our roots spring from Palmyra rather than Cambridge.
>
> We are men of God first and men of letters second, and men of science third and noted men fourth, men of rectitude rather than academic competence. . . . Our academic training must be as impeccable as our lives.
>
> A defection that would pass unnoticed elsewhere is exploited relentlessly when it occurs at BYU.

There are relative truths, and there are absolute truths. The gospel is absolute—its basic functions and teachings do not change. President J. Reuben Clark Jr. wrote:

> The philosopher, in his worldly way, may speak of relative truth in the field of ethics and worldly knowledge, a concept that today and here may be truth, but that tomorrow and there may be error, a truth based upon man's development, his learnings, his ethics, his concepts, his hopes, his aspirations, his God. . . .
>
> As our knowledge is widened, we to Job's incomprehensibles have added almost a universe of unknown physical phenomena. . . .
>
> But we have at our hands unchanging, ultimate truths which God has vouchsafed to us for our guidance, salvation, and exaltation. They are shields against temptation, and are our redemption from sin. They give us the light for our feet; they guide us on our way.

They draw aside for us the curtains of heaven, so that, like Stephen of old, we may see "the glory of God, and Jesus standing on the right hand of God" (Acts 7:55). "They are the rocks upon which we build our house, that the winds and storms wash not away. They are the bridge connecting time with eternity, mortality with immortality; over it, we walk from worldliness into salvation."[6]

Whereas in other institutions there seem to be faculties and administration groups and students who are fighting for supremacy as to the policies and conduct of the university, BYU is entirely different. It is financed and operated and sustained by the tithes of the people—poor and rich. It is governed by the board of trustees, who are General Authorities of the Church. The Prophet, Seer, and Revelator is the interpreter of the doctrines. It must be ever thus.

And Paul warned us, "Beware lest any man spoil you through philosophy and vain deceit, after the tradition of men, after the rudiments of the world, and not after Christ" (Col. 2:8).

It would not be expected that all of the faculty should be categorically teaching religion constantly in their classes, but it is proper that every professor and teacher in this institution would keep his subject matter bathed in the light and color of the restored gospel and have all his subject matter perfumed lightly with the spirit of the gospel. Always there would be an essence, and the student would feel the presence.

Every instructor should grasp the opportunity occasionally to bear formal testimony of the truth. Every student is entitled to know the attitude and feeling and spirit of his or her every teacher. Certainly, a science instructor or a physical education teacher or a math or art teacher could find an opportunity sometimes to mention spiritual experiences or comment on the gospel truths. This would be in harmony with the spirit of Brigham Young's charge to Karl G. Maeser, so often quoted:

> President [Young] looked steadily forward for a few minutes, as though in deep thought, then said: "Brother Maeser, I want you to remember that you ought not to teach even the alphabet or the multiplication tables without the Spirit of God. That is all. God bless you. Good-bye."[7]

That statement has been used over and over, but we must never forget it. If we begin to ape the world and forget this injunction, we are lost. We pay our taxes; we support state schools; therefore, there is no justification whatever for our spending these millions of dollars on this institution unless we mind the purposeful objective given by the prophet.

Many of us have had dreams and visions of the destiny of this great Church university. Joel said, "Your old men shall dream dreams, your young men shall see visions" (Joel 2:28).

Now that we have reached maximum in enrollment, much of the energy formerly given to growth and expansion can now be concentrated on making our dreams come true. With this revolving twenty thousand choice, last-dispensation students from all over the world running into hundreds of thousands through the years, can we not build dream castles in the air and build foundations solidly under them to develop students, faculty, campus, and a university that would eclipse all others within the limitations of our courses?

In our world, there have risen brilliant stars in drama, music, literature, sculpture, painting, science, and all the graces. For long years, I have had a vision of the BYU greatly increasing its already strong position of excellence till the eyes of all the world will be upon us.

President John Taylor so prophesied, as he emphasized his words with this directive: "You will see the day that Zion will be far ahead of the outside world in everything pertaining to learning of every kind as we are today in regard to religious matters. You mark my words, and write them down, and see if they do not come to pass."[8] He further declared: "God expects Zion to become the praise and glory of the whole earth, so that kings, hearing of her fame, will come and gaze upon her glory."[9] With regard to masters, surely there must be many Wagners in the BYU, approaching him or yet to come in the tomorrows— young people with love of art, talent supreme, and eagerness to create. I hope we at BYU may produce men greater than this German composer, Wagner, but less eccentric, more spiritual.

Who of us has not sat spellbound with *Aida, Il Trovatore,* or other of the masterpieces of Verdi? Can there never be another Verdi or his superiors? Could we not find and develop a Bach, to whom some say music, especially organ and choral music, owes almost as much as a religion does to its founder.

Is there anyone here who has not been stirred by the rich, melodic voice of Enrico Caruso, the Italian-born operatic tenor? Surely there have been few voices which have inspired so many. Considered to be the greatest voice of his century by many, year after year, he was the chief attraction at the Metropolitan Opera.

Would someone say that they produce singers best in Italy, in Germany, in Poland, or in Sweden? Remember, we draw our students from all these places. BYU should attract many and stir their blood with the messages of the ages. And they will sing songs of accomplishment, eternal marriage, and exaltation, and we at BYU shall encourage and train them.

And then there was Patti—Adeline Maria Patti—who was scintillating in her accomplishments and her greatness. She is known as an Italian singer, though she was born in Madrid. Not only did Patti have a pure, clear-toned voice, but a wide range that was excelled only by her personal grace and charm, her pure style, her loveliness. Surely at this university we can produce many Pattis in the tomorrows.

Then we remember the celebrated Jenny Lind, the Swedish singer, with such tone faculty, such musical memory, such supremacy, and with such unprecedented triumphs. Do you think there are no more voices like Jenny Lind's? Our day, our time, our people, our generation, our BYU should produce such as we catch the total vision of our potential and dream dreams and see visions of the future.

Brigham Young said, "Every accomplishment, every polished grace, every useful attainment in mathematics, music, and in all sciences and art belong to the Saints."[10]

Many of us can still remember the enchanting Madame Schumann-Heink, the Bohemian-Austrian, later American, lady, who was by many regarded as the greatest contralto of her time and a noble character also. She had sons in World War I on both sides, losing one in the American army and one in the German army.

And here at BYU many times I have been entranced with sweet and lovely voices. I believe that deep in the throats of these BYU students of today and tomorrow are qualities superior, which, superbly trained, can equal or surpass those of these known great singers. There was also Nellie Melba, the great Australian prima donna, the Melba who captivated her audiences as she sang.

BYU certainly must continue to be the greatest university, unique and different. In these fields and in many others, there should be an ever-widening gap between this school and all other schools. The reason is obvious. Our professors and instructors should be peers or superiors to those at any other school in natural ability, extended training, plus the Holy Spirit, which should bring them light and truth. With hundreds of "men and women of God" and their associates so blessed and trained, we have the base for an increasingly efficient and worthy school.

What is the future for BYU? It has long had a strong music department, but we have hardly begun the great work that could be done here. I envision that day when the BYU symphony will surpass in popularity and performance the Philadelphia Orchestra or the New York Philharmonic or the Cleveland Symphony.

One great artist was asked which of all his productions was the greatest. His prompt answer was, "The next."

If we strive for perfection, the best and greatest, and are never satisfied with mediocrity, we can excel. In the field of both composition and performance, why cannot the students from here write a greater oratorio than Handel's *Messiah*? The best has not yet been composed or produced. They can use the coming of Christ to the Nephites as the material for a greater masterpiece. Our BYU artists tomorrow may write and sing of Christ's spectacular return to the American earth in power and great glory and of his establishment of the kingdom of God on the earth in our own dispensation. No Handel or other composer of the past or present or future could ever do justice to this great event. How could one ever portray in words and music the glories of the coming of the Father and the Son and the restoration of the doctrines and the priesthood and the keys unless he were an inspired Latter-day Saint, schooled in the history and doctrines and revelations and with rich musical ability and background and training? Why cannot the BYU bring forth this producer?

George Bernard Shaw, the Irish dramatist and critic, summed up an approach to life: "Other peoples," he said, "see things and say, 'WHY?' But I dream things that never were—and I say, 'WHY NOT?'" We need people here who can dream of things that never were, and ask, "WHY NOT?"

Dom Jae gave us this: "Blessed is the man with new worlds to conquer. For him the future beams with promise. He never attains ultimate success, is never satisfied, is ever on the way to better things. Ahead of him there is always another dream castle glittering in the sun—and what fun it is to build foundations under it!"

Freed largely from expansion and growing pains, we can now pour many firm foundations under our dreams for the future.

And Niccolo Paginini, the Italian violinist! Why cannot we discover, train, and present many Pagininis and other such great artists? And shall we not here at BYU present before the musical world a pianist to excel in astonishing power of execution, depth of expression, sublimity of noble feeling, the noted Hungarian pianist and composer Liszt? We have already produced some talented artists at the piano, but I have a secret hope to live long enough to come to the BYU auditorium and hear and see at the piano a greater performer than Paderewski, the Polish statesman, composer and pianist. Surely all Paderewskis were not born in Poland in the last century; all talented people with such outstanding recreative originality, with such nervous power and such romantic appearance were not concentrated in this one body and two hands! Certainly, this noted pianist with his arduous super-brilliant career was not the last of such to be born!

The Italian painter and sculptor Leonardo da Vinci, with his masterful and wonderful technique, made his portraits, figures, and designs true to life. His *Mona Lisa* is celebrated, and in it he was striving to catch the fleeting manifestations of the secret soul of his attractive and winsome subject. He seems to have given inspiration to Raphael and others of the great.

On our last visit to Copenhagen, we were excited and inspired as we drank in the beauty of Thorvaldsen's *Christ and the Twelve Apostles*. We wondered if any one, any time, could produce a greater masterpiece, and yet time and the BYU may surprise the world. Can you see statues on this campus of the Lord, his prophets and his disciples? There are many of the martyrs and prophets of the centuries who have never been so honored.

Michelangelo thought of himself only as a sculptor. He was called upon in 1505 by Pope Julius II to build a great monument which the Pope desired to have finished within his lifetime.

This monument was never completed, and the controversies which arose embittered a large part of the great artist's life. His thirty-five hundred square foot painting in the Sistine Chapel is said to be the most important piece of mural painting of the modern world.

To be an artist means hard work and patience and long-suffering. This artist said, "I am a poor man and of little merit, who plods along in the art which God gave me. . . . I am more exhausted than ever man was." And when we see Michelangelo's masterpieces of art, we feel as did Habakkuk: "Behold ye among the heathen, and regard, and wonder marvellously: for I will work a work in your days, which ye will not believe, though it be told you" (Hab. 1:5).

But then we ask, Can there never be another Michelangelo? Ah! Yes! His *David* in Florence and his *Moses* in Rome inspire to adulation. Did all such talent run out in that early century? Could not we find an embodied talent like this, but with a soul that was free from immorality and sensuality and intolerance?

Could there be among us embryo poets and novelists like Goethe? Have we explored as much as we should? Of the creator of *Faust,* Emerson said, "The old eternal genius that built the world had confided itself more to this man than to any other." But Goethe was not the greatest nor the last. There may be many Goethes among us even today, waiting to be discovered. Inspired students will write great books and novels and biographies and plays.

Can we not find talent equal to those who gave us *A Man for All Seasons, Doctor Zhivago, Ben Hur?* This latter book I read when a small boy, and many times I have returned to it. Critics might not agree with me, but I feel that it is a great story. *My Fair Lady* and *The Sound of Music* and such have pleased their millions, but I believe we can improve on them.

We have the great Rembrandt, whose style is original, founded on the work of no other artist, whose coloring is somber and reaches its highest achievement in combinations of browns and grays. There are few paintings about which so much has been written as Rembrandt's *Night Watch* or his self-portraits. His morals also have been subject to criticism.

And we have the Italian painter Raphael, generally accepted in the European world as the greatest of religious painters.

It has been said that many of the great artists were moral degenerates. In spite of their immorality, they became great and celebrated artists. What could be the result if discovery were made of equal talent in men who were clean and free from the vices and thus entitled to revelations?

We have scientists who can help harness the limitless powers and turn them to good for all humanity. There have been Pasteur and Curie and Albert Einstein, and there are the Harvey Fletchers, the Henry Eyrings, and there will be greater yet.

Then there is Shakespeare. Everybody quotes Shakespeare. The English poet and dramatist was prodigious in his productions. His *Hamlet* and *Othello* and *King Lear* and *Macbeth* are only prelude to the great mass of his productions. Has anyone other ever been so versatile, so talented, so remarkable in his art? And yet, could the world produce only one Shakespeare?

The Lamanite-Nephite culture means much to the people of the Church, and properly so. Here at BYU, should we not have the greatest collection of artifacts, records, writings, concerning them in the world? Through revelation, we have received much knowledge concerning these peoples. Should not BYU then be preeminent in this field of culture?

Perhaps growing up in a backwoods forest in Indiana or Louisiana or Oregon or Illinois there may be some little deprived boy doing his elementary math on a wooden fire shovel and borrowing books from neighbors and splitting rails who will find his way tomorrow to the BYU and here in the proper departments, get the background, knowledge, and inspiration which will send him skyrocketing to fame and honors, perhaps even to the White House, and a man to be ever after heralded for his wisdom, bravery, conscience, humanity, leadership, and to be quoted till eternity. His name might be Abraham, his mother's name might be Nancy, and could this be written concerning him as was written of his nineteenth-century counterpart?

> Oh, well, send the women,
> Send them there to Nance;
> Poor little young un'
> Born without a chance.

The little Abes could have their chances and their greatest talents improved and perfected, and their notoriety spring from humble but influential BYU.

Oh, how our world needs statesmen! And we ask again with George Bernard Shaw, "Why not?" We have the raw material; we have the facilities; we can excel in training. We have the spiritual climate. We must train statesmen, not demagogues; men of integrity, not weaklings who for a mess of pottage will sell their birthright. We must develop these precious youth to know the art of statesmanship, to know people and conditions, to know situations and problems, but men who will be trained so thoroughly in the arts of their future work and in the basic honesties and integrities and spiritual concepts that there will be no compromise of principle.

For years I have been waiting for someone to do justice in recording in song and story and painting and sculpture the story of the Restoration, the reestablishment of the kingdom of God on earth; the struggles and frustrations; the apostasies and inner revolutions and counterrevolutions of those first decades; of the exodus; of the counterreactions; of the transitions; of the persecution days; of plural marriage and the underground; of the miracle man Joseph Smith, of whom we sing, "Oh, what rapture filled his bosom, for he saw the living God!" and of the giant colonizer and builder Brigham Young, by whom this university was organized and for whom it was named.

The story of Mormonism has never yet been written nor painted nor sculptured nor spoken. It remains for inspired hearts and talented fingers *yet* to reveal themselves. They must be faithful, inspired, active Church members to give life and feeling and true perspective to a subject so worthy. Such masterpieces should run for months in every movie theater, cover every part of the globe in the tongue of the people, written by great artists, purified by the best critics.

Our writers, our motion picture specialists, with the inspiration of heaven, should tomorrow be able to produce a masterpiece which would live forever. Our own talent, obsessed with dynamism from a *cause,* could put into such a story life, heartbeats, emotions, love, pathos, drama, suffering, fear, and courage. In such literature, the great leader—the mighty modern

Moses who led a people farther than from Egypt to Jericho, who knew miracles as great as the stream from the rock at Horeb, manna in the desert, giant grapes, rain when needed, battles won against great odds—the great miracle prophet, the founder of this university, would never die.

Take a Nicodemus and put Joseph Smith's spirit in him, and what do you have? Take a da Vinci or a Michelangelo or a Shakespeare and give him a total knowledge of the plan of salvation of God and personal revelation and cleanse him, and then take a look at the statues he will carve and the murals he will paint and the masterpieces he will produce. Take a Handel with his purposeful effort, his superb talent, his earnest desire to properly depict the story, and give him inward vision of the whole true story and revelation, and what a master you have!

What a great university the BYU now is! A much greater one it can yet become! One of the rich rewards coming from doing great things is the capacity to do still greater things.

The architect Daniel H. Burnham said:

> Make no little plans; they have no magic (there) to stir
>   men's blood
> And probably themselves will not be realized.
> Make big plans; aim high and hope and work,
> Remembering that a noble, logical diagram once recorded
>   will never die,
> But long after we are gone,
> Will be a living thing,
> Asserting itself with ever-growing insistency.
> Remember that our sons and grandsons are going to do
>   things
> That would stagger us.
> Let your watchword be order and your beacon beauty.

The BYU must keep its vessel seaworthy. It must take out all old planks as they decay and put in new and stronger timber in their place. It must sail on and on and on.

And now may we suggest to you as did the commanding officer on the sands of Dunkirk when three hundred thousand troops were hemmed in by enemy tanks and they had to be transported off the beach. Hundreds of men with motorboats and dinghies rushed to help. There were no charts—no time for pep talks or pampering. They were told, "Now off you go and good luck to you—steer for the sound of the guns. No time for loitering. We must be engaged with it."

May God bless this great university and you and us and its impressive student body.

II. Second-Century Address

It was almost precisely eight years ago that I had the privilege of addressing an audience at the Brigham Young University about "Education for Eternity." Some things were said then which I believe, then and now, about the destiny of this unique university. I shall refer to several of those ideas again, combining them with some fresh thoughts and impressions I have concerning Brigham Young University as it enters its second century.

I am grateful to all who made possible the Centennial Celebration for the Brigham Young University, including those who have developed the history of this university in depth. A centennial observance is appropriate, not only to renew our ties with the past, but also to review and reaffirm our goals for the future. My task is to talk about BYU's second century. Though my comments will focus on the Brigham Young University, it is obvious to all of us here that the university is, in many ways, the center of the Church Educational System. President McKay described the University as "the hub of the Church educational wheel." Karl G. Maeser described the Brigham Young Academy as "the parent trunk of the great education banyan tree," and later it has been designated as "the flagship." However it is stated, the centrality of this university to the entire system is a very real fact of life. What I say to you, therefore, must take note of things beyond the borders of this campus but not beyond its influence. We must ever keep firmly in mind the needs of those ever-increasing numbers of LDS youth in other places in North America and in other lands who cannot attend this university, whose needs are real and who represent, in fact, the majority of LDS college and university students.

In a speech I gave to many of the devoted alumni of this university in the Arizona area, I employed a phrase to describe the Brigham Young University as becoming an "educational Everest."

There are many ways in which BYU can tower above other universities—not simply because of the size of its student body or its beautiful campus, but because of the unique light BYU can send forth into the educational world. Your light must have a special glow, for while you will do many things in the programs of this university that are done elsewhere, these same things can and must be done better here than others do them. You will also do some special things here that are left undone by other institutions.

First among these unique features is the fact that education on this campus deliberately and persistently concerns itself with "education for eternity," not just for time. The faculty have a double heritage which they must pass along: the secular knowledge that history has washed to the feet of mankind with the new knowledge brought by scholarly research—but also the vital and revealed truths that have been sent to us from heaven.

This university shares with other universities the hope and the labor involved in rolling back the frontiers of knowledge even further, but we also know through the process of revelation that there are yet "many great and important things" (A of F 1:9) to be given to mankind which will have an intellectual and spiritual impact far beyond what mere men can imagine. Thus, at this university, among faculty, students, and administration, there is and must be an excitement and an expectation about the very nature and future of knowledge that underwrites the uniqueness of BYU.

Your double heritage and dual concerns with the secular and the spiritual require you to be "bilingual." As LDS scholars, you must speak with authority and excellence to your professional colleagues in the language of scholarship, and you must also be literate in the language of spiritual things. We must be more bilingual, in that sense, to fulfill our promise in the second century of BYU.

BYU is being made even more unique, not because what we are doing is changing, but because of the general abandonment by other universities of their efforts to lift the daily behavior and morality of their students.

From the administration of BYU in 1967 came this thought:

> Brigham Young University has been established by the prophets of God and can be operated only on the highest standards of Christian morality. . . . Students who instigate or participate in riots or open rebellion against the policies of the university cannot expect to remain at the university.
>
> The standards of the Church are understood by students who have been taught these standards in the home and at Church throughout their lives.
>
> First and foremost, we expect BYU students to maintain a single standard of Christian morality. . . .
>
> Attendance at BYU is a privilege and not a right, and . . . students who attend must expect to live its standards or forfeit the privilege.[11]

We have no choice at BYU except to "hold the line" regarding gospel standards and values and to draw men and women from other campuses also—all we can—into this same posture, for people entangled in sin are not free. In this university (that may to some of our critics seem unfree), there will be real individual freedom. Freedom from worldly ideologies and concepts unshackles man far more than he knows. It is the truth that sets men free. BYU in its second century must become the last remaining bastion of resistance to the invading ideologies that seek control of curriculum as well as classroom. We do not resist such ideas because we fear them, but because they are false. BYU in its second century must continue to resist false fashions in education, staying with those basic principles which have proved right and have guided good men and women and good universities over the centuries. This concept is not new, but in the second hundred years, we must do it even better.

When the pressures mount for us to follow the false ways of the world, we hope in the years yet future that those who are part of this university and the Church Educational System will not attempt to counsel the board of trustees to follow false ways. We want, through your administration, to receive all your suggestions for making BYU even better. I hope none will presume on the prerogatives of the prophets of God to set the basic direction for this university. No man comes to the demanding position of the Presidency of the Church except his heart and

mind are constantly open to the impressions, insights, and revelations of God. No one is more anxious than the brethren who
stand at the head of this Church to receive such guidance as
the Lord would give them for the benefit of mankind and for the
people of the Church. Thus it is important to remember what
we have in the revelation of the Lord: "And thou shalt not command him who is at thy head, and at the head of the church"
(D&C 28:6).[12] If the governing board has as much loyalty from
faculty and students, from administration and staff as we have
had in the past, I do not fear for the future!

The Church Board of Education and the Brigham Young
University Board of Trustees involve individuals who are committed to truth as well as to the order of the kingdom. I observed
while I was here in 1967 that this institution and its leaders
should be like the Twelve as they were left in a very difficult
world by the Savior: "The world hath hated them, because they
are not of the world, even as I am not of the world. I pray not
that thou shouldest take them out of the world, but that thou
shouldest keep them from the evil. They are not of the world,
even as I am not of the world" (John 17:14–16). This university
is not of the world any more than the Church is of the world,
and it must not be made over in the image of the world.

We hope that our friends, and even our critics, will understand why we must resist anything that would rob BYU of its
basic uniqueness in its second century. As the Church's commissioner of education said on the occasion of the inaugural of
President Dallin Oaks, "Brigham Young University seeks to improve and to 'sanctify' itself for the sake of others—not for the
praise of the world, but to serve the world better."[13]

That task will be persisted in. Members of the Church are
willing to doubly tax themselves to support the Church Educational System, including this university, and we must not merely
"ape the world." We must do special things that would justify
the special financial outpouring that supports this university.

As the late President Stephen L. Richards once said,
"Brigham Young University will never surrender its spiritual
character to a sole concern for scholarship." BYU will be true to
its charter and to such addenda to that charter as are made by
living prophets.

I am both hopeful and expectant that out of this university and the Church Educational System there will rise brilliant stars in drama, literature, music, sculpture, painting, science, and in all the scholarly graces. This university can be the refining host for many such individuals who will touch men and women the world over long after they have left this campus.[14]

We must be patient, however, in this effort, because just as the city of Enoch took decades to reach its pinnacle of performance in what the Lord described as occurring "in process of time" (Moses 7:21), so the quest for excellence at BYU must also occur "in process of time." "Ideals are like stars; you will not succeed in touching them with your hands. But like the seafaring man in the desert of waters, you choose them as your guides, and following them you will reach your destiny."[15]

I see even more than was the case nearly a decade ago a widening gap between this university and other universities both in terms of purposes and in terms of directions. Much has happened in the intervening eight years to make that statement justifiable. More and more is being done, as I hoped it would, to have here "the greatest collection of artifacts, records, writings . . . in the world."[16] BYU is moving toward preeminence in many fields, thanks to the generous support of the tithe payers of the Church and the excellent efforts of its faculty and students under the direction of a wise administration.

These changes do not happen free of pain, challenge, and adjustment. Again, harking back, I expressed the hope that the BYU vessel would be kept seaworthy by taking "out all old planks as they decay and put in new and stronger timber in their place," because the Flagship BYU must sail on and on and on. The creative changes in your academic calendar, your willingness to manage your curriculum more wisely, your efforts to improve general education, your interaction of disciplines across traditional departmental lines, and the creation of new research institutes here on this campus—all are evidences that the captain and crew are doing much to keep the BYU vessel seaworthy and sailing. I refer to the centers of research that have been established on this campus, ranging from family and language research on through to research on food, agriculture, and ancient studies. Much more needs to be done, but you must "not run faster or labor more than you have strength and means provided" (D&C 10:4). While the discovery of new knowledge must increase, there must always be a heavy and primary emphasis on transmitting knowledge—on the quality of teaching at BYU. Quality teaching is a tradition never to be abandoned. It includes a quality relationship between faculty and students. Carry these over into BYU's second century! Brigham Young undoubtedly meant both teaching and learning when he said, "Learn everything that the children of men know, and be prepared for the most refined society upon the face of the earth, then improve upon this until we are prepared and permitted to enter the society of the blessed—the holy angels that dwell in the presence of God."[17]

We must be certain that the lessons are not only taught, but are also absorbed and learned. We remember the directive that President John Taylor made to Karl G. Maeser "that no infidels will go forth from this school."

> Whatever you do, be choice in your selection of teachers. We do not want infidels to mould the minds of our children. They are a precious charge bestowed upon us by the Lord, and we cannot be too careful in rearing and training them. I would rather have my children taught the simple rudiments of a common education by men of God, and have them under their influence, than have them taught in the most abstruse sciences by men who have not the fear of God in their hearts. . . . We need to pay more attention to educational matters, and do all that we can to procure the services of competent teachers. Some people say, we cannot afford to pay them. You cannot afford not to pay them; you cannot afford not to employ them. We want our children to grow up intelligent, and to walk abreast with the peoples of any nation. God expects us to do it; and therefore I call attention to this matter. I have heard intelligent practical men say, it is quite as cheap to keep a good horse as a poor one, or to raise good stock as inferior animals. And is it not quite as cheap to raise good intelligent children as to rear children in ignorance?[18]

Thus we can continue to do as the Prophet Joseph Smith implied that we should when he said, "Man was created to dress the earth, to cultivate his mind, and to glorify God."[19]

We cannot do these things except we continue, in the second century, to be concerned about the spiritual qualities and abilities of those who teach here. In the book of Mosiah we read, "Trust no one to be your teacher nor your minister, except he be a man of God, walking in his ways and keeping his commandments" (Mosiah 23:14).

"I have no fear that the candle lighted in Palestine years ago will ever be put out."[20] We must be concerned with the spiritual worthiness, as well as the academic and professional competency, of all those who come here to teach. William Lyon Phelps said, "I thoroughly believe in a university education for both men and women; but I believe a knowledge of the Bible without a college course is more valuable than a college course without the Bible."[21]

Students in the second century must continue to come here to learn. We do not apologize for the importance of students' searching for eternal companions at the same time that they search the scriptures and search the shelves of libraries for knowledge. President David O. McKay observed on one occasion that "this university is not a dictionary, a dispensary, nor is it a department store. It is more than a storehouse of knowledge and more than a community of scholars. University life is essentially an exercise in thinking, preparing, and living."[22] We do not want BYU ever to become an educational factory. It must concern itself not only with the dispensing of facts, but with the preparation of its students to take their place in society as thinking, thoughtful, and sensitive individuals who, in paraphrasing the motto of your centennial, come here dedicated to love of God, pursuit of truth, and service to mankind.

There are yet other reasons why we must not lose either our moorings or our sense of direction in the second century. We still have before us the remarkable prophecy of John Taylor when he observed, "You will see the day that Zion will be as far ahead of the outside world in everything pertaining to learning of every kind as we are today in regard to religious matters. You mark my words, and write them down, and see if they do not come to pass."[23] Surely we cannot refuse that rendezvous with history because so much of what is desperately needed by mankind is bound up in our being willing to contribute to the fulfillment of that prophecy. Others, at times, also seem to have a sensing of what might happen. Charles H. Malik, former president of the United Nations General Assembly, voiced a fervent hope when he said that

> one day a great university will arise somewhere, . . . I hope in America, . . . to which Christ will return in His full glory and power, a university which will, in the promotion of scientific, intellectual, and artistic excellence, surpass by far even the best secular universities of the present, but which will at the same time enable Christ to bless it and act and feel perfectly at home in it.[24]

Surely BYU can help respond to that call!

By dealing with basic issues and basic problems, we can be effective educationally. Otherwise, we will simply join the multitude who have so often lost their way in dark, sunless forests even while working hard. It was Thoreau who said, "There are a thousand hacking at the branches of evil to one who is striking at the root."[25] We should deal statistically and spiritually with root problems, root issues, and root causes in BYU's second century. We seek to do so, not in arrogance or pride, but in the spirit of service. We must do so with a sense of trembling and urgency, because what Edmund Burke said is true: "The only thing necessary for the triumph of evil is for good men to do nothing."[26]

Learning that includes familiarization with facts must not occur in isolation from concern over our fellowmen. It must occur in the context of a commitment to serve them and to reach out to them.

In many ways, the dreams that were once generalized as American dreams have diminished and faded. Some of these dreams have now passed so far as institutional thrust is concerned to The Church of Jesus Christ of Latter-day Saints and its people for their fulfillment. It was Lord Acton who said on one occasion,

> It was from America that the plain ideas that men ought to mind their own business, and that the nation is responsible to Heaven for the acts of the State—ideas long locked in the breast of solitary thinkers, and hidden among Latin folios—burst forth like a conqueror upon the world they were destined to transform, under the title of the Rights of

Man. . . . The principle gained ground, that a nation can
never abandon its fate to an authority it cannot control.[27]

Too many universities have given themselves over to such massive federal funding that they should not wonder why they have
submitted to an authority they can no longer control. Far too
many no longer assume that nations are responsible to heaven
for the acts of the state. Far too many now see the Rights of
Man as merely access rights to the property and money of others,
and not as the rights traditionally thought of as being crucial to
our freedom.[28]

It will take just as much sacrifice and dedication to preserve these principles in the second century of BYU and even
more than were required to begin this institution in the first
place—when it was once but a grade school and then an academy supported by a stake of the Church. If we were to abandon our ideals, would there be any left to take up the torch of
some of the principles I have attempted to describe?

I am grateful, therefore, that, as President Oaks observed,
"There is no anarchy of values at Brigham Young University."
There never has been. There never will be. But we also know, as
President Joseph Fielding Smith observed in speaking on this
campus, that knowledge comes both by reason and by revelation. We expect the natural unfolding of knowledge to occur as
a result of scholarship, but there will always be that added
dimension which the Lord can provide when we are qualified to
receive and he chooses to speak: "A time to come in the which
nothing shall be withheld, whether there be one God or many
gods, they shall be manifest." And further, "All thrones and
dominions, principalities and powers, shall be revealed and set
forth upon all who have endured valiantly for the gospel of
Jesus Christ" (D&C 121:28, 29).

As the pursuit of excellence continues on this campus and
elsewhere in the Church Educational System, we must remember the great lesson taught to Oliver Cowdery, who desired a
special outcome—just as we desire a remarkable blessing and
outcome for BYU in the second century. Oliver Cowdery
wished to be able to translate with ease and without real effort.
He was reminded that he erred, in that he "took no thought
save it was to ask" (D&C 9:7). We must do more than ask the

Lord for excellence. Perspiration must precede inspiration; there must be effort before there is excellence. We must do more than pray for these outcomes at BYU, though we must surely pray. We must take thought. We must make effort. We must be patient. We must be professional. We must be spiritual. Then, in the process of time, this will become the fully anointed university of the Lord about which so much has been spoken in the past.

We can sometimes make concord with others, including scholars who have parallel purposes. By reaching out to the world of scholars, to thoughtful men and women everywhere who share our concerns and at least some of the items on our agendum of action, we can multiply our influence and give hope to others who may assume that they are alone.

In other instances, we must be willing to break with the educational establishment (not foolishly or cavalierly, but thoughtfully and for good reason) in order to find gospel ways to help mankind. Gospel methodology, concepts, and insights can help us to do what the world cannot do in its own frame of reference.

In some ways, the Church Educational System, in order to be unique in the years that lie ahead, may have to break with certain patterns of the educational establishment. When the world has lost its way on matters of principle, we have an obligation to point the way. We can, as Brigham Young hoped we would, "be a people of profound learning pertaining to the things of this world"[29] but without being tainted by what he regarded as the "pernicious, atheistic influences"[30] that flood in unless we are watchful. Our scholars, therefore, must be sentries as well as teachers!

We surely cannot give up our concerns with character and conduct without also giving up on mankind. Much misery results from flaws in character, not from failures in technology. We cannot give in to the ways of the world with regard to the realm of art. President Romney brought this to our attention not long ago in a quotation in which Brigham Young said there is "no music in hell."[31] Our art must be the kind which edifies man, which takes into account his immortal nature, and which prepares us for heaven, not hell.

One peak of educational excellence that is highly relevant to the needs of the Church is the realm of language. BYU should become the acknowledged language capital of the world in terms of our academic competency and through the marvelous "laboratory" that sends young men and women forth to service in the mission field. I refer, of course, to the Missionary Training Center. There is no reason why this university could not become the place where, perhaps more than anywhere else, the concern for literacy and the teaching of English as a second language is firmly headquartered in terms of unarguable competency as well as deep concern.

I have mentioned only a few areas. There are many others of special concern, with special challenges and opportunities for accomplishment and service in the second century.

We can do much in excellence and, at the same time, emphasize the large-scale participation of our students, whether it be in athletics or in academic events. We can bless many and give many experience, while at the same time we are developing the few select souls who can take us to new heights of attainment.

It ought to be obvious to you, as it is to me, that some of the things the Lord would have occur in the second century of the BYU are hidden from our immediate view. Until we have climbed the hill just before us, we are not apt to be given a glimpse of what lies beyond. The hills ahead are higher than we think. This means that accomplishments and further direction must occur in proper order, after we have done our part. We will not be transported from point A to point Z without having to pass through the developmental and demanding experiences of all the points of achievement and all the milestone markers that lie between!

This university will go forward. Its students are idealists who have integrity, who love to work in good causes. These students will not only have a secular training, but will have come to understand what Jesus meant when he said that the key of knowledge, which had been lost by society centuries before, was "the fulness of the scriptures" (D&C 42:15). We understand, as few people do, that education is a part of being about our Father's business and that the scriptures contain the master concepts for mankind.

We know there are those of unrighteous purposes who boast that time is on their side. So it may seem to those of very limited vision. But of those engaged in the Lord's work, it can be truly said, "Eternity is on your side! Those who fight that bright future fight in vain!"

I hasten to add that as the Church grows global and becomes more and more multicultural a smaller and smaller percentage of all our LDS college-age students will attend BYU, or the Hawaii campus, or Ricks College, or the LDS Business College. It is a privileged group who are able to come here. We do not intend to neglect the needs of the other Church members wherever they are, but those who do come here have an even greater follow-through responsibility to make certain that the Church's investment in them provides dividends through service and dedication to others as they labor in the Church and in the world elsewhere.

> To go to BYU is something special. There were Brethren who had dreams regarding the growth and maturity of Brigham Young University, even to the construction of a temple on the hill they had long called Temple Hill, yet "dreams and prophetic utterances are not self-executing. They are fulfilled usually by righteous and devoted people making the prophecies come true."[32]

So much of our counsel given to you here today as you begin your second century is the same counsel we give to others in the Church concerning other vital programs—you need to lengthen your stride, quicken your step, and (to use President N. Eldon Tanner's phrase) continue your journey. You are headed in the right direction! Such academic adjustments as need to be made will be made out of the individual and collective wisdom we find when a dedicated faculty interacts with a wise administration, an inspired governing board, and an appreciative body of students.

I am grateful that the Church can draw upon the expertise that exists here. The pockets of competency that are here will be used by the Church increasingly and in various ways.

We want you to keep free as a university—free of government control, not only for the sake of this university and the Church, but also for the sake of our government. Our government, state and federal, and our people are best served by free colleges and universities, not by institutions that are compliant out of fears over funding.[33]

We look forward to developments in your computer-assisted translation projects and from the Ezra Taft Benson Agriculture and Food Institute. We look forward to more being done in the field of education, in the fine arts, in the J. Reuben Clark Law School, in the Graduate School of Management, and in the realm of human behavior.

We appreciate the effectiveness of the programs here. But we must do better in order to be better, and we must be better for the sake of the world!

As previous First Presidencies have said, and we say again to you, we expect (we do not simply hope) that Brigham Young University will "become a leader among the great universities of the world." To that expectation I would add, "Become a unique university in all of the world!"[34]

III. Installation of and Charge to the President

Members of the General Authorities and board of trustees, Elder Maxwell, President Holland and faculty, students, and friends of Brigham Young University, greetings. I extend a warm welcome to all of you on this historic and happy occasion—the inaugural of Dr. Jeffrey R. Holland as the ninth president of Brigham Young University.

First, I wish to congratulate and commend my dear friend Dr. Dallin Oaks and his predecessors, who have brought this great university from a small and humble beginning to the high point at which it now stands. Marvelous has been their labor and devoted has been their service. With all our hearts, we thank President Oaks and the great men who preceded him. We honor them and rejoice in their many accomplishments.

My beloved brothers and sisters, it is my responsibility and my privilege to give to President Holland his charge as he begins his presidency at this great university. I do so representing the First Presidency and the Board of Trustees.

May I say to you, President Holland, that we love you and sustain you and rejoice in your worthiness to hold such a responsible position in the Lord's kingdom. Your academic achievements are well known. They, together with your spiritual preparation and your great testimony and faith, will bless the lives of this splendid faculty and the students. We commend your lovely wife and children for their support. They are your greatest treasure and will be a shining example to the youth of this university.

In some remarks I made at this university in 1975, I employed a phrase to describe the Brigham Young University as becoming an "educational Mt. Everest." First, it seems to us, President Holland, that such a term was never more appropriate than it is now, on the occasion of your inauguration, for such is your challenge. There are many ways in which BYU can tower above other universities—not simply because of the size of its student body or its beautiful campus spread out below magnificent mountains—but by the unique light BYU can send forth into the educational world. That light must have a special glow. You will do many things in the programs of this university that are done elsewhere, but you must do them better. At the same time, we expect you to do some special things here at BYU that are left undone by other institutions.

Second, education on this campus deliberately and persistently must concern itself with "education for eternity," not just for mortal time. You and your faculty have a dual heritage which you must pass along: the secular knowledge that history has amassed over the centuries, along with new knowledge brought by scholarly research—but also the vital and revealed truths that have been given to us from heaven.

This university shares with other universities the hope and the labor involved in rolling back the frontiers of knowledge, but we also know that, through divine revelation, there are yet "many great and important things" (A of F 1:9) to be given to mankind which will have an intellectual and spiritual impact far beyond what mere men can imagine. Thus, at this university among faculty, students, and administration, there is, and there must be, an excitement and an expectation about the very nature and future of knowledge. That underlies the uniqueness of BYU.

Third, BYU must be a bastion against the invading ideologies that seek control of curriculum as well as classroom. We do not resist such ideas because we fear them, but because they are false. BYU must continue to resist false and capricious fashions in education, holding fast to those basic principles which have proved true and right and have guided good men and women and good universities over the centuries.

Fourth, I am both hopeful and expectant that from this university there will rise brilliant starts in drama, literature, music, art, science, and all the scholarly graces. This university can be the refining host for many such individuals who, in the future, long after they have left this campus, can lift and inspire others around the globe. We must be patient as well as persistent in this effort because, just as the city of Enoch took time to reach its pinnacle of performance in what the Lord described as occurring "in process of time" (Moses 7:21), so the quest for excellence at BYU must also occur "in process of time."

Fifth, quality teaching is a tradition never to be abandoned. It included a trusting relationship between faculty and students. Continue these in your new administration. We remember the directive that President John Taylor made to Karl G. Maeser: "Whatever you do, be choice in your selection of teachers. We do not want infidels to mould the minds of our children."[35] In the book of Mosiah, we read, "Trust no one to be your teacher nor your minister, except he be a man of God, walking in his ways and keeping his commandments" (Mosiah 23:14).

Sixth, remember that, as the Church grows globally and becomes more and more multicultural, a smaller and smaller percentage of our LDS college-age students will attend BYU or the other Church schools. More and more, it will be a privileged group who are able to come here. Those who are blessed to attend BYU have a great responsibility to make certain that the Church's investment in them provides dividends through service and dedication to others as they labor in the Church and in the world. Your challenge is to assure that this investment does bear fruit, "a consummation devoutly to be wished."[36]

Lastly, it should be obvious to us all that the ultimate future of BYU is partially hidden from our immediate view. Until we have climbed the hills just ahead, we cannot glimpse what lies beyond. And the hills ahead are higher than we think. We cannot be transported over them without meeting demanding challenges. Such will be your challenge, President Holland. You must fortify yourself to guide this great university by wisdom and by inspiration. You will not always be able to see the future, but by drawing close to our Heavenly Father, you will be guided. This is his work. This is his university. You are his servant. You are on his errand.

As previous First Presidencies have said, we say again to you, "We expect—we do not merely hope—that Brigham Young University will become a leader among the great universities of the world." To that expectation, I would add, "Remain a unique university in all the world!"[37] Then, in the process of time, this truly will become the fully recognized university of the Lord about which so much has been spoken in the past.

Your feet are planted on the right path, and you are headed in the right direction! Such academic adjustments as need to be made will be made out of the individual and collective wisdom we find when a dedicated faculty works with a wise administration, an inspired governing board of trustees, and appreciative and responsive students.

Dr. Jeffrey R. Holland, representing the Church Board of Education and the Board of Trustees, I officially install you as the new president of Brigham Young University. I invoke the blessings of our Heavenly Father upon you and your family. May you go forward with enthusiasm and great courage, knowing you are loved by him and by us, your fellow servants.

Part I, "Education for Eternity," was given at the annual faculty workshop at Brigham Young University on September 12, 1967, when Spencer W. Kimball was a member of the Quorum of the Twelve Apostles. Part II, "Second-Century Address," was delivered on October 10, 1975, at the Founder's Day Convocation. Published in *BYU Studies* 16, no. 4 (1976): 445–57. Minor deletions have been made where quotations used in this address were also used in the previous address, "Education for Eternity." Part III, "Installation of and Charge to the President," was given at the inauguration of Jeffrey R. Holland as president of Brigham Young University on November 14, 1980. President Kimball was President of the Church when he gave these last two speeches.

NOTES

[1]David O. McKay, "The Spiritual Life, the True Life of Man," *Instructor* 102 (September 1967): 338.

[2]Brigham Young, in *Journal of Discourses,* 26 vols. (Liverpool: F. D. Richards, 1855–86), 16:77, May 25, 1873 (hereafter cited as *JD*). For more on this topic, see page 68.

[3]Young, in *JD,* 9:369, August 31, 1862.

[4]J. Reuben Clark Jr., source unknown. For a partial citation, see James R. Clark, *Messages of the First Presidency* (Salt Lake City: Deseret Book, 1965), 6:238.

[5]This topic is discussed further on page 65.

[6]J. Reuben Clark Jr., source unknown.

[7]Reinhard Maeser, *Karl G. Maeser* (Provo, Utah: Brigham Young University, 1928), 79.

[8]John Taylor, in *JD,* 21:100, April 13, 1879. See also discussion on page 69.

[9]Taylor, in *JD,* 20:47, August 4, 1878.

[10]Young, in *JD,* 10:224, April and May 1863.

[11]Ernest L. Wilkinson, address delivered at Brigham Young University, July 1967.

[12]See also page 52.

[13]Neal A. Maxwell, "Greetings to the President," address delivered at the inaugural of President Dallin H. Oaks, 1971.

[14]See also pages 55–62.

[15]Carl Schurz, address delivered at Faneuil Hall, Boston, April 18, 1975.

[16]President Kimball quotes his earlier address, "Education for Eternity"; see page 60 above.

[17]Young, in *JD,* 16:77, May 25, 1873. See also page 47.

[18]Taylor, in *JD,* 24:168–69, May 19, 1883. See also page 77.

[19]Joseph Smith Jr., quoted in Leonard J. Arrington, foreword to *Brigham Young University: The First Hundred Years,* ed. Ernest L. Wilkinson, vol. 1 (Provo, Utah: Brigham Young University Press, 1975), ix.

[20]William R. Inge, source unknown.

[21]William Lyon Phelps, *Human Nature in the Bible* (New York: Charles Scribner's Sons, 1923), ix.

[22]David O. McKay, *Gospel Ideals* (Salt Lake City: Improvement Era, 1953), 346.

[23]Taylor, in *JD,* 21:100, April 13, 1887. See also page 55.

[24]Charles H. Malik, "Education and Upheaval: The Christian's Responsibility," *Creative Help for Daily Living,* September 21, 1970.

[25]Henry David Thoreau, *Walden* (New York: Norton, 1966), 51.

[26]Edmund Burke to William Smith, January 9, 1975.

[27]John Emerich Edward Dahlberg, Lord Acton, *The History of Freedom and Other Essays* (London: MacMillan, 1907), 55–56.

[28]See also page 74.

[29]Young, in *JD,* 8:40, April 8, 1860.

[30]Leonard J. Arrington, "Seven Steps to Greatness," *BYU Studies* 16, no. 4 (1976): 461.

[31]Young, in *JD,* 9:244, March 6, 1862.

[32]Wilkinson, *Brigham Young University.*

[33]See also page 71.

[34]See also page 78.

[35]Taylor, in *JD,* 24:168–69, May 19, 1883. See page 68 above for full quotation.

[36]William Shakespeare, *Hamlet,* act 3, scene 1.

[37]See also page 75.

An Eternal Quest—
Freedom of the Mind

Hugh B. Brown

I should like to refer for just a minute to comments that have been made about the Brigham Young University by those who see us from the outside. There is an article called "The Mormons" from a Catholic bulletin of Williston Park, New York.

> In the Nixon cabinet there are two fellows. Tip your hats. David Kennedy and George Romney are Mormons. They are strict. They don't smoke or drink. They give ten percent of all they earn to the Mormon Church. They have earned a lot of money. Romney gave a year of his life to spreading the Mormon faith in England.
>
> Respect the Mormons. Their theology is out of this world. Fantastic. Incredible. But they make men who deserve our respect. In spite of the fact that there are only a few million Mormons . . . maybe it is good that Nixon put these men in positions of power.[1]

That is a nice compliment coming from our Catholic friends. And this is from the *Chicago Tribune*:

> As the dust settles at some campuses and others prepare to meet their own unmakers, it is refreshing to take a look at Brigham Young University in Provo, Utah. . . .
>
> It is a religious school run by the Mormon church and has a long tradition of discipline. We're not saying that every college can or should adopt its rigid rules against drinking and even smoking; but the fact that these

rules are adhered to without riotous protests suggests a respect for authority and tradition that is rapidly disappearing at other institutions with vastly more years and tradition behind them.[2]

I would also like to read some words by the Honorable John Gardner, former secretary of health, education, and welfare under Lyndon B. Johnson, having to do with current problems:

> The possibility of coherent community action is diminished today by the deep mutual suspicions and antagonisms among various groups in our national life.
>
> As these antagonisms become more intense, the pathology is much the same. . . . The ingredients are, first, a deep conviction on the part of the group as to its own limitless virtue or the overriding sanctity of its cause; second, grave doubts concerning the moral integrity of all others; third, a chronically aggrieved feeling that power has fallen into the hands of the unworthy (that is, the hands of others). . . .
>
> Political extremism involves two prime ingredients: An excessively simple diagnosis of the world's ills and a conviction that there are identifiable villains back of it all. . . . Blind belief in one's cause and a low view of the morality of other Americans—these seem mild failings. But they are the soil in which ranker weeds take root . . . terrorism, and the deep, destructive cleavages that paralyze a society.[3]

And James Reston gives us a summary of the situation as it appears today in the United States and other countries: "Almost everywhere we look these days, authority is under challenge: the authority of the family, the church, the university, the community, and the state."

Much has been said on this campus, from this rostrum, and throughout the United States about sustaining authority, upholding elected officials, believing in our own country, and emphasizing the good as against the evil. [President Brown here quotes a lengthy statement from the First Presidency on true patriotism and honoring the law, including serving in the armed forces, dated May 12, 1969. He then quotes Abraham Lincoln on reverence for the law and Dwight D. Eisenhower and other presidents on the United Nations.]

President Hugh B. Brown (center) with President David O. McKay (left) and BYU President Ernest L. Wilkinson (right) at a Church College of Hawaii (now BYU Hawaii) commencement. Courtesy BYU Archives.

One of the most important things in the world is freedom of the mind; from this all other freedoms spring. Such freedom is necessarily dangerous, for one cannot think right without running the risk of thinking wrong, but generally more thinking is the antidote for the evils that spring from wrong thinking. More thinking is required, and we call upon you students to exercise your God-given right to think through every proposition that is submitted to you and to be unafraid to express your opinions, with proper respect for those to whom you talk and proper acknowledgment of your own shortcomings.

We live in an age when freedom of the mind is suppressed over much of the world. We must preserve this freedom in the Church and in America and resist all efforts of earnest men to suppress it, for when it is suppressed, we might lose the liberties vouchsafed in the Constitution of the United States.

Preserve, then, the freedom of your mind in education and in religion, and be unafraid to express your thoughts and to insist upon your right to examine every proposition. We are not so much concerned with whether your thoughts are orthodox or heterodox as we are that you shall have thoughts. One may memorize much without learning anything. In this age of speed, there seems to be little time for meditation.

Dissatisfaction with what is around us is not a bad thing if it prompts us to seek betterment, but the best sort of dissatisfaction in the long run is self-dissatisfaction, which leads us to improve ourselves. Maturity implies the ability to walk alone and not be ashamed within ourselves of the things we do and say.

Progress in maturity may be measured by our acceptance of increased self-responsibility and an increased sagacity in decision making. This transition is not a time of calm enjoyment, but of growth and adaptation.

One matures as a person by responding differently today from the way in which one responded yesterday. We observe restraint so that restraints do not have to be imposed upon us; we do our best to think clearly so that we avoid chasing after false doctrines; we use deliberation so as to see through non-sense; we realize our social duty to the honest opinions of others while maintaining our own principles.

Self-discipline—and that is a subject on which I think I have some right to speak because of my military training and experience—means doing things you would rather not do but having the courage to do them if they are right. When a course of action shows itself to be unprofitable, it is sensible and valorous to drop it.

There is no personal value in making a show of maturity if you do not have it. Affectation of any sort borders on vulgarity, and at the least, it is ridiculous to pretend to feelings and beliefs that do not appeal to your intelligence.

On the other hand, no mature person will be content to sit by the side of the road and watch the world go by. One cannot be merely a bystander, doing nothing but criticize.

When a human being finds a dead end, it is tempting to turn to that last desperate resource of muddled humankind: lawlessness. People do not realize the unprofitableness in delinquency and the low standard of living to which it condemns them. They may even imagine themselves as martyrs in some trivial or irrelevant cause. This hooliganism brings discredit to the peaceful, legitimate, and often courageous protests by young people on great moral issues.

Society is indulgent toward young people, but there are limits to permissibility. Youth is right to repudiate sham and hypocrisy, but to assume that disorder and chaos have merit in themselves is to assume that we are no longer capable of reasoning together in search of the right solution of problems.

You students have strong desires. You are not content to live a merely miscellaneous life, however pleasurable it may be. You dream beyond the actual and think beyond your fingertips. In doing so, you are living up to the great law of culture: that people shall become all that they are created capable of becoming.

While we speak of independence and the right to think, to agree or to disagree, to examine and to question, we must not forget that fixed and unchanging laws govern all God's creations, whether it be in the vastness of the starry heavens, in the minute revolving universe of the atom, or in human relationships. All is law. All is cause and effect, and God's laws are universal. God has no favorites; no one is immune from either life's temptations or the consequences of personal deeds. God is not capricious.

Our reactions to the ever-changing impacts of life will depend upon our goals, our ideals. "The vision that you glorify in your mind, the ideal that you enthrone in your heart, this you will build your life by, this you will become." Every life coheres around certain fundamental core ideas, whether we realize it or not, and herein lies the chief value of revealed religion. But while I believe all that God has revealed, I am not quite sure that I understand what he has revealed. The fact that he has promised further revelation is to me a challenge to keep an open mind and to be prepared to follow wherever my search for truth may lead. You young people have been attending a school presided over by the President of the Church, a school established by a prophet of God, a school where your eternal welfare is ever foremost in the minds of your professors, your administration, the faculty, and others. Our reactions to the ever-changing impacts of life will depend upon our goals and our ideals. And I would like to leave that thought with you to ponder.

Again I emphasize, there is no final goal. Life must continue to expand, to unfold, and to grow, if it is to continue to be a good life. These things are indispensable, and in this connection age makes little difference. There is opportunity for all to expand and to grow and to be and to become.

There are forces at work in our society today which degrade an intellectual quest for knowledge. These forces are nothing new. They have always been powerful. They are anti-intellectual. Forces in this country and in other countries are known and grappled with, but they are making headway. The know-nothings of the last century in this country could be cited as but one example. Germany in the thirties saw the burning of books and the glorification of barbaric emotion as part of the tragedy of Hitlerism.

We have been blessed with much knowledge by revelation from God which, in some part, the world lacks. But there is an incomprehensibly greater part of truth which we must yet discover. Our revealed truth should leave us stricken with the knowledge of how little we really know. It should never lead to an emotional arrogance based upon a false assumption that we somehow have all the answers—that we in fact have a corner on truth, for we do not.

Whether you are in the field of economics or political science, history or the behavioral sciences, continue your search for truth. And maintain humility sufficient to be able to revise your hypotheses as new truth comes to you by means of the spirit or the mind. Salvation, like education, is an ongoing process.

One may not attain salvation by merely acknowledging allegiance, nor is it available in ready-to-wear stores or in supermarkets where it may be bought and paid for. That it is an eternal quest must be obvious to all. Education is involved in salvation and may be had only by evolution or the unfolding or developing into our potential. It is in large measure a problem of awareness, of reaching out and looking up, of aspiring and becoming, of pushing back our horizons, of seeking for answers, and of searching for God. In other words, it is not merely a matter of conforming to rituals, climbing sacred stairs, bathing in sacred pools, or making pilgrimages to ancient shrines. The depth and height and quality of life depend upon awareness, and awareness is a process of being saved from ignorance. Human beings cannot be saved in ignorance.

We today not only enjoy many advantages and comforts unknown to former generations, but we suffer many trials and cope with many problems which did not plague our forefathers. We are puzzled by the frictions and the deficiencies of our society.

I think the expression "Keep it cool" is peculiar to your age, but it means in reality "Do not be impatient." Too many young people are so impatient that when they press an electric button, they can't wait for the answer. They think there is a gap somewhere, and they think it is because of the old folks that don't know enough to press the button.

Historians, philosophers, and scientists all agree that life on this earth has been and is one continuous, never-ceasing process of readjustment.

Your generation is maturing in body and mind at an earlier age than did preceding generations, and as you become aware of that fact, you are inclined to become critical of the older generation—sometimes with justification. We are not here to defend ourselves against you; we are here to let you know some things we have learned the hard way—sometimes by sad experience.

For almost all young people, adolescence means one thing above all else: they must prove that they are no longer children. They are fighting to establish themselves as a person. When choice is to be made of a course of action or a deed, choose that which has significance. Every youth is forced to answer the question in dialogue with himself: "What are the things that I ultimately value?" The answer must come with this thought in mind: "I will have to live with myself all my life, and what I decide now will influence my happiness."

As you go forward in your search for truth and as you espouse principles and establish ideals toward which to work, pray for courage to be true to your loyalties, to your ideals, and to yourself. It has been said that those who know the precepts and neglect to obey them are like those who light a candle in the darkness and then close their eyes. Remember, there is a power greater than yourselves upon which you may call. It is the gospel that Paul declared to be the power of God unto salvation. There is a power available to all which, when understood and utilized, will lead to salvation.

I am going to have to shorten what I had thought of saying, because I want to leave with you at the end a statement from my heart. You are going home shortly, many of you. This, I understand, is the final devotional assembly to be held on the campus this spring. I want you to take with you to your homes and to your families the spirit of the gospel of Christ. It makes it possible for you to participate in the things around you. The organization of stakes and wards on this campus has enabled thousands of young people to become active in the Church and, thereby, to open their eyes and their understanding. This question of participation was impressed upon my own mind years ago, when I was acting as coordinator for servicemen.

I want to tell you this story to emphasize the value of participation.

While I was acting as servicemen's coordinator, I was in London, England. I sent the following telegram to the senior chaplain of a large camp near Liverpool: "I'll be in your camp tomorrow morning at 10:00. Kindly notify all Mormon boys in your camp that we'll hold a meeting."

When I arrived the next morning, I met seventy-five young men, all in uniform. They were delighted to see me, although I knew none of them. They were glad to see someone from home.

There stepped out from the crowd a man who, after shaking hands, said, "I'm the one to whom you sent your telegram. I'm the chaplain of this camp. I didn't get your telegram until this morning [that is, Sunday morning]. Upon receipt of it, I made an inquiry—a careful inquiry. I found there were seventy-six Mormon boys in this camp. Seventy-five of them are here; one is in the hospital."

He said, "I wish you'd tell me, Mr. Brown, how you do it. I have six hundred men in my church in this camp, and if I gave them six months' notice they couldn't meet that record. Tell me how you do it."

"Well," I said, "if you come into our meeting, we'll show you how we do it." And so he accompanied me into the quonset hut, and before us sat these seventy-five young men. I had the minister sit next to me.

I said, "How many of you fellows have been on missions?" Fully 50 percent of them raised their hands. I pointed to six of them and said, "Come here and administer the sacrament." I pointed to six others and said, "Come here and be prepared to speak." I looked at my friend, the minister, and he had his mouth open. He had never seen such a thing.

And then I said, "Fellows, what shall we sing this morning?" And with one voice they said, "Come, Come, Ye Saints!" And I said, "Who can lead the music?" and most of them raised their hands. I selected one. "Who can play this portable organ?" And again there was a fine showing, and one was selected.

We didn't have any books, but the man at the organ sounded a chord, and those young men stood, shoulders back and chins pulled in, and they sang all the verses of "Come, Come, Ye Saints." I have heard that sung all over the Church many times, even by the Tabernacle Choir, to whom I apologize for what I am going to say. I have never heard "Come, Come, Ye Saints" sung with such fervor, such conviction, such power as those young men sang it. When they came to that last verse, "And should we die before our journey's through, happy day, all is well," I tell you it was thrilling. And as I looked at my friend again, I found him weeping.

After the prayer, one of the boys knelt at the sacrament table and said, "O God, the Eternal Father," and then he paused for what seemed to be a full minute before proceeding. At the close of the meeting, I went and looked him up. I put my arm across his shoulder and said, "What's the matter, lad?"

He said, "Why?"

"Well, you seemed to have difficulty in asking a blessing on the bread. Has something happened?"

"Well, sir," he said, "a few hours ago I was over Germany and France on a bombing mission. We had made our run, left our calling cards [meaning the bombs], and when we gained altitude and were about to return across the channel, we ran into heavy flak. My tail assembly was pretty well shot away, one of my engines was out, a number of my crew were wounded, and it looked like a hopeless situation. It seemed like no power in heaven or earth could get us back across the channel to a landing field. But," he said, "Brother Brown, up there I remembered what my mother had said to me. [And this I want to say to this vast audience, both those that are here and those that are listening in.] This is what my mother said, 'If ever you find yourself in a situation where man can't help you, call on God.' I had been told that same thing in Primary, in the seminaries, in Sunday School: 'If ever you need help and man can't help you, call on God.' Although it seemed hopeless and impossible, I said, 'O God, the Eternal Father, please sustain this ship until we get back into England.' . . . Brother Brown, he did just that.

"When I heard of this meeting I ran all the way to get here, and when I knelt at the table and named his name again, I remembered shamefully that I had not stopped to say 'thank you.' And that's the reason I paused, to express my gratitude for the goodness of God."

Well, we went on with our meeting, and these young men spoke, and they spoke with power and conviction. Every one who heard them was thrilled by the evidence of their faith, and my friend, the chaplain, continued to weep. When they had finished talking, I said, "Fellows, we'll have to dismiss." (That meeting was not like this; it had to be dismissed on time.) I said, "We'll have to dismiss, or you won't get any chow."

They said, "We can have chow any time. Let's have a testimony meeting."

"Why," I said, "if you have a testimony meeting, you'll be here another two hours."

They repeated with one voice, "Please let us have a testimony meeting."

I turned to my friend, the minister, and said, "Now I know this is unusual for you. We've been here two hours, and we're going to be here another two hours. We'll excuse you if you prefer to withdraw."

He put his hand on my knee and said, "Please, Sir, may I remain?" And of course I encouraged him to stay, and then for two solid hours those young men, one after another, stood up and bore witness of the truth of the gospel. My only job was to say, "You're next, and then you, and then you," because all of them wanted to get up at once. It was a glorious occasion.

Finally there came an end. We dismissed, and this minister turned to me and said, "Mr. Brown, I have been a minister of the gospel for twenty-one years, but this has been the greatest spiritual experience of my life." And again he said, "How do you do it? How did you know which of those fellows to call on?"

I replied, "It didn't make any difference which one I called on. They are all prepared. And this could happen in any camp anywhere in the world where there are seventy-five young Mormon boys."

I relate this to you, my dear students, that you may realize the value of participation, the value of a conviction of the truth, and that you may take advantage of every opportunity to bear witness to that truth.

I bear my witness to you now, as you leave for home and as time goes on; I do not know that I will be here again, and that doesn't matter much as far as you are concerned. But I want to leave this witness with you. I am too old to try to deceive you— I have one foot in the grave and am waiting to kick the bucket with the other. But this I want to say to you before I leave, and I say it with apologies for holding you a moment.

With all the fervor of my soul, I know that God lives, that he is a reality, that he is a personality; that Jesus of Nazareth is and was and will ever be the Son of God, the Redeemer, and

the Savior of the world. I know that better than I know anything else, and I say with Peter of old who was asked, "Whom
say ye that I am?" He replied, as I reply. He replied with the
same authority with which I speak, "Thou art the Christ,
the Son of the living God." And he was told by the Master
what I have been told by him as well, "Flesh and blood hath
not revealed it unto thee, but my Father which is in heaven"
(Matthew 16:15–17).

God bless you, my dear fellow students.

This address was given to the BYU student body on May 13, 1969,
when Hugh B. Brown was First Counselor in the First Presidency.

NOTES

[1]*St. Aidan's Bulletin,* March 2, 1969.
[2]*Chicago Tribune,* Sunday, May 4, 1969.
[3]John Gardner, *No Easy Victories* (New York: Harper and Row,
1969), 8, 9.

Installation of and Charge to the President

Harold B. Lee

May I begin by citing the Lord's own charge to this Church and the world: "And even so I have sent mine everlasting covenant into the world, to be a light to the world, and to be a standard for my people, and for the Gentiles to seek to it, and to be a messenger before my face to prepare the way before me" (D&C 45:9). When the meaning of this revelation is understood, it should be a reminder that every institution which is a part of the kingdom of God must keep in mind the purpose of the restored gospel—to be that light to the world and a standard for this people and all men to seek.

Brigham Young University, led by its president, must never forget its role in bringing to reality the ancient prophecy—to build the mountain of the Lord's house in the tops of the mountains, so great and so glorious that all nations may come to this place and be constrained to say, "Show us your way that we may walk therein" (see Isa. 2:3).

Constantly remember that profound and oft-repeated admonition of the Apostle James: "If any of you lack wisdom, let him ask of God, that giveth to all men liberally, and upbraideth not; and it shall be given him. But let him ask in faith, nothing wavering. For he that wavereth is like a wave of the sea driven with the wind and tossed" (James 1:5–6).

It will be remembered that obedient to that instruction, the fourteen-year-old boy Joseph Smith, in a quest for truth, was led to seek in fervent prayer to Almighty God the answer to

President Harold B. Lee at the dedication of the J. Willard Marriott
Center, February 1973. Courtesy Mark A. Philbrick/BYU.

a burning question which caused him great concern. The answer to that question, delivered in the Sacred Grove, commenced the ushering in of the dispensation of the fullness of times. This instruction is applicable to all of us as we seek to find the answers to unsolved problems and seek for guidance beyond the wisdom of men. You, too, must many times go to your Sacred Grove in your quest of truth.

As you meet challenging problems, see, as it were, written on the darkened walls of your sequestered chamber, the words of heavenly wisdom, which will give you the assurance that you can place your trust in God and leave the rest with him.

When you stand at the crossroads of two alternative decisions, remember what the Lord said: Study the whole matter in your mind to a conclusion. Before action, ask the Lord if it be right. Attune yourself to the spiritual response—either to have your bosom burn within you to know that your conclusion is right or to have a stupor of thought which will make you forget it if it is wrong. Then, as the Lord has promised, "the Spirit shall be given unto you by the prayer of faith" (D&C 42:14). "Dispute not because ye see not, for ye receive no witness until after the trial of your faith" (Eth. 12:6).

Have before you always the ideals of scholarship in fields of secular knowledge. Never forget those lofty goals to which we have been pointed by our inspired leaders and by the Lord's own revelations. I refer to two very significant inspired declarations: "It is impossible for a man to be saved in ignorance" (D&C 131:6). "A man is saved no faster than he gets knowledge."[1]

But in the interpretation of these quotations, do not make the mistake of assuming that this means that one with an advanced degree in secular learning is more assured of salvation than one with only an elementary schooling.

The Prophet Joseph Smith, speaking on this subject, declared, "Knowledge through our Lord and Savior Jesus Christ is the grand key that unlocks the glories and the mysteries of the Kingdom of Heaven."[2] He also said: "A man is saved no faster than he gets knowledge, for if he does not get knowledge, he will be brought into captivity by some evil power in the other world. . . . Hence, it needs revelation to assist us, and give us knowledge of the things of God."[3]

I quote a paragraph from an address by the late President J. Reuben Clark to impress the characteristics which distinguish this school from other universities:

> The school has a dual function, a dual aim and purpose—secular learning, the lesser value; and spiritual development, the greater. These two values must be always together; neither would be perfect without the other, but the spiritual values, being basic and eternal, must always prevail, for the spiritual values are built upon absolute truth.[4]

The limitless expanse of these truths in their fullness you who teach here must ever have in mind as you counsel the inquiring minds of your students. Have always in mind the ninth Article of Faith: "We believe all that God has revealed, all that He does now reveal, and we believe that He will yet reveal many great and important things pertaining to the Kingdom of God."

It was never intended that the leaders in this Church be an ignorant ministry in the learning of the world, as has clearly been set forth in an admonition to the early elders of the Church. May I quote a few verses to show the immense field which is laid before us, to keep pace with scientists and scholars and the development of modern knowledge:

> Teach ye . . . of things both in heaven and in the earth, and under the earth; things which have been, things which are, things which must shortly come to pass; things which are at home, things which are abroad; the wars and the perplexities of the nations, and the judgments which are on the land; and a knowledge also of countries and of kingdoms—That ye may be prepared in all things when I shall send you again to magnify the calling whereunto I have called you, and the mission with which I have commissioned you. (D&C 88:78–80)

We must never forget that which was impressed by the ancients: "Wisdom is the principal thing; therefore get wisdom: and with all thy getting get understanding" (Prov. 4:7).

This, then, is your law of instruction and a guide to keep before faculty and students—to prepare yourselves for the work of the ministry as they go out to take their places in worldly affairs.

We pass on to you, also, the divine admonition to have those under your tutelage "study and learn, and become acquainted with all good books, and with languages, tongues, and people" (D&C 90:15). Brigham Young University, indeed the whole educational system of this Church, has been established to the end that all pure knowledge must be gained by our people, handed down to our posterity, and given to all men.

We charge you to give constant stimulation to these budding scientists and scholars in all fields and to the urge to push back further and further into the realms of the unknown.

Several years ago, Dr. David Sarnoff, the father of radio and television, was asked to suggest the possibilities of attainments twenty years hence. It was his expectation that within twenty years from that time we would begin to solve the riddle of communication by some electronic device by which we could speak in English and our hearers would understand, each in his own language. With our responsibility to teach the people of the world, think what it would mean to our missionary and teaching efforts if some scholars from this institution were to contribute to this possibility.

We would hope that you would give to the students of this institution the vision of the possibility that the Eyring Science Center could make a significant contribution to the discovery of a cure for cancer—that treacherous disease which took the life of that great scholar, Dr. Carl Eyring, after whom that building was named. Or that from the David O. McKay Building we would continue to graduate great teachers, inspired by the life and superb example of one of the greatest teachers of our day, after whom that building was named.

With the prospect of the J. Reuben Clark Law School, we would hope that this institution might be instrumental in developing statesmen, as exemplified by the life of J. Reuben Clark Jr.—men and women not only with unsurpassed excellence of training in the law, but also with unwavering faith that the Constitution of the United States was divinely inspired and written by men whom God raised up for this very purpose.

Hold up before these students the prophetic statement of the Prophet Joseph Smith—that if and when this inspired Constitution should hang as by a thread, that here well-qualified defenders of the faith of our fathers, elders of this Church, would be prepared to step forth and save the Constitution from destruction.[5]

God Give Us Men

God give us men. A time like this demands
Strong minds, great hearts, true faith and ready hands!
Men whom the lust of office does not kill,
Men whom the spoils of office cannot buy,
Men who possess opinions and a will,
Men who love honor, men who cannot lie.

—J. G. Holland

This institution has a great tradition. Its graduates, as has been well attested, hold positions of distinction in the educational world as well as in many fields of business and politics.

Seek for balanced educational ideals. For example, seek for an education that would bring from the athletic field an athlete who has not only athletic excellence, but also a high degree of intellectual competence. Such a one also would have standards of right living, which would make him or her not only a hero on the playing field, but also one prepared to face the problems of life, which would win the highest respect of his or her associates—one who has learned to be a worthy family member. In short, seek a balanced education that would bring forth an upright, honorable citizen to whom this institution could point with pride as an individual who finds favor not only with others, but also with God.

But again, may we indulge the hope that you may devise a method of discovering the greatness of that soul who, as measured by some arbitrary set of academic measurements, may not be accepted. As an example of what I mean, may I remind you that the great painter James Whistler, as a cadet at West Point, failed in chemistry and was dismissed from that institution. But he was head of his class in drawing and painting. It was a sad blow to him, but he did not repine. Years later he remarked, whimsically, "Had silicon been gas, I would have been a Major General."

With this vision of eternal acceptance in the presence of God constantly before you and fixed in the minds of a dedicated faculty, inspired by the president, and impressed upon the students, thereby is laid the foundation for the awakening of wellsprings of spiritual powers which will bring forth miraculous accomplishments.

To one, like yourself, schooled in the doctrines of salvation and the history of the Restoration and with a testimony of the divine origin of this Church, we would remind you that the acquiring of knowledge by faith is no easy road to learning. It will demand strenuous effort and a continual striving by faith.

We need only to remind you of the means by which Daniel learned the secret of Nebuchadnezzar's vision or how Joseph Smith had to prepare himself for his prophetic calling.

David Whitmer, one of Joseph's intimate associates in the early days, gives us a glimpse as to why Joseph could obtain learning by faith. "Joseph Smith was a good man when I knew him," said Whitmer. "He had to be or he could not go on with his work."

In short, learning by faith is no task for a lazy man. Someone has said, in effect, that such a process requires the bending of the whole soul, the calling up of the depths of the human mind and linking them with God—the right connection must be formed. Then only, comes "knowledge by faith."

As I conclude, I remind you of that oft-repeated charge of President Brigham Young to the first principal of this school, Karl G. Maeser. This charge summarizes, in one sentence, the spiritual admonition which has done more to guide teachers and students alike in their attitudes and their labors in this institution than has ever come from those of scholarly wisdom of the world. That profound educational formula was "not to teach even the multiplication tables without the Spirit of God."

So may we say to you, never hesitate to declare your faith as did the apostle Paul that "the gospel of Christ . . . is [indeed] the power of God unto salvation" (Rom. 1:16).

Again, we charge you to set a proper example in your own personal conduct. See that your family and home life are in proper order. Do not neglect your wife and family. They are your most prized possessions. Hold your family home evenings.

Keep always before the youth of this institution a deep sense of gratitude for their pioneer heritage, a love for this country, and a deep-seated reverence for the Constitution of the

United States to the end that they will never forget their civic and political obligations. Now that the voting age has been lowered to eighteen, this becomes all the more imperative.

Your great joy will come as, in the years that lie ahead, you see the graduates from this school become honored citizens in their communities and active participants in building up the kingdom of God.

On this, one of the great moments of your career—your inauguration as the president of Brigham Young University—we, as the First Presidency, the Church Board of Education, and the Board of Trustees, assure you that you have our full confidence.

I give you this final charge—that you will reach into that spiritual dimension for answers which, if you seek earnestly, will secure for you the sublime witness in your heart that your acts, your life, and your labors have the seal of approval of the Lord and Creator of us all.

This address was given on May 4, 1971, at the inauguration of Dallin H. Oaks as president of Brigham Young University. Harold B. Lee was First Counselor in the First Presidency.

NOTES

[1]Joseph Smith Jr., *History of The Church of Jesus Christ of Latter-day Saints,* ed. B. H. Roberts, 2d ed., rev., 7 vols. (Salt Lake City: Deseret Book, 1971), 4:588.

[2]Smith, *History of The Church,* 5:389.

[3]Smith, *History of The Church,* 4:588.

[4]J. Reuben Clark Jr., Inauguration Services of Howard S. McDonald as President of Brigham Young University, November 14, 1945. Special Collections and Manuscripts, Harold B. Lee Library, Brigham Young University, Provo, Utah, 12.

[5]Preston Nibley, "What of Joseph Smith's Prophecy That the Constitution Would Hang by a Thread?" *Church News,* published by *Deseret News,* December 15, 1948.

Academic Responsibility

Robert K. Thomas

At an educational conference a few years ago, a speaker told of sitting in a bus on his way home from work and over-hearing a conversation between two laborers who were in the seat in front of him. They were obviously elated at the thought of some overtime work that had been promised them, and they were hard at work trying to figure out what next week's pay-check would be. One man listed the hourly rate that they were being paid and, to the side, the number of hours of work that had been promised to them.

At this point he turned to his companion and asked, a bit dubiously, if his friend knew how to multiply. After a moment's hesitation, the friend took the paper and pencil, wrote the num-ber of hours beneath the hourly rate, drew a line under both, and placed an x to the side. Then he waited expectantly; they both waited. Nothing happened. Finally, the one who had hoped to set the multiplication in motion by writing an x to the side of his problem crumpled the paper in disgust and said to his companion, "That's what's wrong with multiplication; you've got to know the answer before you begin the problem."

Begin at the Beginning

We smile sympathetically at such frustration because we share it whenever we fail to begin at the beginning. If we have not learned to add, the relative sophistication of multiplying will escape us. If we neglect faith—the first principle of the gospel—true repentance is simply not generated. If we would be skilled and dedicated Latter-day Saints, we must prepare ourselves to succeed.

We are told, poetically, that "the thoughts of youth are long, long thoughts." As good poetry always should, this suggests more than it seems to say. For while it bids us to appreciate the vision of youth, it also hints at a major limitation of the juvenile: a willingness to be satisfied with a single dimension. "Long" thoughts may be profound, but they are often only tenuous. The breadth and depth that make an adult out of an adolescent, that unite vision with judgment, are earned—and learned. There are no shortcuts and few substitutions. Apprenticeship precedes mastery, and first steps may not be very sure.

All steps are really first steps if our vision matches our developing ability. It is some comfort to take tentative steps together, and formal schooling provides the security of growing with our peers. In this sense, college should be both culmination and promise. We assemble as a community of faculty and students in a university setting, as the scriptures suggest, to "teach one another." (See D&C 38:23; 88:77, 118.)

In a truly dynamic learning situation, nothing escapes change. For the instructor, teaching can be a continuing intellectual implosion. The material that is being studied comes to fruition, and the student is released from the bondage of ignorance and superstition. For the moment, however, let me concentrate on what can happen to the student who is "anxiously engaged" in collegiate education. To begin with, attitude, far more than training, distinguishes the halfhearted pupil from the aspiring scholar.

Ordinary Student or Scholar?

The ordinary student finds his or her relationship with faculty and administration both vague and awkward. They tend to become symbols: the teacher becomes a grade, and the administration a big stick. At the risk of sounding defensive, I believe that most teachers sincerely regret this arrangement and are eager to achieve at least an intellectual rapport with those

Robert K. Thomas, right, confers with Elder Neal A. Maxwell, left, at the Annual University Conference, August 1975. Courtesy Mark A. Philbrick/BYU.

whom they instruct. But here the teacher's authority works against him or her. Since the teacher can command, the invitation is suspect. Yet even when a student voluntarily meets with an instructor or administrative officer, real communication rarely takes place. For one who comes to such an interview to *learn,* a hundred come to *explain.*

Too many young people today believe the defensive assertions that attempt to justify student dereliction. They have been told so often that they are not responsible causes—they are only unfortunate results—that they believe it. After all, a result does not have a future, only a past. The establishment is to blame, or the Vietnam war, or broken homes, poor teachers, or comic books. Such a list becomes a litany of extenuation.

In a rather moving poem, John Holmes tells of his boyhood experiences with an old, deaf New England shipbuilder who provided him with some of the profoundest "talk" he ever heard—without speaking a word. As young Johnny watched the skilled hands of the old craftsman, it suddenly came to him with the force of a voice shouting in his ear that, no matter how you build it, "your ship has to float: you can't explain to the ocean."

How many students have come to me to "explain to the ocean." Their work will be late; they have not been feeling well lately; or—a reflection of our mind-obsessed times—they have always had a psychological block against spelling or grammar. The ultimate, or perhaps nadir, of all such "explanations" in my experience occurred when a student, a mite plaintively, excused his absence from my daily ten o'clock class by telling me that he needed to have his teeth fixed and that ten o'clock was the only "free period" he had.

How significantly different are the attitudes of the student-scholar. He or she recognizes in the administration not discipline so much as direction, and the teacher is not an opponent, but a component in a dynamic process. The student turned scholar expects, nay insists, on being inspired by the instructor—and is not often disappointed. The material is always ready; the teacher is usually ready. But when the material, student, and teacher are ready, there is fusion, not the amalgamation that we often rather unctuously call education.

In the real learning experience, the teacher is not outside or above or detached; he or she is an integral part of the reaction and is never quite the same afterward. How easy it is for the student to settle for something less than scholarship on his or her own part and in so doing make it impossible for the teacher to provide more than mechanical direction.

When a student gives the instructor grudging attention, the instructor becomes the police; fawning upon the instructor tends to corrupt. Even the least student, however, can never completely escape the gnawing realization that dull students are invariably taught by dull teachers, and scholars are taught by scholars. A student will never know how much steel there is in the instructor's mind unless his or her own mind is file hard!

Three Rs for Our Day

May I now shift for a moment to those in the audience who are teachers. Our forefathers fought for the three *R*s of elementary education. May I today suggest an additional three that have distinguished the best teachers I have known and that seem particularly appropriate for our day. Almost reluctantly I have come to believe a statement that struck me as overstated when I first heard it: "It is better to be loved than understood." I am sure that this statement was meant to shock a little, perhaps even provoke that opposition out of which knowledge can come.

In retrospect, the people who have influenced me most were not those who provided me with the most information. I remember these people with gratitude—just as I remember some books with a feeling of obligation. But those who have helped me hear the key in which I was trying to compose the little tune that I would sing throughout my life gave me more than information. Over the years I have tried to decide what they did give me. I am now convinced that it was not so much what they gave—the gift varied—but that they all shared the memorable quality of *radiance*.

Radiance

Radiance is not merely enthusiasm; this is only one of its manifestations. One of its basic meanings is *root*, for radiance is always more than surface sparkle. In a relative world, it rests on ultimates. As we grow through experience and training, we realize more and more that all problems are finally theological ones, that the unproven premise precedes every rational conclusion. A formal religious commitment provides that premise for most of us. Radiance is also a philological cousin of our word *twig*—that oft-spoken metaphor of one person's influence upon another. But no connotation that this word carries is so meaningful as its suggestion of *light*.

A few years ago, a relatively uneducated contractor who was installing refineries in India was having astounding success in training natives to operate highly technical equipment. Since his success was not shared by others similarly engaged, he was asked to reveal the tests that he used to discriminate between those who could and could not be trained as technicians. Insisting that he really did not have a formal test, the contractor said that he would be happy to demonstrate his method of selection.

At a central employment center, he simply asked applicants for work to file by him slowly. From time to time, he pulled a man out of line. Finally, pointing to those whom he had chosen so informally, the contractor said, "I just look at the eyes. If they shine, that person can be taught anything. If they don't, I can't take a chance on him."

Granting the questionable validity of such subjective evaluation, I yet submit that almost all eyes shine in kindergarten and in Primary. I am sure that many factors combine to dull them, but lackluster teaching would not be far down the list. I insist that large classes and inadequate facilities compromise radiant teaching only slightly. In a telling description, Thoreau talks about what he means to be awake: "To be awake is to be alive. I have never met a man who was quite awake. How could I have looked him in the face?"

Thoreau goes on to say that the highest of arts is to affect the quality of each day. Radiant people not only affect the quality of the day, they also change the direction of lives. I am not sure that radiance can be taught, but I believe it can be evoked and nurtured. I submit to you that no teaching function is so critical as inspiring students. Teachers will never inform as successfully as a library. We will always be overmatched at calculation by the computer. But in the blazing radiance of our own conviction, we can kindle fires that will warm and light generations.

Respect

My second *R* is *respect*—a word with an old-fashioned ring. Yet, love that is more than infatuation or indulgence must add respect to affection to achieve wholeness. I cringe a little when I hear that a teacher has established himself or herself as a "pal" to students. I think it revealing that such a description usually comes from the teacher and not from the students themselves. The generation gap may be receiving faddish attention today, but it can be real.

To begin with, there is a security in respect that counters some of the self-consciousness that deters needed growth. Unfortunately, phrases such as "demanding respect" emphasize only coercion. Real respect is never demanded successfully. You can force conformity, but obedience is always given. This is not to imply that conformity is wholly negative. In most situations, the Old Testament ideal of conformity to law must precede the New Testament doctrine of obedience to love. Awareness of this may keep the beginning teacher from pleading for cooperation with unruly students who translate their guilt into dislike for the teacher who indulges them.

Fairness is the ethic of the young. Youngsters do not have the thoughtless adult's reverence for consistency. If the phrasing is beyond them, all children get the point of Emerson's dictum that "a foolish consistency is the hobgoblin of little minds." The explanation of many teachers, "If I did it for you, I would have to do it for everyone," strikes most youngsters as being ridiculous, which it is. Such a statement is neat, and it has the aura of fairness; but no child is fooled. The teacher is simply saying, "I don't have enough respect for you to hear your story or to evaluate the special circumstances you would like to plead."

No two cases are the same; rarely are they more than superficially similar. The student instinctively knows this and is resentful at being lumped with others to suit a teacher's convenience. It just will not work to explain that the size of your class precludes your taking time to hear a student out. You must make your decision in the light of fact, instead of expedient similarity, to retain a student's respect. Faced with any other attitude on your part, the student feels driven to fall back on the tactic that is used so successfully at home—whining. If you think that listening to a student's reasoned plea takes time, just try cutting off a whiner.

Perhaps one of our difficulties is that we lack respect for our own ignorance. Possibly, the creeping security of advanced degrees blunts the sensitivity that keeps us aware of what we really do not know. I suspect that I am as guilty as anyone, but I would like to cite as an example our willingness to measure students. Dramatic cases of misjudgment are commented upon disapprovingly, and educational journals grow shrill in their defense of individual differences. It is a rare teacher, however, who has such respect for human potential and such an awareness of his or her own limitations that he or she remains flexible and alert to budding abilities and groping sensitivities.

Restraint

The final *R* is *restraint*. To action-oriented contemporaries, impatient with any system and heady with success as a result of direct involvement, restraint is almost synonymous with cowardice or a lack of integrity. I feel that I have a special competence to speak about restraint because of my own undergraduate experience. My alma mater, Reed College, underwent twenty-five years ago what many campuses are just coming to.

While I was not really a participant, I was part of a militant student body that not only negotiated in strength with the administration, but also defied local and federal authorities in a massive demonstration against the draft, war, and any restriction upon personal lives. Most of the students involved were very bright, overwhelmingly articulate, and determined to change the world *now*. As I read the papers today, I often have the eerie sensation of living over my youth. The very slogans are the same—and those intense, imploring faces.

I do not remember those years in disgust; I remember them in sorrow. They were far from useless—the intellectual challenge was immense—but those years were not ones of controlled growth. Students throbbed when they should have meditated. They marched when they might have examined. They learned to live by symbols—and, although they would have denied it then, the simpler the symbol the better. They were skillful scorners and rabid partisans. Their adrenaline ran all the time. Whatever else they were, they were not apathetic. The teachers they usually followed were graying copies of the students they aroused. They were not all that way, however.

The teachers who are now unforgettable, whose features do not blur into the mass and whose words still tingle, never took the easy, emotional way of mob power. They tried to help me see that uncontrolled effort is essentially wasted. It may seem to solve immediate problems, but in fact, it sets up antagonisms and solidifies stances until only surface agreements are possible. Alexander took the activist's part in solving the riddle of the Gordian knot when he contemptuously cut it, but it needs to be noted that he ruined the rope.

Now, I would not be misunderstood. Restraint is not retreat. Just complaints must be heard, and problems are not solved by ignoring them. If, however, you turn your relations with those that you attempt to instruct into adversary proceedings, you license their rebellion.

Education is always a matter of discrimination, a skillful selection of alternatives. Significant innovation may begin in intuition, but it must be established in order. No one ever learned order in fomenting disorder. A teacher's self-discipline sets the behavioral tone in classes. Teachers who lose their temper turn respect for authority into a struggle for power.

Yet the most profound results of restraint on the part of the teacher lie not in keeping control, advancing order. The teacher who embodies and teaches restraint can also inculcate taste—an attribute fast disappearing under the aggressively gross onslaught of mass entertainment. An ancient proverb warns us that tastes are not to be disputed, but we have almost made this point irrelevant in our capitulation to the tasteless.

Yet taste is only an expanded term for that sensitivity which makes civilization possible. Laws cannot be detailed enough to settle every dispute. Technology cannot surround us with riches so great that all will have enough. It is only taste that helps us recognize the unspoken yearning of another's dreams—and leads us to call decent that which builds community and makes love more than lust. A teacher at BYU might well help a student develop what James Russell Lowell has called "that good taste which is the conscience of the mind, and that conscience which is the good taste of the soul."

A Teacher's Responsibility

The teacher, by training and by opportunity, must help the young person set knowledge in a moral and social context that cannot always be spelled out. But the restraint that helps the student function as a truly human being, capable of a developing interaction with peers and a willingness to earn a part in society, must be taught.

It is the enviable opportunity of the teacher to help reveal gradually, but irresistibly, the exciting world that is the province of cultured knowledge. Not all such opportunities are restricted to the classroom. I remember a brief exchange during World War II with a welder on my crew in a shipyard. As our graveyard shift was coming to an end, the dawn broke in a soft flush over the water; I quoted some lines from Homer. My unlettered friend found Homer's phrase "rosy-fingered dawn" interesting but inadequate. Yet it stirred him to his own fresh but somewhat awkward description of the coming day. As we punched out, he casually inquired, "What was the name of that fellow who talked about the dawn's hands?" Homer may not have gained an immediate admirer, but something besides the sun was dawning that morning.

I also remember the young cowboy from Montana who came to BYU some years ago. I was new at the university, and he was in a freshman English class that I was instructing. His lack of preparation for the class was almost outrageously obvious. He had very little concept of coherence and no skill at all in developing an idea. We suffered together. One day, after class, he handed me a much folded piece of paper and confessed that it was a poem that he had written. The thought of this boy subjecting himself to the discipline of poetry was almost beyond belief, but I assured him that I would like to read his poem and that I would be happy to talk with him about it.

I am afraid that the opening lines were about what I had expected. And yet, on down the page, as he tried to tell me what it was like to be in a summer thunderstorm out on the ranch of which he was a part, suddenly out of that page came a line of unmistakable poetry. He wrote about thunder "rumbling, bumbling, grumbling like a God in disgrace." I envied that line, and it suddenly occurred to me that this boy perhaps only lacked preparation and that I—who manifestly was not a poet—might yet teach one.

In the Vanguard

Finally, may I speak a word for those administrative officers of the university whose duties give them little time to be students or to experience again the exhilaration of teaching. Perhaps some of you are aware of the investigative teams that descend upon the university and whose often uncivil questions must be answered civilly—and interminably. Some of you may even realize the hours that are spent in adjudicating trivial complaints or just listening to those who would help run the university but who have seldom seen any of the ramifications of their suggestions.

At national conventions, identification as a BYU representative is usually good for an exhortation or two from utter strangers. We are constantly asked to assume roles for which we have neither the inclination nor the authority. BYU cannot speak for the Church—nor do we want to—but in the cross fires of controversy, the administration is fair game for all sides.

Lest such an assertion claim more sympathy than I intend, let me hasten to add that most of us are here because we think that this is the greatest opportunity in the world to unite professional training and religious commitment. We deeply appreciate the sensitive concern of our board of trustees, and we want them to know that we serve gladly. May I lift a brief experience from my own youth to speak for us all.

On the evening of the day that Pearl Harbor was attacked, I sat by a radio in the town on the coast of southern Oregon where I had spent most of my youth. It was the only deep-water port between San Francisco and Portland, and its harbor was well known to hundreds of Japanese seamen who had loaded lumber at its docks. We sat in darkness and heard our local radio station report that a Japanese cruiser had been sighted off northern California headed toward Oregon.

In a thousand homes there was but one thought: we were liable to be under attack before morning. Suddenly, Pearl Harbor seemed very near, and the war was no longer a distant abstraction. The radio announcer, trying to keep his voice calm, suggested that the local sporting goods stores open and distribute what ammunition they had.

I pulled out my hunting rifle, which had never been fired in anger, and then set it down again, remembering the size of the guns on the Japanese cruisers that had often visited us. Through the night I reflected that I was not disposed for battle, but I knew that there was no place in the world that I would rather have been that night than sitting in that room, in that city, at that time. What was to come would find me willingly in the vanguard.

We share with all of you a love for BYU—that for which it has stood and now stands—and that for which it is destined to be. We pledge to you the concerted, best efforts of faculty and administration to support the cause in which we all serve.

This Maeser Awards Assembly address was given at BYU on April 27, 1971. Dr. Thomas was Academic Vice-President and Professor of English at Brigham Young University. Published in *BYU Studies* 11, no. 3 (1971): 293–303.

A House of Faith

Dallin H. Oaks

The theme of my remarks is "a house of faith, a house of learning" (D&C 88:119). I will focus on the first half of that theme, pointing to the ideal of Brigham Young University as "a house of faith."

In his "Second-Century Address," delivered in 1975, President Spencer W. Kimball helped us see Brigham Young University, present and future, through the eyes of a living prophet. He saw the need and challenged us to increased effort and accomplishment in our various responsibilities. He saw the need and exhorted us to greater spirituality and worthiness in our individual lives. Then, with prophetic insight, he concluded with this promise, which identifies our goal and reminds us that we have not yet arrived: "Then, in the process of time this will become a fully anointed university of the Lord about which so much has been spoken in the past."[1]

How are we to achieve that prophetic destiny as "the fully anointed university of the Lord"? (1) We must understand this university's role in the kingdom of God, (2) we must be worthy in our individual lives, (3) we must be fearless in proclaiming the truths of the gospel of Jesus Christ, (4) we must be exemplary in efforts understandable to the world, and (5) we must seek and heed the inspiration of God in the performance of our individual responsibilities.

BYU President Dallin H. Oaks at a BYU forum address, July 5, 1976.
Courtesy Mark A. Philbrick/BYU.

The University in the Kingdom

The first and greatest revelation of this dispensation on the subject of education was Doctrine and Covenants 88, given December 27, 1832. The Lord directed the Saints to build a temple in Kirtland: "Organize yourselves; prepare every needful thing; and establish a house, even a house of prayer, a house of fasting, a house of faith, a house of learning, a house of glory, a house of order, a house of God" (D&C 88:119).

This revelation also directed the Saints to begin a school of the prophets. This school, which Joseph Smith promptly established in Kirtland in the winter of 1833, more than three years before the dedication of the temple, was the forerunner of all educational efforts in The Church of Jesus Christ of Latter-day Saints. Doctrine and Covenants 88, which defined the objectives of the School of the Prophets and gave related commandments, counsel, and knowledge, is still the basic constitution of Church education. It defines Brigham Young University's role in the kingdom.

The immediate purpose of the School of the Prophets was to train the restored Church's earliest leaders for the ministry, especially for missionary work. The Church's first educational effort was also intimately related to the teachings to be communicated in the temple. The school was intended to be housed in the temple (see D&C 95:17).

The commandments and knowledge communicated in the eighty-eighth section concern the temple, the school, and the work of the ministry as an inseparable and unified whole. That is their eternal relationship. The laws and conventions and shortsightedness of man currently compel us to separate these activities for some purposes, but to a Father in Heaven who has given no temporal law and to whom all things are spiritual (D&C 29:34), the work of temple, school, and ministry must all be seen as the unified work of the kingdom.

Often in the last three years, I have stood at the window of my office, looking out across the northern part of the campus to the Missionary Training Center and the temple. I tell the visitors who share this sight that these three institutions—university, mission, and temple—are the most powerful combination of institutions on the face of the earth. They make this place unique in all the world. Now, after studying the eighty-eighth section, I see even more clearly the common origins of all three institutions in a single great revelation. I am grateful that it has been during the period of our service that the servants of the Lord have united in one sacred location the Lord's university, the Lord's temple, and the school where his missionaries become "acquainted with . . . languages, tongues, and people" (D&C 90:15).

We are all familiar with the comprehensive curriculum the Lord outlined in section 88. He directed these early Saints to "teach one another the doctrine of the kingdom" and the "law of the gospel" (D&C 88:77, 78). Beyond that, he commanded them to teach "all things that pertain unto the kingdom of God" (D&C 88:78). They must "diligently" seek "out of the best books words of wisdom" (D&C 88:118). They should be instructed in

> things both in heaven and in the earth, and under the earth; things which have been, things which are, things which must shortly come to pass; things which are at home, things which are abroad; the wars and the perplexities of the nations, and the judgments which are on the land; and a knowledge also of countries and of kingdoms. (D&C 88:79)

Two months after the school commenced, the Lord reinforced this breadth of instruction by commanding the Prophet to "study and learn, and become acquainted with all good books, and with languages, tongues, and people" (D&C 90:15).

The Lord also revealed that the technique of learning was to reach beyond the conventional pedagogy of that day (or this). Those who studied in the School of the Prophets were to "seek learning, even by study and also by faith" (D&C 88:118).

All these verses from the eighty-eighth section are familiar and have often been used to stress the universal concern of our inquiries at Brigham Young University—comprehending the secular as well as the spiritual—and our special approach to learning—comprehending conventional study and the acquisition of insights from the Spirit through faith. But this great revealed charter of the Church Educational System contains much more.

At the beginning of the eighty-eighth section, the Lord instructed his little flock in the most fundamental principle of all learning: all things were made by the power and glory of God and his son Jesus Christ (vv. 4–5, 7–19). He is the source of the light of the sun and of the light that quickens our understandings (vv. 7, 11). It is through Jesus Christ that we receive "the light which is in all things, which giveth life to all things, which is the law by which all things are governed, even the power of God, . . . who is in the midst of all things" (v. 13). What could be more basic to a learning effort than this knowledge that God is the power by which all things were made and governed and that he is in all things, comprehends all things, and is the source of all enlightenment?

This revelation also declares the purpose of learning in the Church Educational System. It is that we "may be prepared in all things" when the Lord shall send us to magnify the calling whereunto he has called us and the mission with which he has commissioned us (D&C 88:80). In other words, we receive enlightenment as stewards with a duty to use that knowledge to go out into the world to warn and bless the lives of others and "to prepare the saints for the hour of judgment which is to come" (D&C 88:81, 84).

The attitude that should motivate all our efforts in education is specified in the sixty-seventh verse: our eye should be single to the glory of God. That short verse also contains the most significant promise ever given pertaining to education: "And if your eye be single to my glory, your whole bodies shall be filled with light, and there shall be no darkness in you; and that body which is filled with light comprehendeth all things." In other words, those who achieve singleness of purpose in love of God and service in his kingdom are promised that they will ultimately comprehend all things. The manner of learning that would fulfill this unique promise was revealed to the Prophet Joseph Smith six years later in Liberty Jail: "God shall give unto you knowledge by his Holy Spirit, yea, by the unspeakable gift of the Holy Ghost, that has not been revealed since the world was until now" (D&C 121:26).

One of the most distinctive characteristics of Brigham Young University in this day is our proud affirmation that character is more important than learning. We are preoccupied with behavior and consider personal worthiness an essential ingredient of our educational enterprise. That educational philosophy was revealed by God. Again and again the eighty-eighth section stresses the importance of worthiness for teacher and student. "Prepare yourselves, and sanctify yourselves," the Lord commands; "yea, purify your hearts, and cleanse your hands and your feet before me, that I may make you clean" (v. 74). "Therefore, cease from all your light speeches, from all laughter, from all your lustful desires, from all your pride and light-mindedness, and from all your wicked doings" (v. 121). Again: "Abide ye in the liberty wherewith ye are made free; entangle not yourselves in sin, but let your hands be clean, until the Lord comes" (v. 86). Another verse of commandment concludes with a promise that ties the purifying effort directly to the process and objective of learning: "Cease to be idle; cease to be unclean; cease to find fault one with another; cease to sleep longer than is needful; retire to thy bed early, that ye may not be weary; arise early, *that your bodies and your minds may be invigorated*" (v. 124; italics added).

Soon after the beginning of the School of the Prophets and as a direct result of experiences in the meetings of the school, the Lord gave Joseph Smith the revelation designated as "a Word of Wisdom" (D&C 89:1). This was also a commandment with a promise. Those who observed its proscriptions, "walking in obedience to the commandments, shall receive health in their navel and marrow to their bones" (D&C 89:18), and "shall run and not be weary, and shall walk and not faint," and "the destroying angel shall pass by them, as the children of Israel, and not slay them" (D&C 89:20–21). But the promised spiritual blessings were of at least equal importance, especially for those involved in learning: "And all saints who remember to keep and do these sayings, walking in obedience to the commandments, . . . shall find wisdom and great treasures of knowledge, even hidden treasures" (D&C 89:18–19).

The teacher in the School of the Prophets was commanded to be worthy, prepared, reverent, and exemplary in conduct. The Lord commanded that the teacher "should be first in the house, . . . that he may be an example" (D&C 88:130). He should also "offer himself in prayer upon his knees before God, in token or remembrance of the everlasting covenant" (D&C 88:131).

The students must also be worthy. When a student entered the School of the Prophets, the teacher was commanded to salute him "in the name of the Lord Jesus Christ, in token or remembrance of the everlasting covenant," in fellowship, and in a determination to be a friend and brother and "to walk in all the commandments of God blameless, in thanksgiving, forever and ever" (D&C 88:133). If students were unworthy of this salutation and of the covenant, the Lord commanded that they "shall not have place among you" (D&C 88:134).

Finally, the Lord made a promise in the eighty-eighth section to all who would participate in the important educational work of his kingdom. This promise applies to efforts in our day just as it did then: "Draw near unto me and I will draw near unto you; seek me diligently and ye shall find me; ask, and ye shall receive; knock, and it shall be opened unto you. Whatsoever ye ask the Father in my name it shall be given unto you" (D&C 88:63–64).

The acquisition of knowledge is a sacred activity, pleasing to the Lord and favored of him. That fact accounts for what President Kimball called "the special financial outpouring that supports this university."[2] "The glory of God is intelligence, or, in other words, light and truth" (D&C 93:36). The holiest places on earth, the temples of God, are places of instruction. From the beginning of this dispensation, the Lord has associated the temple, the school, and the ministry, a trio now brought together in this spot. Under the direction of the servants of the Lord, Brigham Young University's role is to be a "house of faith" (D&C 88:119), a sanctified and fully effective participant in the revealing and teaching and reforming mission of the kingdom of God. When we can perform this university's calling in a manner fully acceptable to the Lord and his servants, we will become what President Kimball has called "the fully anointed university of the Lord."[3]

Worthiness

If we are to achieve that prophetic destiny, we must follow the general charter of Church education as revealed in the

Doctrine and Covenants and the more recent and more specific
direction of the living prophets. Each of these authorities has told
us that our first challenge is to be worthy in our personal lives.

In the eighty-eighth section, the Lord commanded his
educators to be pure, worthy, prayerful, and exemplary in all
things. In his great address to BYU faculty and staff a decade
ago (September 12, 1967), "Education for Eternity," President—
then Elder—Kimball declared: "BYU is dedicated to the building of character and faith, for character is higher than intellect,
and its teachers must in all propriety so dedicate themselves."[4]
More recently, President Kimball explained that we cannot make
the progress needed at BYU

> except we continue . . . to be concerned about the spiritual
> qualities and abilities of those who teach here. In the book
> of Mosiah, we read, "Trust no one to be your teacher nor
> your minister, except he be a man of God, walking in his
> ways and keeping his commandments" (23:14). . . . We must
> be concerned with the spiritual worthiness, as well as the
> academic and professional competency, of all those who
> come here to teach.[5]

One of the conditions of employment at Brigham Young
University is observance of all the principles of our code of
honor. We cannot expect less of ourselves than we expect
of our students.

> Each worker in this University—and especially those
> who are in teaching positions, formal or informal—must
> be a role model for the young people who study here.
> Individuals whose personal lives cannot meet that high
> standard of example are honor bound to repent speedily,
> seeking the help of their bishop and/or their University
> supervisor as the circumstances warrant, or to obtain
> other employment.[6]

Our annual interviews with all university personnel seek to
encourage and assure that worthiness. They must be carried out
faithfully by both parties.

I am always humiliated when a bishop or stake president
contacts me or another university official to say that there is a
BYU teacher or administrator or staff member in his ward or

stake who refuses to take Church assignments, is not faithful in attending Church meetings, or does not pay a full tithing.

> The payment of an honest tithing is an expectation of employment at Brigham Young University. How could it be otherwise, when about two-thirds of the University's budget comes from appropriations from the tithes of the Church? These sums are paid in a freewill offering by members of the Church throughout the world, often at great sacrifice. Many of these members have standards of living and income far below what is enjoyed by the employees of this university.[7]

The Church holds us up as examples of faithful Latter-day Saints whose lives are worthy of emulation. If leaders or members of our wards know that we are not, our continued employment at BYU is a trial to the faith of those who know us, an insult to the standards of this institution, and an affront to the Church. None of us can afford to be in that position. While we do not expect perfection, we do expect that all our BYU personnel will observe all the principles of our code of honor, and that all of us who are members of the Church will be worthy of a temple recommend and will be conscientiously working to preserve and improve our spirituality. We expect the same high standards of personal worthiness of our workers who are not members of our Church, except that they are not expected to pay tithing and they have no responsibility of attendance or activity in our Church.

Workers at BYU are also expected to be worthy examples of Christian living in the performance of all their duties at the university. From time to time, we are grieved to receive evidence of dishonesty by BYU employees, including instances where persons have stolen the property or the time of the university. The theft of university time is far more common than and just as deplorable as the theft of property. We are also grieved to hear reports of profanity or abusive language by BYU personnel. Foul language of any kind is deeply resented by students and others and has no place on the job at BYU. The same is true of untruthful reports, backbiting, evil speaking, and excessive displays of anger.

I am always saddened when I hear that supervisors or others at the university have "chewed out" a fellow worker in a degrading manner or held someone up to public ridicule in the eyes of colleagues, students, or others. We must have high performance from our university workers, and when a person's performance does not measure up to standards, he or she must be corrected, including, if necessary, being dismissed from a position or from university employment. All of this will be necessary, just as it is in other employment and, indeed, in Church positions. But we should be consistent with the examples of priesthood leadership, and correction and changes should be accomplished without anger, rancor, or public embarrassment.

We must be especially exemplary in our communications with persons who telephone us or come to the campus as guests. Let us strive to be Christlike in all our personal dealings, always showing gentleness, love, and consideration for all. Only by this means can we be worthy residents and teachers in the household of faith.

Testimony and Gospel Teaching

All who study, teach, or work in a "house of faith" (D&C 88:119) should be fearless in proclaiming the truth of the gospel of Jesus Christ. By the power of the Holy Spirit, we should testify of God the Father and his son Jesus Christ. That faith and testimony should be paramount in our lives and in our teachings.

We must be more explicit about our religious faith and our commitment to it. In doing so, we will fill a demonstrated need. Pollster George Gallup recently observed that Americans are "spiritually hungry." Increasing numbers are disillusioned with the secular world, have rejected rationalism, and are turning to "the life of the spirit for guidance."[8] Our students share that hunger, and we must see that they receive spiritual food.

When a student entered the School of the Prophets, the teacher was commanded to salute him in the name of the Lord as a token of their mutual determination to keep the commandments of God (D&C 88:132–33). To serve that same purpose, our teachers and others in a position of authority at BYU should find occasion to bear their testimonies to students and fellow workers, to express their faith, and to be explicit about the relevance of the gospel in their lives. These commitments and attitudes should be explicit in our teaching. President Kimball underlined the importance of that subject in these words:

> I would expect that no member of faculty or staff would continue in the employ of this institution if he or she did not have deep assurance of the divinity of the gospel of Christ, the truth of the Church, the correctness of the doctrines, and the destiny of the school.
>
> . . . Every instructor knows before coming to this campus what the aims are and is committed to the furthering of those objectives.
>
> If one cannot conscientiously accept the policies and program of the institution, there is no wrong in his moving to an environment that is compatible and friendly to his concepts.[9]

A teacher's most important possession is his or her testimony of Jesus Christ. It is more important than the canons and theories of any professional field. We should say so to our students. Similarly, we ought not to present ourselves as teachers at Brigham Young University unless we are living so that we are entitled to the continuous companionship and guidance of the Holy Ghost. In my opinion, the Lord's statement that "if ye receive not the Spirit ye shall not teach" (D&C 42:14) has very literal application to the teaching activities of this university.[10]

Our testimonies are important to our students and to our fellow workers as our most important common bond. We are privileged to use expressions of faith in our teaching and other associations. In public institutions, teachers are less free.

Each teacher must decide how gospel values will be made explicit in his or her own teaching. Some subjects can be permeated with gospel truths and values. In other subjects, reference to the gospel is more difficult. But in every class in this university, a teacher can at least begin the teaching effort by bearing testimony of God, by expressing love and support for his servants, and by explaining the importance of the gospel truths in his or her life. And it would always be desirable for a teacher at BYU to affirm publicly the great truth expressed by

President Joseph Fielding Smith that "knowledge comes both by reason and by revelation." As President Kimball explained,

> It would not be expected that all of the faculty would be categorically teaching religion constantly in their classes, but it is proposed that every professor and teacher in this institution would keep his subject matter bathed in the light and color of the restored gospel, and have all his subject matter perfumed lightly with the spirit of the gospel. Always there would be an essence, and the student would feel the presence.
>
> Every instructor should grasp the opportunity occasionally to bear formal testimony of the truth. Every student is entitled to know the attitude and feeling and spirit of every teacher.[11]

This is the responsibility of our non-LDS teachers as well, and many fulfill it admirably. We know of several instances where non-LDS BYU faculty members have been among our most effective practitioners and teachers of wholesome Christian values, surpassing some of their LDS colleagues in showing how these principles can and should be pervasive in our teaching and associations at BYU.

In my remarks to the faculty two years ago, I suggested that in order to be effective at teaching secular subjects and at integrating gospel concepts, we must be "bilingual." I urged that we had to be fluent in the language of scholarship in order to command the respect of the secular world and that we also had to speak in the special language of our faith to communicate our adherence to the gospel values that illuminate our learning efforts and justify our existence as a university. I was pleased when President Kimball used this same metaphor in his "Second-Century Address" and that the idea of being "bilingual" and the phrases "language of scholarship" and "language of faith" are becoming a familiar part of our vocabulary. But much remains to be done before BYU has met this challenge with the needed array of solid achievements in public and private communications.

I now feel prompted to add another dimension. The challenge to be bilingual involves more than the ability to speak both languages. That is a terrestrial skill at best. To be bilingual in the celestial sense, we must use the appropriate combination of the language of scholarship and the language of faith to assure that what we communicate is the whole truth as completely as we perceive it with the full combination of our scholarly and spiritual senses. That is the culmination of being bilingual. That is what President Lee meant when he said that one purpose of our Church schools was "to teach secular truth so effectively that students will be free from error, free from sin, free from darkness, free from traditions, vain philosophies, and the untried, unproven theories of science."[12]

If we are to communicate at the highest level of the bilingual, we must be thoroughly prepared in our individual disciplines and also deeply schooled in the gospel.

A student wrote me to complain that we "are not using the teachings of the prophets . . . in our classrooms as we could."[13] He criticized our teaching, especially in one particular department, as having a lack of balance. He described the prototype of a professor who "has a Ph.D. in his academic discipline and the equivalent of an eighth grade education in the Gospel." Although this student did not apply that description to any particular teacher, I would like to consider it as a challenge to each of us. If any teacher at BYU has a doctorate in his or her discipline but only grade-school preparation in the gospel, that teacher needs some spiritual development. The reverse is also true: a doctorate-level knowledge of the gospel will not suffice if we are poorly prepared in our individual discipline.

In this university, we are free to seek the truth—a "knowledge of things as they are, and as they were, and as they are to come" (D&C 93:24). As President Kimball observed, at BYU we have "real individual freedom. Freedom from worldly ideologies and concepts unshackles man far more than he knows. It is the truth that sets men free."[14] Each of us should pursue that truth by study and by faith. Each of us should increase our qualifications to communicate that truth by an inspired combination of the language of scholarship and the language of faith. And each of us should gain a doctorate-level knowledge of the gospel as well as of our individual disciplines.

Excellence in Secular Terms

In his "Second-Century Address," President Kimball also challenged us to excel in terms understandable to the world in our teaching, our creative work, and in all our activities. "While you will do many things in the programs of this university that are done elsewhere," he said, "these same things can and must be done better here than others do them."[15]

We can measure up to that challenge only with solid individual effort. "We must do more than ask the Lord for excellence," President Kimball declared. "Perspiration must precede inspiration; there must be effort before there is excellence. We must do more than pray for these outcomes at BYU, though we must surely pray. We must take thought. We must make effort. We must be patient. We must be professional. We must be spiritual."[16] Thus, when President Kimball challenged us to excel at literacy and the teaching of English as a second language, he reminded us that our efforts must be "firmly headquartered in terms of unarguable competency as well as deep concern."[17]

All this reminds us that we cannot expect to be instruments in advancing the truth in our individual disciplines merely through studying theology and living righteous lives. When the Lord sends us to spread the gospel in all parts of the world, he expects us to use modern technology in transportation and communication. He has revealed these for our use. But isn't it significant that he revealed these scientific wonders through natural channels, to persons who were pursuing learning by secular means and for secular purposes?

There have been inspired men and women in every discipline. The Lord expects us to learn what we can from what he has previously revealed. We do not begin by rejecting what we sometimes call "the learning of men." The learning of men, when it is true, is inspired of God. We must put our own efforts into paying the price of learning, of degrees, and of all intermediate steps necessary to acquire depth in our individual disciplines and skills. Future revelation in a particular discipline or skill is most likely to come to one who has paid the price of learning all that has previously been revealed. A lawyer is not likely to be inspired with the key to the energy crisis, nor a physicist with new truths about the science of government.

Inspiration to Assist Us

While we must not begin by rejecting the learning of men, we must not be confined by it. We must not be so self-satisfied and so deep in our own disciplines that we cannot be open to the truths contained in the scriptures or the illumination communicated by the Spirit. Can we afford to gloss over the scriptures when the prophet has testified that they "contain the master concepts for mankind"?[18] Can we afford to make no attempt to use inspiration, when that is our designated access to the source and author of all truth? In his "Second-Century Address," President Kimball declared:

> This university shares with other universities the hope and labor involved in rolling back the frontiers of knowledge even further, but we also know that through the process of revelation there are yet "many great and important things" [A of F 1:9] to be given to mankind which will have an intellectual and spiritual impact far beyond what mere men can imagine.[19]

In light of what the Prophet has said, how can we at Brigham Young University do our part "in rolling back the frontiers of knowledge even further"? We will not achieve this goal by the casual use of gospel insights implied in the phrase "philosophies of man, mingled with scripture." If we limit ourselves to the wisdom of men, we will wind up like the Nephites, who, boasting in their own strength, were destroyed because they were "left in their own strength" (Hel. 4:13).

If we are to qualify for the choicest blessings of God—if we are to become the "house of faith" (D&C 88:119) described in the revelation—our ultimate loyalty must be to the Lord, not to our professional disciplines. Elder Neal A. Maxwell illustrated that principle with the metaphor of the passport: "The orthodox Latter-day Saint scholar should remember that his citizenship is in the Kingdom and that his professional passport takes him abroad into his specialty. It is not the other way around."[20] The Lord once rebuked the Prophet Joseph Smith for a violation of his principle of loyalty. "Behold," he declared, "how oft you have transgressed the commandments and the laws of God, and have gone on in the persuasions of men. For, behold, you should not have feared man more than God" (D&C 3:6–7).

How would we stand in a conflict between the wisdom of man and the inspiration of God? Do we go on "in the persuasions of men"? Do we fear man more than God? Do we have our citizenship in the professional world and teach or do other work at BYU by virtue of a passport? I suggest that question for prayerful consideration in all our professional work.

This question not only calls on us to identify our ultimate loyalty—which I think each of us would quickly affirm is to the Lord—but it also calls on us to authenticate our commitment in a way that is evident in our day-to-day professional work. Consider the implications of President Kimball's charge that "we must not merely 'ape the world.' We must do special things that would justify the special financial outpouring that supports this university."[21] He explains one implication of that principle as follows: "We must be willing to break with the educational establishment (not foolishly or cavalierly, but thoughtfully and for good reason) in order to find gospel ways to help mankind. Gospel methodology, concepts, and insights can help us to do what the world cannot do in its own frame of reference."[22]

Are we secure enough in our professional preparation and attainments and strong enough in our faith that we can, as President Kimball says, "break with the educational establishment . . . for good reason in order to find gospel ways to help mankind"? Although we are beginning to see some brilliant examples of gospel approaches in secular subjects at BYU, many of us are not yet ready to be this bold and this creative. As more and more of us acquire superior professional preparation and unshakable faith, we will see our overall performance improve. And when it does, the results will be spectacular.

Our Father in Heaven has invited us to "cry unto him" over our crops and our flocks "that they may increase" and "that [we] may prosper in them" (Alma 34:20, 24, 25). He has also told us through his prophet, "Counsel with the Lord in all thy doings, and he will direct thee for good" (Alma 37:37). Our

Father in Heaven will teach us and help us and magnify us, if we will only place our faith in him and seek the inspiration of his Spirit. "Draw near unto me," he said in that great charter of learning, the eighty-eighth section, "and I will draw near unto you; . . . ask, and ye shall receive. . . . Whatsoever ye ask the Father in my name it shall be given unto you" (D&C 88:63–64). Only by this means, with the Lord's help, sought and received, can we fulfill President John Taylor's remarkable prophecy: "You will see the day that Zion will be as far ahead of the outside world in everything pertaining to learning of every kind as we are today in regard to religious matters."[23]

If we qualify by professional excellence, by worthiness, by loyalty, and by spirituality, we can receive the inspiration of God in our professional work. "We expect the natural unfolding of knowledge to occur as a result of scholarship," President Kimball observed, but then he made this significant promise: "There will always be that added dimension which the Lord can provide when we are qualified to receive and he chooses to speak."[24]

The First Presidency illustrated this principle in a special message published only a month ago: "Members of the Church should be peers or superiors to any others in natural ability, extended training, plus the Holy Spirit which should bring them light and truth."[25] As Latter-day Saints, we are therefore *privileged* to augment our individual creative efforts with the insights of the gospel and the guidance of the Spirit. But as Brigham Young University faculty and staff, we are *responsible* to do so.

If we are to become the "fully anointed university of the Lord,"[26] we *must* make use of those gospel insights and values "in order to find gospel ways to help mankind." We must have access to "that added dimension which the Lord can provide when we are qualified and he chooses to speak."[27] We must make use of those gospel insights and values and those spiritual powers in our teaching, in the selection and development of our creative efforts, and in all our work at the university. I have had that experience in my work, others have enjoyed it also, and I know it is available for those who have not yet experienced it.

On one occasion, the Prophet Joseph Smith described the spirit of revelation in this manner: "A person may profit by noticing the first intimation of the spirit of revelation; for instance, when you feel pure intelligence flowing into you, it may give you sudden strokes of ideas . . . and thus by learning the Spirit of God and understanding it, you may grow into the principle of revelation."[28] On a choice occasion early in my service at BYU, when we faced an important and far-reaching decision on our academic calendar, I experienced that kind of revelation as pure intelligence was thrust upon my consciousness. I treasure that experience. It stands as a vivid testimony of the fact that when the matter is of great importance to his children and to his kingdom, our Father in Heaven will assist us when we are qualified and seeking.

At other times, I have felt the promptings of the Spirit to stay my hand from a course of action that was not in the best interest of the university. I was prevented from signing a legal document on one occasion and a letter on another. In each instance, we reexamined the proposed action and within a few weeks could see, with the benefit of additional information not available to us earlier, that the restraining hand of the Spirit had saved us from an irreversible error. On another occasion, I was prompted to accept a speaking appointment I would normally have declined, and the fulfillment of that assignment turned out to be one of the most significant public acts of my period of service and has led to many other important invitations, publications, and influences. At other times, in connection with my scholarly work on law and legal history, I have been restrained from publishing something that later turned out to be incorrect, and I have been impressed to look in obscure places where I found information vital to guide me to accurate conclusions in matters of moment in my work.

In all of this, I have been blessed beyond my own powers and have received an inkling of what the Lord can do for us if we qualify and reach out for his help in the righteous cause in which we are engaged.

When we in the "household of faith" have paid the price of excellence in our preparation and in our individual efforts, when we have become thoroughly schooled in the gospel, when we have qualified by worthiness and spirituality, and when we are seeking for his guidance continually, as he chooses to speak, and are fully qualified to press on with demonstrable excellence when he leaves us to our own best judgment, we will be making the progress we must make in order to become "the fully anointed university of the Lord."[29] Let us reach upward for this higher plane, and let us do so proudly, confidently, and speedily, taking heart in the question and promise of the Apostle: "If God be for us, who can be against us?" (Rom. 8:31). May God help us to do what I believe he would have us do.

This address was given to BYU employees at the 1977 Annual University Conference. Dallin H. Oaks served as president of Brigham Young University from 1971 to 1980.

NOTES

[1]Spencer W. Kimball, "Second-Century Address," *BYU Studies* 16, no. 4 (1976): 453. See pages 63–75 in this volume.

[2]Kimball, "Second-Century Address," 448.

[3]Kimball, "Second-Century Address," 453.

[4]Spencer W. Kimball, "Education for Eternity," address given September 12, 1967, at Brigham Young University, 8. See pages 43–63 in this volume.

[5]Kimball, "Second-Century Address," 450.

[6]Dallin H. Oaks, "Annual Report on the University," *Second Century: On with the Task,* Brigham Young University Conference Speeches 1976, 24.

[7]Oaks, "Annual Report," 25.

[8]"Gallup Says Americans 'Spiritually Hungry,' Reject Rationalism," *Washington Post,* May 13, 1977, E6.

[9]Kimball, "Education for Eternity," 8.

[10]See also Dallin H. Oaks, "Annual Report to the Faculty," Brigham Young University Conference 1974, 17.

[11]Kimball, "Education for Eternity," 11–12.

[12]Harold B. Lee, *Ye Are the Light of the World* (Salt Lake City: Deseret Book, 1974), 104.

[13]Student letter received August 12, 1977.

[14]Kimball, "Second-Century Address," 447.

[15]Kimball, "Second-Century Address," 446.

[16]Kimball, "Second-Century Address," 453.

[17]Kimball, "Second-Century Address," 454.

[18]Kimball, "Second-Century Address," 455.

[19]Kimball, "Second-Century Address," 446.

[20]Neal A. Maxwell, *Deposition of a Disciple* (Salt Lake City: Deseret Book, 1976), 15.

[21]Kimball, "Second-Century Address," 448.

[22]Kimball, "Second-Century Address," 453–54.

[23]John Taylor, in *Journal of Discourses,* 26 vols. (Liverpool: F. D. Richards, 1855–86), 21:100, April 13, 1879.

[24]Kimball, "Second-Century Address," 453.

[25]Spencer W. Kimball, "The Gospel Vision of the Arts," *Ensign* 7 (July 1977): 3.

[26]Kimball, "Second-Century Address," 453.

[27]Kimball, "Second-Century Address," 453.

[28]Joseph Fielding Smith, comp., *Teachings of the Prophet Joseph Smith* (Salt Lake City: Deseret News Press, 1943), 151.

[29]Kimball, "Second-Century Address," 453.

By Study and Also by Faith

Rex E. Lee

We gain understanding by two processes. I will refer to them as the rational process and the extrarational process. My theses are that each of these processes plays an important role in our fulfilling that ancient and all-important mandate to "get understanding" (Prov. 4:7), that there is no inherent inconsistency between the two processes, and that our eventual achievement of total perfection will require the use of both processes.

The rational process is the one that you are accustomed to using in your academic work. Its tools should be familiar to all of you: reading, analysis, research, criticism, and, generally, problem resolution by thoughtful inquiry. Properly applied, it is a strenuous, taxing, and frequently frustrating experience. It is my belief that the difficulties and frustrations of the rational process are inextricably interlaced with the plan of eternal progress and that a principal objective of this plan is to achieve a facility and, eventually, mastery of its use.

At the time that the era of free agency was ushered in, God informed Adam, "In the sweat of thy face shalt thou eat bread" (Gen. 3:19). That metaphor has far broader application than the relationship between physical work and the achievement of the necessities of life. Just as hard labor or exercise strengthens our muscles and makes them more useful, so also the hard, frustrating straining of our mental abilities to the point that— symbolically, at least—they ache just as a muscle would ache results in the strengthening of our ability to use these processes.

It is not easy to become a great football player, weight lifter, or discus thrower; no one ever achieved greatness in these endeavors without extensive and continuous sweat of the face. Similarly, no one ever achieved excellence of the mind without really pushing himself or herself. The requisite mental effort is difficult, frustrating, and often tormenting, but it is an inseparable aspect of the law of eternal progress. Only by the sweat of our intellectual faces can we taste the bread of contentment that comes from having successfully challenged and mastered the rational process.

The acquisition of understanding through the rational process takes on a special dimension for members of The Church of Jesus Christ of Latter-day Saints. The restoration of the gospel has provided many of the answers to life's great questions. Since the answers to these questions have come through the only infallible source of knowledge—direct revelation from God—there is no need to resolve them rationally.

Take an example that is of perhaps lesser substantive importance but provides a cogent illustration of the point. I don't smoke tobacco, and I don't drink alcoholic beverages. The question whether I would smoke or drink, even in moderation or on isolated occasions, for the achievement of certain social or business objectives is simply not an open question. The answer to that question has been provided for me by God himself in a revelation given to Joseph Smith, February 27, 1833 (D&C 89:5, 8). For other people, the question whether to smoke or not to smoke involves the kind of balancing of interests that is characteristic of the rational process, weighing such considerations as the probable shortening of life by a decade or so against the delightful smell that tobacco smoke imparts to the clothes of its users.

Similarly, we hear a lot these days to the effect that confining sexual relations to the marriage context is outmoded and society would be better off if this idea were discarded. Much can be said and ought to be said in rational opposition to these suggestions. But you and I, as members of The Church of Jesus Christ of Latter-day Saints, do not really approach that issue on a rational basis. The Lord has revealed to us that the misuse of our powers of creation is an offense second only to the shedding of innocent blood. That kind of knowledge supersedes any

Rex E. Lee speaks at the J. Reuben Clark Law School about 1986.
Courtesy Janet Lee.

possible conclusions of human beings, no matter how brilliant and no matter how skilled in the use of rational processes.

There are other examples: we baptize by immersion at eight years of age; we meet once a week to partake of the sacrament; we confer the priesthood upon those who qualify at age twelve; and we do vicarious ordinance work for the dead. As to these practices and these beliefs, the rational processes are simply irrelevant. Even if I should conclude that I would be a happier person if I smoked and that the delightful smell on my clothes and the aura of distinction and dignity that surrounds smokers is more important than ten or fifteen years added to my life, I still would not smoke. I don't need to concern myself with whether eight years is really the best age for baptism, or twelve the optimum age to receive the priesthood. These for me are not questions which are subject to the rational process.

From the accepted premise that the gospel provides the complete answer to many of life's great questions, we sometimes make the mistake of assuming that the gospel forecloses from the rational process a rather vast segment of problems which we ought to resolve for ourselves and which, from my understanding of the plan of eternal progress, really require that we resolve for ourselves—issues such as whether I should be a Republican or a Democrat; whether we should have an income tax and, if we do, whether the rate should be progressive; whether our units of local government should fluoridate their water supply; whether we should be selling grain to communist countries; and so on. There are many questions such as these which the discharge of our obligations as American citizens requires us to work out for ourselves by the application of our own intellectual abilities. They are the kinds of issues on which two members of the Church can reach opposite conclusions without impairing the Church standing of either. And they are the kinds of problems to which, in my view, the law of eternal progress anticipates that we will apply rational processes if we are to achieve the corresponding development.

I turn now to the acquisition of understanding through extrarational processes. The methods are not the same. The results are much surer, though they are not as susceptible to our own control.

For centuries, men have been debating about the nature of God. On occasion, hundreds of the world's best scholars assembled for the purpose of resolving the issue by application of their combined intellectual talents. Out of these centuries of rational effort by the world's finest minds evolved the prevailing Christian concept of God—centuries, if you will, of application of the finest minds in the world to this important question! And yet, in the space of just a few minutes, a boy of fourteen years learned more about the true nature of God than had come from centuries of the best rational effort of the world's best minds. The process was extrarational. It did not depend on study, thought, or contemplative inquiry. It came through revelation, through direct contact between a mortal man and his Father in Heaven.

Joseph Smith's experience is the most outstanding example of extrarational learning that has occurred since the resurrection of the Savior, but it is not the only instance. Though of less dramatic surrounding circumstances, the opportunity is available to every earthly creature to gain understanding through the extrarational process.

Extrarational learning takes a great variety of forms: the quiet, serene confidence of total assurance that can accompany the reading of the scriptures, particularly the Book of Mormon; the ring of truth that is detected upon hearing another person's testimony; the quiet, yet overwhelming inner conviction that the work in which one is engaged is truly the restored kingdom of Jesus Christ. May I share with you a personal experience involving learning by extrarational means.

The experience occurred in a suburb of Mexico City, Colonia Moctezuma. My companion and I had returned on one hot afternoon to discuss what was then the third lesson (dealing with the Restoration) with a widow and her daughters. The first two lessons had been rather sterile and innocuous. We had been treated with courtesy but not much interest, and frankly, I was somewhat surprised that we had been invited back the third time. The Restoration lesson is distinctive in its almost complete reliance on individual testimony. At least as we were presenting it at that time, there were practically no scriptural references. By that time, we had already explained the need for apostles and prophets and the fact that these had been taken from the earth in ancient times. The Restoration lesson consisted simply of recounting the contacts that had been made between heaven and earth during the restoration period, and then bearing our testimonies that we knew that these things had really happened.

The third visit with this family started out much as the two preceding ones. And then, something happened that I will remember as long as I live. I began to recount the restoration of the Aaronic Priesthood, how it was that John the Baptist had appeared to the Prophet Joseph Smith and Oliver Cowdery, laid his hands upon their heads, and restored the lesser priesthood. As I began to speak, the thought occurred to me: This is really true. The same man who baptized the Savior himself and cried repentance in the wilderness really did come to this earth, some eighteen centuries later, and actually laid his hands upon the heads of Joseph and Oliver, bringing to the earth once again the authority to do what he himself had done in the meridian of time—perform the foundational ordinance of baptism. As this overwhelming impression came over me—that what I was saying was really true—I could tell that I was conveying the same impression to the members of that family. And the means of conveyance was not just the spoken word. The words that were coming from my mouth were not materially different from the words that I had spoken on hundreds of prior occasions. And yet I could tell that this same impression, this realization of truth which I was personally finding so compelling, was also being conveyed to this widow and her daughters. I had witnessed a manifestation of that great principle articulated by the prophet Nephi, that "when a man speaketh by the power of the Holy Ghost the power of the Holy Ghost carrieth it unto the hearts of the children of men" (2 Ne. 33:1). Before I finished speaking and before any of the family members had expressed their own impressions, I knew that conversion had occurred. I knew that these people knew that John the Baptist on May 15, 1829, had personally made a visitation to this earth and that his visitation was one integral part of the restoration of the kingdom of God. I knew that from that point forward it was only a matter of time until the family would be baptized. And this is in fact what happened.

Having examined briefly some of the essential characteristics of each of these processes, let us turn now to some of the basic relationships between the two. Two great learning processes: What are their interrelationships? Or are there any?

First, of the two methods, the extrarational gives the surer results. It does not follow, however, that anyone who has had hands laid on his head and been given the promise of the constant companionship of the Holy Ghost, contingent on his worthiness, has no need to apply his mental skills to acquire learning. No matter how righteous you are, no matter how carefully you cultivate the companionship of the Holy Ghost, there are vast amounts of knowledge which you need to acquire and which you are not going to receive through revelation. The great plan of eternal progress anticipates our growth and development through use of our mental skills, the kind of progress that can come only through the strenuous application of our reasoning abilities.

Second, there occasionally exists the tendency among those who achieve proficiency in either of these processes to downplay the importance of the other. There is a corollary tendency to assume that excellence in the use of one of these methods forecloses the need to develop excellence in the other. The oft-repeated observation that "we have something that no one else has" is undeniably true. But the fact that we have the gospel should not be used as an excuse to fail to do the very thing that the gospel commands, to expand our knowledge of all truth. The eighty-eighth section of the Doctrine and Covenants is explicit on this point. It does not enjoin us to seek learning "either by study or by faith." Neither does it state that "if ye have achieved learning by faith, ye are thereby permanently exempted from study." Rather, the commandment is to obtain learning and to obtain it both "by study and also by faith" (D&C 88:118). And I say to you that no man is truly learned whose learning experiences exclude either the rational or the extrarational method.

Again, the experience of the Prophet is instructive. Unquestionably, his was the prime example of extrarational learning by a mortal. It is interesting, and in my view significant, that his was an experience that was preceded by extensive rational effort as well as prayer. Similarly, the famous instruction given by the Lord to Oliver Cowdery in the ninth section of the Doctrine and Covenants—and through Oliver Cowdery to all of us—involves a combination of the two processes: "You must study it out in your mind; then you must ask me if it be right, and if it is right I will cause that your bosom shall burn within you; therefore, you shall feel that it is right" (D&C 9:8).

We should be both scholarly and spiritual, and we should discard any notion that there is any inconsistency in the two methods. The true intellectual is one whose intellect is sufficiently developed that he recognizes not only the great potential, but also the limitations of his intellectual capacity. Conversely, there is no need for the person who has acquired understanding through spiritual insights to be suspicious of those who acquire learning by study. The scriptural mandate is that both processes be used. The most learned people I know—and there are many of them—are people who find no inconsistency between study and faith and who have achieved a proficiency in each. We should feel equally at home in the academy and in the chapel; we should recognize each as a center of learning. We know that the day will come when the lamb will lie down with the lion. We need not await the Millennium for the scholar to be a patriarch and the patriarch to be a scholar.

Third and finally, I have expressed the view that there is no inconsistency between the rational method and the extrarational method. This does not mean that the conclusions reached by each of these methods will always be consistent. Indeed, it is almost inevitable that there will be some instances in which the rational method will lead us to some conclusion—not many, but some—which is at odds with what we know to be true because it has been revealed from God. Now what do you do when you encounter such instances? (And I reiterate: encounter is almost inevitable.) The answer is not to stop struggling with the matter on a rational level. But we must recognize that our rational processes, marvelous as they are, have limited capabilities. Therefore, the underlying approach must be that in those few instances in which we find disparity between the conclusions reached by our rational and extrarational processes, the extra-rational must prevail. We must recognize that in those few instances the seeming inconsistency is attributable to the fallible nature of our rational capacity. The answer is not to stop the rational struggle with the problem, but rather to recognize the fallible nature of the rational process, the infallible nature of the extrarational process, and the inescapable conclusion that where inconsistencies in results occur—until such time that they can be reconciled—it is the extrarational that must prevail.

The inadequacies of my own mental abilities were impressed upon me early in life. As a young boy growing up, I would gaze from my perch on a sawmill into the clear, starry night, unable to comprehend what was out there. My Sunday School teacher told me that space is without end. My brain was unable then, and is still unable, to comprehend that fact. I simply lack the capacity to perceive how it is that space can continue on and on and never come to an end. And yet my mind is sufficiently developed to comprehend that the alternative is totally unacceptable. If there is some point out there where it all comes to an end, then what is on the other side? These questions concerning space and their equally perplexing counterparts relating to time supply the most cogent examples of which I am aware, and other examples give me a rational basis for my conclusion that in those few instances in which the rational and extrarational processes yield inconsistent results, we must rely on the extrarational.

This address was given to the J. Reuben Clark Law School about 1982, when Rex E. Lee was Solicitor General of the United States. He was the founding dean of the law school and served as president of Brigham Young University from 1989 to 1995.

BYU President Jeffrey R. Holland at a BYU devotional, September 1988. Courtesy Mark A. Philbrick/BYU.

A School in Zion

Jeffrey R. Holland

I, the Lord, am well pleased that there
should be a school in Zion. (D&C 97:3)

Late last winter I was feeling pretty blue about something or other that didn't seem quite right at the university and found myself wondering if all the effort was really worth it. As is so often the case with such monumental matters, I don't even remember now what it was—but whatever it was, it made those winter days a bit darker than usual.

That led to a question I found myself asking late one night in the darkened study of the President's Home: "Should the Church even have a university at all?" Did it justify the effort, the expense, the toil, the tithing—and was it worth the pain? After all, the Church had disengaged from a number of operations, which included not only hospitals and hotels, but of far more interest to us, schools. Should the Church, I wondered, continue to fund BYU if resources are limited, an increasing number of students cannot attend, and individuals at the university—or in any way the university collectively—could not measure up to the expectations that so many generations have had for us?

I sat there that night thinking of what I said on August 26, 1980, when you were kind enough to sit through the very first of these nine messages from me. I said then that I was trusting everything I had, in whatever the Holland administrative years would be, on one single and preeminent principle. That cardinal supposition, that consuming vision, was that we could be an excellent university, indeed a truly great university, an "educational

Mt. Everest," if you will, and still be absolutely, unequivocally, forever faithful to the gospel of Jesus Christ and to His restored Church that sponsors us. In fact, we would accomplish the one *because* of the other, never *in spite* of it. My presidential belief, the only one that seemed to me to justify BYU's existence, was that we could have it both ways, that superb scholarship and rock-solid faith were as inextricable in our future as they were essential to it. I spoke that day of "scholar-saints" who could make this university one of the latter-day wonders of the world.[1]

From that first meeting to this very hour, I have believed that such idealism, such passion for the ultimate possibility, was incumbent upon us all. "'Tis but a base ignoble mind/That mounts no higher than a bird can soar," Gloucester reminded Suffolk.[2] I believed we could somehow, in some way, mount higher, and I was certain God expected our minds to soar. Henry Thoreau had mused by the side of his woodland pond that "in the long run, men hit only what they aim at."[3] So not failure, but low aim would be the most severe indictment of a Latter-day Saint fortunate enough to be at BYU.

Surely we of all people are moved by that "indomitable urge"—that's Ortéga y Gasset's phrase—to expand life, to enlarge it, to improve it. That is our hope, our heritage, our theology. From the beginning, ours has been a soul-stretching belief. "Thy mind, O man!" said the Prophet Joseph Smith, "if thou wilt lead a soul unto salvation, must stretch as high as the utmost heavens, and search into and contemplate the darkest abyss, and the broad expanse of eternity."[4] Only then, he said, could we "contemplate the mighty acts of Jehovah in all their variety and glory."[5]

"The mighty acts of Jehovah"? I have believed that BYU should be one of the "mighty acts of Jehovah." To be less than that for his purposes and his people seemed to me a blasphemy.

With such aspirations for us all, I suppose it isn't surprising that sometimes in the dark of the night I feel we are not measuring up. Soaring is, after all, difficult work. And yes, I did remember that Nauvoo, the city of Zion, had been laid out to feature two Latter-day Saint monuments: a temple and a university. But I also knew that scholastic tension between the sacred and profane had marked most of this world's history, and if the dream weren't *really* attainable, then why have a BYU at all? The fraction of the Church's youth we can serve decreases dramatically each year; we have a fixed BYU student numerator and an exploding Church membership denominator. So the only challenge we can ever address is the qualitative one. And if we can't win that war—if Jerusalem really can't find and fellowship Athens and seal her firmly into the family group sheet—then let's stop holding all these cottage meetings in Provo.⁶

Would it not, I wondered, be better to use the tithing resources of the Church in a more fundamental way—missionary work or temple building or humanitarian aid, say—and let our students attend any one of a thousand other universities that don't pretend to such millennial aspirations? If BYU were ever to look and act just like any other university, who needs it? Not, I was certain, the tithe payers of the Church.

Those are awfully dark thoughts—but then I've learned that most thoughts at one or two o'clock in the morning are pretty dark. (Thank heavens for sleep. Surely the Lord knew what he was doing when he put a night between two days. But back to the study in the President's Home.)

Thanks to my wife, I long ago established the habit of reading at least some scripture every night before retiring, however late it might be. So after such dark thoughts, I turned a lamp back on and reached for my scriptures. For whatever reason, I decided not to pursue the sequential reading that I do most nights. I simply felt inspired to open the scriptures at random and find something fresh and unfamiliar. This night I opened the book without prejudice and with, I think, a special measure of hope in my heart. Literally and truly the first words on which my eyes fell were these in section 97 of the Doctrine and Covenants: "Behold, I say unto you, concerning the school in Zion, *I, the Lord, am well pleased that there should be a school in Zion*" (D&C 97:3; italics added).

The words hit me like a jackhammer. I chilled and blushed and chilled again. I stood up and walked around the room. I'm not embarrassed to tell you I was emotional—you know me well enough to have assumed that; I blubber if the sun comes up. And there across the street, just a few yards from our home,

I thought I saw the statue of Karl G. Maeser smile. (Karl wears a pretty stern look all day there atop his pedestal, so perhaps he smiles every morning at about 1:30 just to relax, but *I* hadn't seen him do it before!)

So I took something of a lightning strike that night, and I almost felt required to apologize. "Lord, I really *don't* harbor doubts about why we have BYU, even on the bad days. Think of it as a joke, a kind of bad joke, I was playing on my neighbor over there, President Maeser. *Please* don't garnish my wages or my salvation. And *please* don't send me with President Cluff to search on horseback for Zarahemla."[7] I even considered singing the school song. "There has to be a 'school in Zion,'" I thought, "because perhaps *there can be no Zion without it!*" By this time, I suspected that the Brigham Young statue was smiling, too.

Now I know the school referred to in section 97 is technically *not* BYU. But BYU *is,* nevertheless, a legitimate academic descendant of the School of the Prophets, and I got a pat on the backside that night which suggested I stop whining and go to work; there was an inheritance to be claimed.

So today I stand before you a repentant man and now presume to answer in some detail my own dark and fleeting question. I would like to suggest why I think the Lord is well pleased that there be a "school in Zion" and why his servants have kept a Brigham Young University when almost all other Church academies are gone, why I think we need it yet, and why I am committed more than ever to its rightful destiny, a university worthy to place before the all-searching eye of God.

As I have already said, the most conspicuous *and* fundamental reason for a "school in Zion" is plainly and simply because it is our theology. You know the verses: "Do the work of printing, and of selecting and writing books for schools in this church, that little children also may receive instruction before me as is pleasing unto me" (D&C 55:4). "Teach ye diligently and my grace shall attend you, that you may be instructed more perfectly in . . . things both in heaven and in the earth, and under the earth; things which have been, things which are, things which must shortly come to pass; . . . a knowledge also of countries and of kingdoms" (D&C 88:78–79).

"Seek ye out of the best books words of wisdom; seek learning, even by study and also by faith" (D&C 88:118). "Study and learn, and become acquainted with all good books, and with languages, tongues, and people" (D&C 90:15). Such knowledge will rise with us in the Resurrection, we are told, and most sobering of all is the warning "It is impossible for a man to be saved in ignorance" (D&C 131:6), for "the glory of God is intelligence, or, in other words, light and truth" (D&C 93:36), and "light and truth forsake that evil one" (D&C 93:37). So part of the message of that restored gospel of Jesus Christ, part of the light now shining into what had been dark ages indeed, is the divine counsel that "to be learned is good if [we] hearken unto the counsels of God" (2 Ne. 9:29).

Surely the most powerful and compelling of all the glorious principles to reenter the world by way of Palmyra was the doctrine of inherent deity. Dare we think it? Could we say it? Would we be labeled blasphemers and heretics for believing it— that we are all literally the spiritual offspring of God, his rightful daughters and sons, who through a kind of divine DNA and the atoning mediation of that greatest of all heirs, the Lord Jesus Christ, have been given the chance to somewhere, someday by "diligence and obedience" (D&C 130:19) know what God knows and do what God does? From those most humble beginnings in Fayette to the magnificence of the final Follett sermon, the Prophet Joseph kept rolling back the firmament, kept letting us glimpse, however myopically, into the vast expanse of our own eternity.

"God has created man with a mind capable of instruction," he wrote, "and a faculty which may be enlarged in proportion to the heed and diligence given to the light communicated from heaven to the intellect."[8] No wonder we would be "ardent friends of learning," as President George Q. Cannon described the Latter-day Saints. No wonder we would be "true seekers after knowledge."[9] No wonder Joseph would leave warning, "A man is saved no faster than he gets knowledge."[10]

It would be axiomatic that some truths matter *much* more than others, but an educated LDS mind would know that, and having gathered all truth into one great whole, it would order and integrate and prioritize truth, using knowledge to emphasize virtue, love, and the saving ordinances of God. In reflecting on the atrocities of the Holocaust, George Steiner observed, "We know now that a man can read Goethe or Rilke in the evening, that he can play Bach and Schubert, and go to his day's work at Auschwitz in the morning. . . . [What grows] up inside literate civilization [that seems to lead to] barbarism?"[11]

"What grows up . . . is information without knowledge, knowledge without wisdom, and wisdom without . . . compassion."[12] So a Latter-day Saint would read Goethe at sundown, play Bach in the evening, and the next morning *die* for his fellowmen, if necessary.

"The Lord requireth the heart *and* a willing mind," Joseph taught (D&C 64:34; italics added). Your mind and heart must expand together. "You must enlarge your souls towards each other," he pled. "Let your hearts expand [as you learn], let them be enlarged towards others."[13] The heart *and* a willing mind.

And what of Brigham Young? The longer I live and the more I read, the more fitting I find it that this largest and nearly last remnant of the academies established under his pioneer leadership still bears and perpetuates his name. As his advocate Hugh Nibley says, "There never was a man more undeviatingly consistent and rational in thought and utterance."[14]

Brigham Young's metaphor for life was the academy, and the principal schoolmaster was his beloved Joseph Smith. Of Joseph he said, "He took heaven, figuratively speaking, and brought it down to earth; and he took the earth, brought it up, and opened up, in plainness and simplicity, the things of God; and that is the beauty of his mission."[15] How plain was that view of life? How simple? To Brigham Young, quite simple. "What are we here for?" Brigham asks, then answers, "To learn to enjoy more, and *to increase in knowledge and in experience.*"[16] "The object of this existence is to *learn,*" he taught.

> How gladly would we understand every principle pertaining to science and art, and become thoroughly acquainted with every intricate operation of nature. . . . What a boundless field of truth and power is open for us to explore! We are only just approaching the shores of the vast ocean of information that pertains to this . . . world, to say nothing of that which pertains to the heavens.[17]

Hugh Nibley says, "The treasures of the earth are merely to provide us with room and board while we are here at school."[18] And Brigham Young, speaking of property and possessions, said, "They are made for the comfort of the creature, and not for his adoration. They are made to sustain and preserve the body while procuring the knowledge and wisdom that pertain to God and his kingdom, in order that we may preserve ourselves, and live for ever in his presence."[19] "And when we have lived millions of years in the presence of God and angels, . . . shall we then cease learning? No, or eternity ceases."[20] "We shall never cease to learn, unless we apostatize. . . . Can you understand that?"[21]

Obviously that kind of effort would be a struggle, but it was a struggle Brigham was always willing to ask for. He must have anticipated all the demands on our time at BYU. Stay anxiously engaged, he said. Actually, what he said is this: "After suitable rest and relaxation there is not a day, hour or minute that we should spend in idleness, but every minute of every day of our lives we should strive to improve our minds and to increase [our] faith [in] the holy Gospel."[22] "The more knowledge the Elders have the better."[23]

And, of course, for him knowledge meant knowledge of everything. "This is the belief and doctrine of the Latter-day Saints. Learn everything that the children of men know."[24] "Every true principle, every true science, every art, and all the knowledge that men possess, or that they ever did or ever will possess is from God. We should take pains and pride to . . . rear our children so that the learning and education of the world may be theirs."[25] "Teach the children, give them the learning of the world *and* the things of God."[26] "Mothers, . . . we will appoint you a mission to teach your children their duty; and instead of ruffles and fine dresses to adorn the body, teach them that which will adorn their minds."[27]

"We are trying to teach this people to use their brains," he said.[28] "Whatever duty you are called to perform, take your minds with you, and apply them to what is to be done."[29] Apparently Brigham had an experience or two when someone must have forgotten that. "In things pertaining to this life, the lack of knowledge manifested by us as a people is disgraceful."[30] "I have seen months and months in this city when I could have wept like a whipt child to see the awful stupidity of the people."[31]

But that pain was the pain of a prophet, not merely a pedagogue. He knew *why* we needed to be intelligent. "All our educational pursuits are in the service of God, for all these labors are to establish truth on the earth, . . . that we may increase in knowledge, wisdom, understanding in the power of faith and in the wisdom of God, that we may become fit subjects to dwell in a higher state of existence and intelligence than we now enjoy."[32] "If men would be great in goodness, they must be intelligent," he would say.[33]

So it was theology. But surely one need not have a school to learn. No, and many didn't, including Joseph and Brigham themselves, but they knew that made it harder and maybe a lot less likely. They wanted structure and synergism for their young scholars. They needed, in short, a place in which to assemble and intensify their education; ergo, reason number two: they needed a "school in Zion"—as we need BYU. It may be too much to call ourselves Zion in our day, but we can be not only a place of gathering for an academic family five times the population of the southern Utah city in which I was born, but a gathering place for the knowledge and "treasures surviving in the earth from every age and culture."[34]

Immediately after arriving in the valley, President Young initiated such a gathering. "[Secure] at least [one] copy of every valuable treatise on education," he told the Saints, "every book, map, chart, or diagram that may contain interesting, useful, and attractive matter, to gain the attention of children, and cause them to love to learn to read." This would include, he said, "every historical, mathematical, philosophical, geographical, geological, astronomical, scientific, practical, and all other . . . useful and interesting writings."[35]

> It is the business of the Elders of this church . . . to gather up all the truths in the world pertaining to life and salvation, to the Gospel we preach, to mechanism[s] of every kind, to the sciences, and to philosophy, wherever [they] may be found in every nation, kindred, tongue, and people, and bring it to Zion.[36]

> Every accomplishment, . . . every useful attainment . . . in all science and art belong to the Saints.[37]

> [They must] rapidly collect the intelligence that is bestowed upon the nations, for all this intelligence belongs to Zion. All the knowledge, wisdom, power, and glory that have been bestowed upon *[all]* the nations of the earth, from the days of Adam till now, must be gathered home to Zion.[38]

And of course, gathering the stuff of learning, the things of learning, or even the students of learning was not enough. So reason number three. What any true Zion would need—and the present world needs even more—is those educated and spiritual and wise who will sort, sift, prioritize, integrate, and give some sense of wholeness, some spirit of connectedness to great eternal truths. At the turn of the twentieth century, Josiah Royce, writing about the great intellectual achievements of our time, observed that man has, "through the richness of the intellectual quest, become more knowing, more clever and more skeptical." But we have not, Royce warned, "become more profound or more reverent. Nor have we found a way to put our learning in the context of the eternal."

Everyone in this room knows as well as I that from Royce's day to this, the problem with higher education has been the perpetuation of dividedness, separateness, departmentalization, specialties, subspecialties, and subspecies of subspecialties. Universities in this nation are disasters, informational Nagasakis, higher educational Hiroshimas. The "watchmen on the tower" cry out for those who will integrate, coalesce, clarify, and give both order and rank to important human knowledge. This generation has students who may not dare to ask the great human questions because their answers appear to be somewhere in the bottom of an academic dumpster, one nearly exploding at the seams from curricular cramming. "The connectedness of things is what the educator [must pursue]," said Mark Van Doren. "No human capacity is great enough to permit a vision of the world as simple, but if the educator does not aim at the vision no one else will, and the consequences are dire when no one does."[39]

So I am convinced that the Lord needs a "school in Zion" now, even more than a century ago, to help a generation, indeed to help an entire Church membership, sort through

much intellectual nonsense that is inevitably in an inert swamp
of facts. More than any time in human history our students
need—as Matthew Arnold needed—a Latter-day Saint Sopho-
cles to teach them, to whom they would gladly give "special
thanks [for an] even-balanced soul, / . . . Who saw life steadily,
and saw it whole."[40]

Is not BYU the restored gospel's designated place to "see
life steadily and see it whole"? Shouldn't it be here that no less
an intellect than Albert Einstein could find what he called that
"vivid sense of the [truly] beautiful, [that vivid sense of the]
morally good"?[41] Could that not be one of the functions of "the
Zion of the mind," as Professor Allen Bergin referred to
the university in light of his own conversion to the Church and
decision to come to BYU? A place not only to love the truth
and gather it, but to organize and integrate it as well. A place
for connectedness, for true community. A place for "even-
balanced souls."

But even as I make this appeal for us to help our students
and ultimately our church, I fear that we often can hardly help
ourselves toward such wholeness and integration. Whether we
are plumbers or professors, clerks or clinicians, we find it very
hard to transcend our departments and specialties. Heaven only
knows we find it hard to transcend the trivia of administration.
Let me use a homely example.

Last year in this setting, I referred to a book on education
by Allan Bloom, *The Closing of the American Mind,* which has
since been on the *New York Times* best-seller list, hard cover
and paperback, for some sixty weeks. I said then that it was perhaps the most unlikely best-selling book of modern times—
filled with philosophy and erudite allusions, written on a dull
subject like the responsibility of university presidents and professors. Whoever else might be interested in such matters (and
apparently a surprising number were), the provocative title *The
Closing of the American Mind* and the even more provocative
subtitle *How Higher Education Has Failed Democracy and Im-
poverished the Souls of Today's Students* could *not,* I think, be
more compelling or insistent to the eye of a university population.

On the basis of the title *alone,* would not our professional
loyalties, or just the immensely heated discussion the book has

stimulated for more than a year, almost *force* us to read it—at least a chapter or two? Without being either patronizing or prescriptive, may I just wonder aloud how many in our community have sampled it. I realize it is not required reading. I also realize that its scope doesn't fall neatly into a department. Indeed, the writer may have a background and behavior that do not square with ours. Best of all, I realize that one might argue *against* the book at least as vigorously as one would argue *for* it, but how are we supposed to know?

We are, you and I, accused in a runaway best seller of closing minds, of failing democracy, and of impoverishing souls! Those are terrible indictments. People have been pouring into bookstores in unprecedented numbers to watch one man slap, for all intents and purposes, every university in the nation with a gigantic slab of tuna. What are we to do? Hunker down deeper into our departments? I wonder.

The author says the book is "a meditation on that state of our souls." Does it succeed?

- Is, as he says, the crisis in the university "the profoundest crisis" modern nations face? Why?

- What of his argument that the U.S. Constitution is something more of moral order than of rules of government?

- What does he mean when he says, "Nature is the standard by which we must judge our lives"? Isn't the natural man an enemy to God?

- Does he believe that science can or cannot deal with issues of "the good"?

- Is every Frenchman—and perhaps every human being anywhere—born either Cartesian or Pascalian, and why on earth would it matter?

- What of his principal tension in the book, that of freedom v. openness? Do such distinctions amount to anything?

- How does he feel about the home and family? Would Latter-day Saints generally agree or disagree?

- Is watching a PBS program "the high tide of American intellectual life"?

- How does he feel about psychologists and psycho-analysis? Do they rank higher or lower than econo-mists and economics? Does he have the slightest idea what he is talking about in either field?

- What distinctions, pro or con, does he give to phrases like "moral instinct," "moral reasoning," "moral training," "moral education," and "moral action"?

- Why does he say it is easier to grasp the condition of a student's soul in the Louvre than in a university classroom? How so?

- Is our critic for or against more movies about Sir Thomas More and Mohandas Gandhi?

- What course at the university is most likely to give a student "the lasting image of a perfect soul"?

- Of what does he speak when he quotes Saul Bellow saying, "It's a kind of ghost town into which anyone can move and [immediately] declare himself sheriff"?

- What role does music play in what the author calls "the one regularly recognizable distinction between the educated and uneducated in America"?

- What is the unique significance the author gives to the word *modesty,* and how does it reflect on a fic-tional character like Anna Karenina or a real one like St. Augustine?

- Is it, in fact, any big deal that America has never had to "kill a king" or "overthrow a church"?[42]

Enough of this. So we're not particularly interested in this book. Maybe we don't need to be. It certainly isn't the lost 116 pages of the Book of Mormon manuscript, and no one needs to tell me how precious time is. Choices are inevitable.

But I think how wonderful it would be if, as a true com-munity, we all read something together and talked about it, something broad and provocative and fun. If Bloom is too far down the alphabet, I'd settle for Aeschylus. I think it would be delightful if every person in this room would read tonight *Prometheus Bound, Agamemnon,* and *The Seven against Thebes.* That's about forty-two pages. And then over a paintbrush or pizza or pair of pinking shears, wherever we gather together, we could discuss them, gospel insights and all.

How might we cultivate the larger sense of connectedness *and* community here? I *do* worry about faculty, staff, and administrative segmentation that keeps us from being a full-fledged "school in Zion." Fortunately, those aspirations I spoke of earlier work in our favor. The ennobling climb toward an Everest allows us—indeed requires us—to take the high ground, gives us a place to view the broader, more liberating, more eternal "general" education, if you will, that is so fundamental to the growth of the human mind and development of the human soul.

That is the *real* merging we someday have to do here—not only organizing and pruning and prioritizing the world's knowledge all about us, but also fusing gospel insights and gospel perspectives into every field and discipline of study. One faculty member recently wrote me saying, "We need—without arrogance but with energy and daring—to try [to] integrate faith and scholarship in our writing and in our teaching and improve it until it stands on its own merit. . . . We especially need to get over merely trying to imitate others or win their approval. Too many [here] are still worrying whether what they write or say will pass the judgment of [a particular university] (of all places!)."

"We ought," he concludes, "to more fully find a way, a unique way, to combine the best of traditional scholarship with the religious and moral questions and perspectives *intrinsic* to that scholarship *and* to the restored gospel. That ought to be not an avocation, but a central part of our scholarly work."[43]

The echo of President Kimball's inaugural charge is in the air. "[Your] light must have a special glow. You [must] do many things [here] that are done elsewhere, but you must do them better."[44]

I would quickly note that some disciplines probably lend themselves a little more directly to gospel insights and influence than others, so please spare me the sardonic questions whether there is a Mormon mathematics or a consecrated chemistry. There probably isn't, but I *would* say there are Mormon mathematicians and consecrated chemists and endowed engineers and historians who are high priests or Church auxiliary leaders. That *should* be an advantage in our integration of truth.

I am making an unabashed appeal for a distinctly LDS approach to education—an approach best featured on this campus by our present university-wide efforts in religious, honors, and general education.

I do not want my next statement to be misunderstood. Please, do *not* misunderstand. I do not believe that Brigham Young University, at least with current policies on both funding and mission, *will* or *should* ever aspire to be a great research university as the nation defines research universities. I do believe with all my heart, however, that we should aspire to become the finest undergraduate university on the face of the planet. The misunderstanding I don't want is a knee-jerk, unwarranted assumption that we will therefore have no serious scholarship required of us nor have a significant, albeit careful selection of graduate and professional programs. I did *not* say we would be a four-year college. I said we would be a *university*.

But we will never, I think, be an MIT or a Cal Tech, nor should we. However, to be a world-class undergraduate teaching university, we have to be a lot smarter and a lot better than we are now. For the purposes of an absolutely unequaled liberal arts general and religious education, we must have teachers who investigate and integrate and know something, who are ambitious about godly growth—what Joseph Smith would call "enlargement." We must have teachers who are growing in precisely the same manner we expect students to grow—and that means significant scholarship.

In this day and age when books like those of Bloom and Boyer and Hirsch and a score of others lament the state of public education, and lay the blame squarely at the feet of the universities and their colleges of education who train and place teachers in those public schools, isn't there something that BYU can uniquely do, some way in which we not only can but should "stand and shine," to use John Masefield's description of a true university?[45]

Don't we have both the advantage *and* the duty to step forward and rally the whole country in this time of national challenge? If BYU is to lend something unique to The Church of Jesus Christ of Latter-day Saints in this last dispensation, something *we* can do that makes us a city set on a hill, a light that cannot be hid, wouldn't it be to produce just such an unequaled—and unfragmented and undivided—"school in Zion"? To be known as *the* place where one can obtain a grand, consummate, unparalleled, and integrated undergraduate education, with whatever other graduate and professional programs we can afford, is a reputation I confess to coveting. That is the mission we wrote for BYU eight years ago, and it is our mission still.

Then why aren't we doing better than we are? Well, in many ways we are doing superbly. I am thrilled, for example, with the increasingly vigorous contributions in Religious Education. Our colleagues there have developed a strong core curriculum founded on the standard works, have been very diligent in not letting it get watered down, offer a truly dramatic array of symposia and publications from the Religious Studies Center, and perhaps most gratifying of all have designed a scintillating Book of Mormon seminar for transfer faculty who teach that course. Some of our finest faculty on campus have told me that this seminar ranks among the most stimulating and rewarding faculty experiences they have *ever* had. That is wonderful news to me, to Religious Education, to the students who take those classes, and to the integrating general education climate on our campus. Indeed, our fourteen hours of religious education ought to be seen as the very heart of our general education experience. I have viewed it that way in the years I have been an administrator at BYU. I commend and applaud all those who help make that happen.

As for the Honors and General Education programs themselves, I consider them crown jewels at the very heart of the most important contributions BYU can make to the world of higher education. A great deal that excites me is happening in these university-wide programs, and more will happen. Our

sisterhood and brotherhood and gospel-based goodwill give us
a distinct GE advantage at BYU in our ability to cross disciplin-
ary and departmental lines. We simply have a very muscular
leg up on the rest of the academic world. We must seize that
advantage. Having focused for several years primarily on
structural arrangements, curricular issues, and winning faculty
support, we should be free to pursue informed, inspired, liberating education.

To do so, we must organize, encourage, evaluate, and reward good teaching. You will have noted that in addition to our
Alcuin awards, we have recently awarded professorships to
strong scholar-teachers who have made a major commitment
to undergraduate education. I have announced today the creation
of a Distinguished Teacher Award, as one of the university's two
highest faculty honors. Exciting, demanding, stretching, challenging, well-organized, and well-taught courses are at the heart
of what we do here. No amount of structural fussing or regula-
tory tinkering will compensate for stale, sterile lectures.

In the curriculum, we must constantly resist the centrifugal
force that habitually plagues GE programs and target our limited resources on a relatively small number of very significant
offerings. Furthermore, we need to guard carefully against the
tendency to let general education offerings become mere intro-
ductory courses to a discipline. They simply must remain more
universal than that.

May I suggest that we also must do a better job of commu-
nicating the very practical value of general education—to our
students and to the public. I think it is very important for us not
to create an unnecessary cleavage between the world of the
academy and the world of work, especially not in the minds of
tuition-paying parents and higher education's increasing number of critics. We need to do a better job of showing the crucial
link between general education and vocation.

"If . . . members of a democracy are to be . . . effective con-
tributors [to the community]," writes Professor Steven Cahn,

> each should be provided with the necessary skills, social
> orientation, and intellectual perspective to succeed in some
> wide field of occupational endeavor. But such [true] voca-

tional education must not be confused with narrow job-training. Animals are broken in and trained; human beings ought to be enlightened and educated. An individual [trained but not educated] is unable to adjust in the face of changing conditions and is thus stymied by a world in flux. Sidney Hook [adds]: "There is a paradox connected with vocational training. The more vocational it is, the narrower it is; the narrower it is, the less likely it is to serve usefully in earning a living." [Therefore] broadened vocational preparation is not only of use to the future worker himself; its benefit to society is apparent to anyone who has ever been forced to deal with the mechanized mind of a bureaucrat.[46]

Professor Douglas Tobler once said to me, "A good general education is the most practical thing I know. How to use the mind may be the ultimate vocational skill."

Lastly, across the breadth of our university effort we must respect and elevate the status of the students themselves. They must be seen as more than what Henry Rosovsky called at Harvard "the lumpenproletariat." She is someone's perfect daughter, he is someone's precious son, and they are certainly brothers and sisters to us all. Furthermore, they are coming to us better prepared than ever before, so we need to expect more of them and of ourselves while they are here.

Missionary-like, we need to make this the best four years of their lives. We need to give them personal attention and treat them with great respect, not only in class but in administrative and staff contacts as well. We need to advise them thoughtfully and mentor them professionally as an earlier generation of educators used to do. That may be difficult with some of our larger classes and challenging student-teacher ratios, but a good experience in a large class surely beats a bad experience in a small one. I speak from personal experience.

I have always loved Elder Marion D. Hanks's telling of the John Trebonious story. John Trebonious used to take off his hat on entering the classroom when it was the Germanic custom of the day for professors to keep them on. When asked why he was so needlessly kind to his pupils, he replied, "'These little boys will some day be men, and I do not know but that there

sits among them one who will change the destiny of mankind.
I take off my hat in deference to what they may become.'" Sitting in his classroom, watching the ways of that gentle man, was
the young and future Martin Luther.[47]

A fourth reason for a "school in Zion" is essentially a symbolic one, but a symbol with genuine substance. Elder John A.
Widtsoe once wrote:

> The whole of life is education. . . . No wonder, therefore,
> that in the correct philosophy of life, schools and other
> devices for the training of man's powers are foremost.
> Education is and must be carried onward fully and abun-
> dantly in the Church of Christ. The support of education
> is, indeed, one test of the truth of the Church.[48]

That is a stunning affirmation of our earlier comments
about the LDS doctrine of learning. But what happens when the
true church grows so large and has such call upon its resources
that it can perhaps support only the idea, only the concept of
education rather than actual schools in which to provide it?

In such a time of growth and need, could not the *one* true
Church profit magnificently from at least *one* gleaming evidence of the Church's "support of education," *one* university
sparkling, however distantly, for those Saints who now cluster
in their localities with a somewhat altered sense of gathering
than Zion once had? Could not BYU, both symbolically and
substantially, be an unparalleled, incomparable blessing to *every
one* of those Saints, from Nigeria to Newfoundland, who may
never set foot on BYU soil, let alone dream of having one of
their own? Could it not be a house of hope and glory to every
member of the Church everywhere who is trying to grow, trying
to learn, trying to be strong and safe and spiritual in a very secular world? I should surely think so. We could, for the whole
church, provide what the doughboys called "pride in the out-
fit." And we could provide for them in the process an increasing
array of leadership, example, service, and protection.

Without deifying him prematurely, consider what our own
Hugh Nibley has done to strengthen faith for people far, far
away from Provo—a place from which he almost never travels.

And consider, if you will, his fairly biting indictment of some of the rest of us as he praises the university's namesake.

> [We are] only too glad to settle for the outward show, the easy and flattering forms, trappings and ceremonies of education. . . .
>
> As a result, whenever we move out of our tiny, busy orbits of administration and display, we find ourselves in a terrifying intellectual vacuum. Terrifying, of course, only because we might be found out. But that is just the trouble: having defaulted drastically in terms of President Young's instructions, [some of us] stand as a brainless giant, a push-over for any smart kid or cultist or faddist or crank who even pretends to have read a few books. . . . We . . . stand help-lessly and foolishly by dangling our bonnet and plume while hundreds of students and missionaries, [hundreds] of mem-bers and enemies of the Church alike, presume to challenge and reject the teachings of Joseph Smith on evidence so flimsy that no half-educated person would give it a second thought. . . . No one has ever told them what it means to lay a proper foundation essential to any serious discussion of the things they treat so glibly and triumphantly. . . .
>
> Whether we like it or not, we are going to have to return to Brigham Young's ideals of education; we may fight it all the way, but in the end God will keep us after school until we learn our lesson.[49]

And defending the faith intelligently is only one kind of aid we might offer our far-flung brothers and sisters, albeit surely the most important one. There are, it seems to me, scores of other kinds as well, in virtually every discipline of the uni-versity. And it will not require our physically going to them or bringing them physically here to us. We cannot do much of that. No, in most cases it means *writing*—good writing, strong writ-ing, in all of our disciplines. Please let us never separate "skillful writing" from "good teaching" at BYU.

Let me close by returning to that original "school in Zion" and, in so doing, come full circle. To do that, we have to go to the upper room just moments before Gethsemane and Golgotha.

As part of the strengthening preparation the Savior pro-vided for his Apostles, Apostles who did not and could not comprehend what lay immediately ahead of them, Christ rose from that paschal meal and, girding himself with a towel, poured water into a basin. He then knelt, alone, and washed the feet of the Twelve.

There is a profound gesture of humility and love in this act. During what would be the most anguished evening in human history, when someone might well have attended a bit more to him, the Prince of Peace knelt serving others, leaving an unforgettable lesson on the real meaning of "Master."

Peter tried to resist the Lord's selflessness. "Thou shalt never wash my feet," he recoiled—to which Jesus simply replied, "If I wash thee not, thou hast no part with me." And of course, marvelous Peter then pled, "Lord, not [then] my feet only, but also my hands and my head" (John 13:8–9).

"If I wash thee not, thou hast no part with me." What could that *possibly* have to do with schools and education and learning? Maybe everything.

As the Lord issued the commandment to organize the School of the Prophets, he prefaced it all with what must have been the first of these worthiness interviews still a part of the BYU tradition for faculty, staff, administrators, and students. You must "sanctify yourselves," the Lord said, "yea, purify your hearts, and cleanse your hands and your feet before me, that I may make you clean" (D&C 88:74).

No one was to be in that unique academy unworthily. That is still true for us today.

Gathering, uniting, learning. Community, cleanliness, communion. One in feeling and sentiment and purpose—a basin, a circle, a bond. Humility and service. Strong faith and order. A school in Zion.

Why have the gospel of Jesus Christ at the heart of BYU? I will tell you why: "So that Satan cannot overthrow us, nor have any power over us here."[50] Remember: "The glory of God is intelligence, or, in other words, light and truth. [And] light and truth forsake that evil one" (D&C 93:36–37).

May it be so for us this year and always.

This address was given at the Annual University Conference Address on August 22, 1988. Jeffrey R. Holland served as president of Brigham Young University from 1980 to 1989.

NOTES

[1]Jeffrey R. Holland, "The Bond of Charity," Annual University Conference, August 1980, 2–12.

[2]William Shakespeare, *King Henry VI, Part* 2, act 2, scene 1, lines 13–14.

[3]Henry David Thoreau, *Walden,* reprint ed. (New York: Viking Penguin, 1983), 69.

[4]Joseph Fielding Smith, comp., *Teachings of the Prophet Joseph Smith* (Salt Lake City: Deseret Book, 1938), 137.

[5]Smith, *Teachings,* 163.

[6]See James Nuechterlein, "Athens and Jerusalem in Indiana," *American Scholar* 57 (summer 1988): 353–68, for a more thorough treatment of the Athens-Jerusalem metaphor.

[7]See Ernest L. Wilkinson and W. Cleon Skousen, *Brigham Young University: A School of Destiny* (Provo, Utah: Brigham Young University Press, 1976), 151–62.

[8]Smith, *Teachings,* 51.

[9]George Q. Cannon, *Gospel Truth: Discourses and Writings of George Q. Cannon,* comp. Jerreld L. Newquist (Salt Lake City: Deseret Book, 1987), 461.

[10]Smith, *Teachings,* 217.

[11]George Steiner, *Language and Silence* (New York: Atheneum, 1967), ix, x.

[12]Ernest Boyer, quoting Steiner in an address to BYU General Education Workshop, June 1988.

[13]Smith, *Teachings,* 228.

[14]Hugh Nibley, "Educating the Saints—a Brigham Young Mosaic," *BYU Studies* 11, no. 1 (1970): 62; reprinted in *Brother Brigham Challenges the Saints,* vol. 13 of *The Collected Works of Hugh Nibley* (Salt Lake City: Deseret Book, 1994), 306–45.

[15]Brigham Young, in *Journal of Discourses,* 26 vols. (Liverpool: F. D. Richards, 1855–86), 5:332, October 7, 1857 (hereafter cited as *JD*).

[16]Young, in *JD,* 14:228, September 16, 1871; italics added.

[17]Young, in *JD,* 9:167, January 26, 1862; italics added.

[18]Nibley, "Educating the Saints," 65.

[19]Young, in *JD,* 8:135, July 29, 1860.

[20]Young, in *JD,* 6:344, July 31, 1859.

[21]Young, in *JD,* 3:203, February 17, 1856.

[22]Young, in *JD,* 13:310, April 17, 1870.

[23]Young, in *JD,* 8:54, April 25, 1860.

[24]Young, in *JD,* 16:77, May 25, 1873.

[25]Young, in *JD,* 12:326, January 10, 1869.

[26]Young, in *JD,* 14:210, August 13, 1871; italics added.

[27]Young, in *JD,* 14:220–21, August 27, 1871.

[28]Young, in *JD,* 11:328, February 10, 1867.

[29]Young, in *JD,* 8:137, July 29, 1860.

[30]Young, in *JD,* 11:105, May 15, 1865.

[31]Young, in *JD,* 2:280, May 27, 1855.

[32]Young, in *JD,* 13:260, October 6, 1870.

[33]Manuscript History of the Church, September 22, 1851, vol. 21, Archives Division, Historical Department, The Church of Jesus Christ of Latter-day Saints, Salt Lake City, 88.

[34]Nibley, "Educating the Saints," 69.

[35]*Millennial Star* 10 (March 15, 1848): 85.

[36]Young, in *JD,* 7:283–84, October 9, 1859; italics added.

[37]Young, in *JD,* 10:224, April and May 1863.

[38]Young, in *JD,* 8:279, June 3, 1860; italics added.

[39]Mark Van Doren, *Liberal Education* (Boston: Beacon Press, 1943), 115.

[40]Matthew Arnold, "To a Friend."

[41]See Otto Nathan and Heinz Norden, eds., *Einstein on Peace* (New York: Simon and Schuster, 1960).

[42]See Allan Bloom, *The Closing of the American Mind* (New York: Simon and Schuster, 1987).

[43]Eugene England, letter to author.

[44]Spencer W. Kimball, "Installation of and Charge to the President," Inaugural Addresses, November 14, 1980, Special Collections and Manuscripts, Harold B. Lee Library, Brigham Young University, Provo, Utah, 9.

[45]See John Masefield, "The University," a speech delivered at the University of Sheffield on June 25, 1946.

[46]Steven M. Cahn, *Education and the Democratic Ideal* (Chicago: Nelson-Hall, 1979), 11.

[47]Marion D. Hanks, *The Gift of Self* (Salt Lake City: Bookcraft, 1974), 126.

[48]John A. Widtsoe, *A Rational Theology* (Salt Lake City: Deseret Book, 1937), 176.

[49]Nibley, "Educating the Saints," 86–87.

[50]Joseph Smith Jr., *History of The Church of Jesus Christ of Latter-day Saints,* ed. B. H. Roberts, 2d ed., rev., 7 vols. (Salt Lake City: Deseret Book, 1971), 2:309.

Spiritual Orientation: Three Addresses

Boyd K. Packer

I. The Edge of the Light

Shortly after I was called as a General Authority, I went to Elder Harold B. Lee for counsel. He listened very carefully to my problem and suggested that I see President David O. McKay. President McKay counseled me as to the direction I should go. I was very willing to be obedient but saw no way possible for me to do as he counseled me to do.

I returned to Elder Lee and told him that I saw no way to move in the direction I was counseled to go. He said, "The trouble with you is you want to see the end from the beginning." I replied that I would like to see at least a step or two ahead. Then came the lesson of a lifetime: "You must learn to walk to the edge of the light, and then a few steps into the darkness; then the light will appear and show the way before you." Then he quoted these eighteen words from the Book of Mormon: "Dispute not because ye see not, for ye receive no witness until after the trial of your faith."

Those eighteen words from Moroni have been like a beacon light to me. Let me put them in their setting:

> And it came to pass that Ether did prophesy great and marvelous things unto the people, which they did not believe, because they saw them not. And now, I, Moroni, would speak somewhat concerning these things; I would show unto the world that faith is things which are hoped

for and not seen; wherefore, dispute not because ye see not, for ye receive no witness until after the trial of your faith. (Ether 12:5–6)

During the twenty-nine years following that experience, I have learned over and over again that all of us must walk by faith—near the edge of the light. Like Nephi, who said, "I was led by the Spirit, not knowing beforehand the things which I should do" (1 Ne. 4:6), each of us must learn to take a few steps into the darkness of the unknown.

A desire to learn is one thing. An expressed willingness to be taught and to be corrected is quite another. I have found, and we have taught our children, that there is always someone older and experienced who knows much about the challenges you face, whether they be spiritual or temporal. It is worth inviting them to help you.

While there is great value in seeking a personal interview to receive counsel, what I am talking about is something else. It is an unstructured process, with counsel and suggestions offered in bits and pieces and you responding with thanks. That process survives only where there is a genuine desire to learn and an invitation to those who can teach and correct you. That invitation is not always in words, but more in attitude. Could that be the reason that the scriptures counsel "Ask and ye shall receive" more than any other statement? I believe the priceless gift of the Holy Ghost, which can be a constant companion, operates on those terms.

Once when I returned from a mission tour totally exhausted, my wife said to me, "I have never seen you so tired. What is the matter; did you find a mission president who wouldn't listen?" "No," I replied, "it was just the opposite. I found one who wanted to learn."

Many will say they want to learn but feel threatened if there is the slightest element of correction in what they are given. I have learned that few respond when that kind of teaching or correction is offered and fewer still invite it. If you are willing, a teacher will spread a cloth and share nourishing morsels from his or her store of experience.

In 1965, Elder Harold B. Lee taught me to take counsel from courage rather than from my fears. At that time, there

Elder Boyd K. Packer at a BYU commencement, April 1994. Courtesy
Mark A. Philbrick/BYU.

were an impressive 2,235,000 members in the Church. Today, the Church is even larger and continues to grow rapidly. Literally thousands of them dream of enrolling at BYU. Most of them cannot be admitted simply because of enrollment ceilings imposed by limits on space and funds. During these years of very rapid growth in membership in the Church, the enrollment at this university has remained constant. It cannot grow as the Church grows, and the growth of the Church cannot be held back. The competition for admission to Church colleges and universities grows ever more intense.

General Authorities frequently receive letters from young people all over the world, begging for the opportunity for an education, wanting desperately to come to a Church-sponsored college. I have just now received one from a young woman in the Philippines. She wants to be a doctor. "I've the grade," she wrote, "but money I've nothing. I kept on praying asking Him, whom will I ask to help . . . and you know what? My heart says it's you, Elder Packer, who can understand what I feel, so here I am asking the Apostle of God to help me."

How painful it is for us to see so many worthy ones for whom there is no room. It is little wonder that the First Presidency would want to "ensure that students who are active Church members are not excluded through enrollment ceilings while inactive members enjoy the blessing of attending Church schools. . . . Students who have not been endorsed may not register for university or college classes for the next academic year." The Church Board of Education and the BYU Board of Trustees are struggling now to update our policy on admission. We have no choice but to make some adjustments to accommodate the growth of the Church. The administrators of Church colleges and universities have no choice but to enforce those policies; they are not free to do otherwise. Entrance requirements cannot be based on grades alone. Church schools are not solely for the academically gifted.

That word *trustee* is worth a comment. In a public institution, trustees are responsible to the taxpayers. In the Church, we are responsible to tithe payers and to the Lord. We presently have institutes of religion at 1,711 colleges and universities across the world. The institutes enroll 126,000 Latter-day

Saints. In this way, we are able to bring religious education, the one discipline essential to the mission of the Church, to our members of college age without the expense of duplicating the whole secular curriculum. High quality education is widely available at state and private colleges and universities.

Notwithstanding the institute program, frequently at stake conferences we face a parent or a Church leader who desperately wants some student to be admitted to BYU. They always ask, "Are the Brethren planning to build another university?" to which we must answer, "They are not." Next question: "Why?" I simply meet that question with one of my own: "Do you have any idea how much money it costs to mow the lawns and wash the windows at BYU?"

Never could we keep pace with the growth of the Church. Education is a very expensive undertaking. The operation of a large university in this country is not possible on a budget of millions or tens of millions of dollars annually. It requires the expenditure of hundreds of millions of dollars each year.

Some time ago, I was sent to inspect a college campus, smaller than this but as modern and beautifully constructed as is this campus. It had been offered to the Church for the taking, with the single requirement that we continue its operation as a college. But we declined, even though it was in a center of Church population. Such offers have come more than once.

We are not only trustees for our school, we must balance the resources of the Church so that the central mission of the Church will be accomplished. Did you know that there are members of this Church who eat only one meal a day? We help them all we can, considering political barriers. We face some very sobering choices. If we must choose between giving more and more to those already well favored and helping them less, we will do just as you would do.

The Church once owned and operated a system of hospitals, a very defensible endeavor. In 1974 the First Presidency stated, "Because the operation of hospitals is not central to the mission of the Church, the Church has . . . decided to divest itself of its extensive hospital holdings." And they were given away.[1]

Question: Are colleges and universities central to the mission of the Church? I might answer, "That all depends."

In his statement to you, President Rex Lee quoted a predecessor, Dallin H. Oaks, who said:

> Religious activities in the BYU stakes are . . . vital to what is unique about this university. [Moreover,] the LDS student who takes no significant part in the religious life of this campus is occupying a place . . . that excludes another Latter-day Saint who is anxious to be admitted and to participate in the entire range of campus activities. This is unfair and an unwise use of the unique resources of this institution.

You will contribute to the central mission of the Church only when you receive and maintain a testimony of the restored gospel to complement an education of superior quality. And there need be no choice between the two, for we can meet, even surpass, the academic standards of those organizations established to improve and accredit colleges and universities.

Why would anyone feel unsettled at a review of your worthiness to remain at a Church college? It is no different than the test to measure your academic progress, no different than the requirement that you maintain a certain grade point average.

BYU is owned by the Church. It was paid for from tithes and offerings of the Saints and other generous donors. We have kept ourselves free from being supported by public funds in order to remain independent. If government funds ever are accepted, it is on a quid pro quo basis. Everything from the pinnacle of the Carillon Tower to the utility tunnels under the earth belongs to the Church. All were paid for from Church resources.

None of this belongs to you or to us. We are but trustees. It was here before we came; it will serve generations after we have gone. For the present, it is placed at our disposal so that as students we may study and as teachers we may teach in an environment that is clean, both spiritually and temporally. It is made available to us at far below the operating costs. That demands that we respect both the property and the purposes for which it was established.

Tuition and fees do not make up one-fourth of the per-student cost of running this university. More than 70 percent comes from the tithes of the Church, from the widow's mite. There is too much toil and faith and self-denial represented in those funds to expend them on one who is unappreciative of the opportunities afforded to progress both spiritually and academically.

How can we justify expending those sacred funds on a student who will dishonor the agreement he or she signed at the time of admission or on the salary of a faculty member who has his or her own agenda which is at variance with the central mission of the Church, particularly when there is a lineup, ever growing, of both students and teachers waiting and anxious to come to learn or to teach and advance the mission of the university and the central mission of the Church?

As to the student body—the lot of you—what a miracle! Where on earth, now or in any past generation, could you assemble such a student body? Individually, you are impressive; together you are powerful, compelling. We admire you! You are unbelievable to the stranger who comes among you. You are a witness of the restoration, you are a joy to your parents, to all of us. You are the object of approval before him who is the father of our spirits and his son who is our Redeemer.

Granted there may be a few among you who feel uncomfortable with the conservative philosophy at Church schools. Each has that choice. If it is a different life-style you choose, you are not chained here. There are plenty of places to find whatever life-style you desire. But together with you, we will maintain this university with a style of its own. We who love this university will not allow some few to alter the life-style here. And, with your help, we will maintain to the best of our ability an environment that is totally free from the use of narcotics, the abuse of prescription drugs, from steroids and stimulants, from gambling or any other destructive addiction; where chastity and decency and integrity are fostered; where their opposites are subject to correction or expulsion.

Always there are those who chafe under standards and guidelines and restraints and want them lowered or loosened or lifted. Always they play on the word *freedom* and ask, "Is not *free agency* a basic doctrine of the gospel?" Those who think standards contradict their agency may wish to read the seventy-eighth verse of section 101 in the Doctrine and Covenants. They will find that the agency vouchsafed to us from God is a *moral* agency and that everyone is accountable. There can be no *freedom* without *choice*. We are determined to maintain standards and guidelines and restraints so those who want to live under them may have that choice.

Now about the faculty and staff. What a miracle. Where on this earth now or in any generation past has there been assembled a faculty and staff of men and women like this, who have achieved the highest academic degrees. Many have been acclaimed for outstanding accomplishments, and at once you are men and women of humility and faith. You of the faculty and staff are exemplary of the fact that on this campus there need be no choice between academic achievement, intellectual inquiry, and simple faith and reverence.

While that balance may be difficult to achieve and a challenge to maintain, are not these the brightest of minds and the most refined of spirits, these teachers and administrators, upon whom the Lord can depend? Does not every soul of you have the supernal gift of the Holy Ghost to be your companion and teacher? You of the faculty and staff, perhaps more than any other, will answer the question, "Can a university contribute to the central mission of the Church?" As with the students, there are perhaps a few faculty and staff who are restless over the conservative philosophy of education in the Church.

There should be no reticence in relating secular truths to revealed truths. Indeed, that is what President McKay gave as the sole purpose of this university. Nor should there be a problem with teaching *about* any topic or philosophy or subject for we should seek all truth. However, to advocate an unworthy philosophy, rather than to teach about it, to appoint one's self as an alternate voice, is out of harmony with the purpose of Church schools and with the central mission of the Church.

In the early thirties, there developed what might be termed a drift from fundamental moorings in the Church schools. Two things are symbolic of such a drift. One of them is apparent when the teachers of other disciplines look upon the teaching of religion as having less stature than they accord themselves. The other is when teachers or administrators develop agendas of their own and adjust the course from the compass bearing which has been set by the trustees, to a course which is a degree or two worldward. This usually in order to gain, if they can, more approval of the world. Such things do not go unnoticed by those whose compass is sensitive to eternal things.

Concerned over what was happening then, the First Presidency organized a summer school. President J. Reuben Clark Jr. was assigned to speak for the First Presidency. He spoke of course settings and compasses and said, "I shall bring together what I have to say under two general headings—the student and the teacher. I shall speak very frankly, for we have passed the place where we may wisely talk in ambiguous words and veiled phrases. We must say plainly what we mean, because the future of our youth, both here on earth and in the hereafter as also the welfare of the whole Church are at stake."[2] I commend this address to every student and every teacher. Read it carefully, for we are not free from the possibility of such a drift today.

In conclusion, a final lesson. There is one category of experiences which by long-standing rule I do not speak of in public. However, I am going to set aside that rule and tell you a part at least of one such experience. I do so because it has to do with light and darkness and may fix in your minds the lesson I have been trying to teach.

In 1971, I was assigned to stake conferences in Western Samoa, including the organization of the Upolo West Stake. After the necessary interviews on Upolo Island, we chartered a plane to the Island of Savaii to hold a midweek stake conference of the Savaii Stake. There were in our party besides myself and John H. Groberg, now of the First Quorum of Seventy and who was then a Regional Representative; President Wayne Shute of the Samoan Mission, now a professor of education here at BYU; Mark Littleford, superintendent of Church schools in Samoa; and Brother Laeausa, a Samoan talking chief who would represent us in some ceremonies.

The plane landed on a grass field at Faala and was to return the next afternoon to take us back to Apia on Upolo Island. The next afternoon it was raining a little. Knowing the plane would not land on the grassy field, we drove to the west end of Savaii where there was a runway of sorts atop a coral water-break. We waited until dark; no plane arrived. We were finally able to learn by radiophone that it was storming on Upolo Island and that the plane could not take off. We were able as well to tell them we would come by boat and to have someone meet us at Mulisanua. We then drove about three hours back around the island to Saleleloga. There President Tuioti, a counselor in the Savaii Stake presidency, arranged for a boat and obtained the necessary police permit to make the night crossing.

As we pulled out of port, the captain of the forty-foot boat, the *Tori Tula,* asked President Shute if he happened to have a flashlight. Fortunately he did and made a present of it to the captain. We made the thirteen-mile crossing to Muli-sanua on Upolo Island on very rough seas. None of us realized that a ferocious tropical storm had hit Upolo Island.

At Mulisanua, there is one narrow passage through the reef. A light on the hill above the beach marked that narrow passage. There was a second lower light on the beach. When a boat was maneuvered so that the two lights were one above the other, it was lined up properly to pass through the reef.

But that night, there was only one light. Someone was on the landing waiting to meet us, but the crossing took much longer than usual. After waiting for hours, watching for signs of our boat, they tired and fell asleep in the car, neglecting to turn on the lower light.

The captain maneuvered the boat toward the single light on shore while a crewman held a flashlight off the bow. It seemed like the boat would struggle up a mountainous wave and then pause in exhaustion at the crest of it with the propellers out of the water. The vibration of the propellers would shake the boat nearly to pieces before it slid down the other side.

We could hear the breakers crashing over the reef. When we were close enough to see them with the flashlight, the cap-tain frantically shouted reverse and backed away to try again to locate the passage through the reef. After many attempts, he knew it would be impossible to find the opening. All we could do was try to reach the harbor in Apia, twenty miles away. We were helpless against the ferocious power of the elements. I do not remember ever being where it was so dark.

We were lying spread-eagled on the cover of the cargo hold, holding on with our hands on one side, with our toes locked on the other to keep from being washed overboard.

Mark Littleford lost hold and was thrown against the low iron rail. His head was cut front and back, but the rail kept him from being washed away.

As we set out for Apia Harbor, I kept a post on the rail in line of sight with the one light on shore. We made no progress for the first hour even though the engine was full throttle. Eventually we moved ahead and near daylight pulled into Apia Harbor. Boats were lashed to boats several deep at the pier. We crawled across several of them, trying not to disturb those sleeping on deck. We made our way to Pesanga, dried our clothing, and headed for Vailuutai to organize the new stake.

I do not know who had been waiting for us at Mulisanua. I refused to let them tell me. Nor do I care now. But it is true that without that light, the lower light—the light that failed—we all might have been lost.

There is in our hymn book a very old and seldom-sung hymn that has very special meaning to me.

> Brightly beams our Father's mercy
> From his lighthouse evermore,
> But to us he gives the keeping
> Of the lights along the shore.
> Let the lower lights be burning;
> Send a gleam across the wave.
> Some poor fainting, struggling seaman
> You may rescue, you may save.
>
> Trim your feeble lamp, my brother;
> Some poor sailor, tempest-tossed,
> Trying now to make the harbor,
> In the darkness may be lost.[3]

What has happened since 1830 did not come about because we followed the wisdom of men. It came because we followed the light described in the scriptures as "a light that shineth in the darkness and the darkness comprehendeth it not" (see D&C 6:21; 10:58; 34:2; 39:2; 45:7; 88:49; 88:67).

"Behold, I am Jesus Christ, the Son of God. I am the same that came unto mine own, and mine own received me not. I am the light which shineth in darkness, and the darkness comprehendeth it not" (D&C 6:21).

I bear witness of Him. He lives; this is his church. The universities and colleges and schools and institutes and seminaries are his.

I pray, oh how I pray, for our Church schools. I feel contrary breezes blow and see dark clouds appear; it is then that I cry out in my prayers at night, "O Lord, bless our youth, bless those who teach them!"

God grant that when you stand at the edge of the light you may say as the Psalmist said, "Thy word is a lamp unto my feet, and a light unto my path" (Psalm 119:105).

II. "I Say unto You, Be One"

As a mission president, I taught the missionaries to ask a few questions about the town in which they were to labor. Where did the town get its name? When was it settled and why? "Then," I told them, "you will know more about the town than even those who have lived here all of their lives." Most people do not know the very simple and, ofttimes, fascinating things about the community in which they live.

You come to Brigham Young University from all over the world. It is my purpose to tell you things about this great community of learning that you do not know. I will tell you things about the past, why it is unique; why and how this university was founded; something about the present, how it is governed; and something of the future, what we must do if we are to keep faith with those who founded it. Most of what I tell you, you will not find written in books.

Church Education in the Early Years

From the beginning, the Church has fostered both spiritual and secular learning, for that is in the revelations. The Lord revealed that "the glory of God is intelligence, or, in other words, light and truth. Light and truth forsake that evil one. [Ye are commanded] to bring up your children in light and truth" (D&C 93:36–37, 40). Another revelation tells us that "whatever principle of intelligence we attain unto in this life, it will rise with us in the resurrection" (D&C 130:18). There are other scriptures which emphasize the importance of both religious and secular learning. One of them includes a promise: "Teach ye diligently and my grace shall attend you, that you may be instructed more perfectly in theory, in principle, in doctrine, in the law of the gospel, in all things that pertain unto the kingdom of God, that are expedient for you to understand" (D&C 88:78).

As the early Saints moved to Ohio, Missouri, and Illinois, they established elementary and secondary schools in each settlement. Schools of the Prophets were organized for adult leaders in Kirtland, Ohio, in 1833, and other such schools were organized even after the settlement here in the West. I know they had a school of the prophets in Brigham City, for instance. In 1840, a university had been established in Nauvoo.

During the trek to the Rocky Mountains, elementary classes were conducted in the camps. In the fall of 1847, within three months of arriving in the valley, the first schools were organized. Three years later, the University of Deseret was founded.

There is another chapter. In fairly recent times, elementary and secondary schools were established many places in the world where schools were not available to our members. When public education became available, more than a hundred schools, including a university, junior colleges, academies, secondary and elementary schools, were transferred to state governments or were closed.

In order to coordinate the programs and growth of Church schools, a general Church board of education was organized in 1888, consisting of selected local Church leaders—stake presidents, for instance. Karl G. Maeser was named the first superintendent of Church schools, a position that later became the commissioner of Church education.

Working As One

In recent years, the board of education of the Church and the board of trustees for Church colleges and universities has been the First Presidency, six members of the Quorum of the Twelve, a member of the Presiding Bishopric, and the presidents of the Relief Society and the Young Women of the Church.

I can best tell you how you are governed today, how the board of trustees functions, by explaining the principles and procedures we follow in the meetings of the First Presidency and Quorum of the Twelve Apostles. These procedures protect the work from the individual weaknesses apparent in all of us.

When a matter comes before the First Presidency and the Quorum of the Twelve Apostles in a temple meeting, one thing that is determined very quickly is whether it is of serious consequence or not. One or another of us will see in an apparently innocent proposal issues of great and lasting consequence.

It is clear from the revelations that the decisions of the presiding quorums "must be by the unanimous voice of the same; . . . unless this is the case, their decisions are not entitled to the same blessings" (D&C 107:27, 29). In order to ensure that to be the case, matters of consequence are seldom decided in the meeting where they are proposed. And, if the proposal is a part of a larger issue, sufficient time is taken to "bring us all along" so that it is clear that each of us has either a clear *understanding* of the issue or, as is often the case, has a very clear *feeling* about it.

The Doctrine and Covenants instructs us: "Let not all be spokesmen at once; but let one speak at a time and let all listen unto his sayings, that when all have spoken that all may be edified of all, and that every man may have an equal privilege" (D&C 88:122). It would be unthinkable to deliberately present an issue in such a way that approval depended upon how it was maneuvered through channels, who was presenting it, or who was present or absent when it was presented.

Often one or more of us is away during regular meetings. We all know that the work must proceed and will accept the judgment of our Brethren. However, if a matter has been studied by one of the Quorum in more detail than the others or he is more familiar with it either by assignment, experience, or personal interest, the matter is very often delayed until he can be in on the discussion. And always, if one of us cannot understand an issue or feels unsettled about it, it is held over for future discussion. I remember occasions when a delegation was sent to the hospital to discuss with a member of the Council who was ill some urgent matter that should not be delayed but which needed that "unanimous consent." There are occasions, as well, when one of us will leave the meeting temporarily to call one of our number who is abroad to get his feelings on a matter under discussion.

There is a rule we follow: A matter is not settled until there is a minute entry to evidence that all of the Brethren in council assembled (not just one of us, not just a committee) have come to a unity of feeling. Approval of a matter in principle is not considered authority to act until a minute entry records the action taken—usually when the minutes are approved in the next meeting.

Sometimes an afterthought keeps one of us restless over a decision. That is never dismissed lightly. It cannot be assumed that that restless spirit is not in fact the Spirit of Revelation.

That is how we function—in council assembled. That provides safety for the Church and a high comfort level for each of us who is personally accountable. Under the plan, men of very ordinary capacity may be guided through counsel and inspiration to accomplish extraordinary things.

Even with the best of intentions, it does not always work the way it should. Human nature may express itself on occasion but not to the permanent injury of the work. I have a deep, even a sacred, regard for councils; inspiration is evident in them. If ever another course has been followed, trouble has followed as surely as night follows day.

If we are to meet the great challenges now facing this university, we must respect these principles. The Lord said, "I say unto you, be one; and if ye are not one ye are not mine" (D&C 38:27). And the Lord added: "I give unto you directions how you may act before me, that it may turn to you for your salvation. I, the Lord, am bound when ye do what I say; but when ye do not what I say, ye have no promise" (D&C 82:9–10). And I repeat, "I say unto you, be one; and if ye are not one ye are not mine" (D&C 38:27).

While secular achievements deserve and receive our respect, as indicated by what the members of the board of trustees have done in their fields, they are not the qualifications on which we place the *highest* values. Those of higher value relate to the qualities of character which establish a balance in education and have to do with moral stability.

We know the method of learning associated with the working of the Spirit. We treasure the gift of the Holy Ghost which has been conferred upon every member of the Church and which can influence others who are seeking the truth. We know the voice of the Lord when he speaks; we know the processes of revelation and how to teach them to those who want to learn. These qualifications we *do* talk about constantly and strive ever to measure up to them.

"By Study and Also by Faith"

Now listen carefully! It is crucial that you understand what I tell you now. There is danger! Church-sponsored universities are an endangered species—nearly extinct now. The January 1991 journal of the New York–based Institute on Religion in Public Life was devoted to the de-Christianizing of American universities. I quote from their editorial, entitled "The Death of Religious Higher Education."

> The beginning of wisdom on this subject is to recognize that the road to the unhappy present was indeed paved with good intentions. To be sure, there were relevant parties who made no secret of their hostility to religion. But, for the most part, the schools that lost, or are losing, their sense of religious purpose, sincerely sought nothing more than a greater measure of "excellence." The problem is that they accepted, uncritically, definitions of excellence that were indifferent to, or even implicitly hostile to, the great concerns of religion. Few university presidents or department chairmen up and decided one day that they wanted to rid their institutions of the embarrassment of religion. It may reasonably be surmised that most believed that they were advancing a religious mission by helping their schools become like other schools—or at least more like the "best" of other schools. The language of academic excellence is powerfully seductive.[4]

IF, if we succeed in keeping BYU in faith with the founders, we will do something very few others have done. And the survivors are well on toward such a separation.

Our best protection is to ensure that the prerogatives of this unique board of trustees are neither diluted nor ignored. Boards of education, trustees, and regents are venerable and indispensable institutions in education in the free world. They are not to be taken lightly. Theirs, and theirs alone, is the right to establish policies and set standards under which administrators, faculties, and students are to function. Standards of both conduct and of excellence.

It is not unusual for highly trained professionals to smart under the necessity of working under a lay board whose members may not be as highly educated as they consider themselves to be. But the future of education in the free world, and of this unique university, depends on safeguarding the prerogatives of the boards of education.

The ties between universities and churches that founded them have been severed because of the constantly recurring contention between the spiritual and the temporal; the never-ending controversy between a narrow view of science and religion; the ancient conflict between *reason* and *revelation*.

There are two opposing convictions in the university environment. On the one hand, "Seeing is believing"; on the other, "Believing is seeing." Both are true! Each in its place. The combining of the two individually or institutionally is the challenge of life. Neither influence will easily surrender to the other. They may function for a time under some sort of a truce, but the subtle discord is ever present. They mix like oil and water mix—only with constant shaking or stirring. When the stirring stops, they separate again. It takes a catalytic process to blend them. This requires the introduction of a third ingredient, a catalyst, which itself remains unchanged in the blending process.

Each of us must accommodate the mixture of reason and revelation in our lives. The gospel not only permits, but *requires* it. An individual who concentrates on either side solely and alone will lose both balance and perspective. History confirms that the university environment always favors reason, with the working of the Spirit made to feel uncomfortable. I know of no examples to the contrary.

Spirituality, while consummately strong, reacts to very delicate changes in its environment. To have it present at all and to keep it in some degree of purity requires a commitment and a watch care which can admit to no embarrassment when compared with what the scholarly world is about.

The moral and spiritual capacity of the faculty and what they shall give, and the spiritual atmosphere in which students are to learn and what they receive, will not emerge spontaneously!

They happen only if they are *caused* to happen and thereafter maintained with unwavering determination. We at BYU can be competent in both and at once merit the respect of those charged with the accreditation of institutions of higher learning.

Some have envisioned BYU as a great graduate research university as opposed to an undergraduate teaching university. A few years ago, the term "the Harvard of the West" was tossed about, and moves were made to recast BYU in that image. But that transformation was not initiated by the board of trustees.

Recently, lengthy discussions on the future role of BYU have been held between the board of trustees and the administration. They have led in the direction of defining BYU as an "academically selective, teaching-oriented, undergraduate university, offering both liberal arts and occupational degrees, with sufficiently strong graduate programs and research work to be a major university."[5] When that role is finally defined, it will be determined by the board of trustees, whose fundamental credentials were not bestowed by man and whose right and responsibility it is to determine policy and "approve *all* proposed changes in basic *programs* and *key personnel*" and establish standards for both faculty and students.[6]

We spoke of the catalytic process where two seemingly antagonistic influences can merge and each give strength to the other. The essential catalyst for the fusion of reason and revelation in both student and faculty is the Spirit of Christ. He is "the true light that lighteth every man that cometh into the world" (D&C 93:2). The blending medium is the Holy Ghost, which is conferred upon every member of the Church as a gift.

The blending of opposites is everywhere present in life. A base metal, fused with a precious one, can produce an alloy stronger and with more resilience than either component alone. Such a blending is seen in the priesthood of God, ordained to be conferred upon the ordinary man who must live in the base, workaday world, where reason and the muscles of his body are the substance of his livelihood. The blending in of revelation will make him anything but ordinary. While such a man must remain *in* the world, he is not *of* the world. Marriage is the wedding of opposites, the union of the man (who faces the world) with woman (who is often the more refined in spirit). When neither seeks to replace the other, the complementing differences in their nature are fostered. Then, in expressions of love, life itself is conceived, and together they receive a fullness of joy. The fusion of reason and revelation will produce a man and woman of imperishable worth.

On the one hand is reason: the thinking, the figuring things out, the research, the pure joy of discovery, and the academic degrees which man bestows to honor that process. On the other is revelation, with the very private and very personal, the very individual, confirmation of truth. The combining of them is *the* test of mortal life!

"The spirit *and* the body are the soul of man" (D&C 88:15; italics added).

> For man is spirit. The elements are eternal, and spirit and element, inseparably connected, receive a fulness of joy; And when separated, man cannot receive a fulness of joy. . . . The glory of God *is* intelligence, or, in other words, light and truth. Light and truth [*will*] forsake that evil one. . . . [We are commanded] to bring up [our] children in light and truth. (D&C 93:33–34, 36, 40; italics added)

Now, all of that is but a preface, an introduction, to my message, which I present in two short sentences.

To you of the administration and faculty, I repeat the counsel given to Dr. Karl G. Maeser by President Brigham Young when he sent him here to start this school: "You ought not to teach even the alphabet or the multiplication tables without the Spirit of God. That is all. God bless you."[7]

To you students, I quote a revelation to you from the Lord: "As all have not faith, seek ye diligently and teach one another words of wisdom; yea, seek ye out of the best books words of wisdom; seek learning, even by study and also by faith" (D&C 88:118).

I give to you my sure witness of the Lord and pray that he will protect this great university as together we move into the perilous years ahead.

III. The Snow-White Birds

With the faculty, staff, and administration present in this audience, only the students are missing. It is in their interest that I have entitled my message "The Snow-White Birds."

President Rex Lee has urged me to reminisce about my years of association with Brigham Young University.

President Harold B. Lee told me once that inspiration comes easier when you can set foot on the site related to the need for it. With a very sincere desire to be guided in preparing what I should say to you, early Sunday morning, before you were about, I stood in the Maeser Building, and I found that President Lee was right.

In one sense, this is a graduation. President Rex Lee has reported periodically to the public on the condition of his health, most often with Janet at his side. The Lees have served faithfully and well. They both have our commendation and affection.

In another sense, I too am graduating tonight. After thirty-four years on the board of trustees for BYU, most of it on the executive committee, I have been released. Members of the Quorum of the Twelve will now be rotated on the board.

Since the future of the Church rests with our youth and since the budget for their education is the second largest of all Church appropriations (the budget for BYU alone is in the hundreds of millions of dollars), you deserve the responsible attention of all of the Twelve. And I am sure you will have that.

It has been said that *young* men speak of the future because they have no past, and *old* men speak of the past because they have no future. Responding to President Lee's request, I will act my age and reminisce.

Our first visit to this campus was forty-eight years ago this month. Donna and I were returning from our honeymoon. Seven years later, I walked into the Maeser Building, then the administration building, to an office I was to occupy as chairman of a summer school for all seminary and institute personnel. There were problems, and so we had been called in for some reinforcement, some shaping up.

Our instructor was Elder Harold B. Lee of the Quorum of the Twelve Apostles. He invited guest lecturers. President J. Reuben Clark Jr. came more than once. President Joseph Fielding Smith, Elders Spencer W. Kimball, Mark E. Petersen, Marion G. Romney, LeGrand Richards, Delbert L. Stapley, and Richard L. Evans; President Belle S. Spafford of the Relief Society (one of the greatest women of our time); and others came.

For two hours a day, five days a week, for five weeks we were taught at the feet of the Apostles. The influence of those days is still evident in our lives and in Church education.

The following year, as a supervisor of seminaries and institutes, I returned to the Maeser Building. I occupied an office there until the administration moved to the newly completed Smoot Building.

In 1958, A. Theodore Tuttle, the other supervisor of seminaries, was called as a member of the First Council of the Seventy. In October 1961, I was called as an Assistant to the Twelve. One of my first assignments was to the Church Board of Education, the BYU Board of Trustees, and the executive committee.

I can remember Presidents Franklin S. Harris, Howard McDonald, and Acting President Christen Jensen. I have had a close association with Presidents Wilkinson, Oaks, Holland, and Lee.

I remember as well Sunday, January 8, 1956. To understand why that is memorable to me, we must go back to 1910.

George Brimhall, having already served nineteen years as president of BYU, determined to establish a recognized teacher's college. He had hired three professors: one with a master's degree from Harvard, one with a doctorate from Cornell, and the other with a doctorate from Chicago. They hoped to transform the college into a full-fledged university. They determined that practicality and religion, which had characterized the school, must now give way to more intellectual and scientific philosophies.

The professors held that "'the fundamentals of religion could and must be investigated by extending the [empirical] method into the spiritual realm,'" and they "considered evolution to be a basic, spiritual principle through which the divinity in nature expressed itself."[8] The faculty sided with the new professors, and the students rallied to them.

Horace Cummings, superintendent of Church schools, became concerned because they were "'applying the evolutionary theory and other philosophical hypotheses to principles of the gospel and to the teachings of the Church in such a way as to disturb, if not destroy the faith of the pupils,'" and he wrote, "'Many stake presidents, some of our leading principals and teachers, and leading men who are friends of our schools have expressed deep anxiety to me about this matter.'"[9] Superintendent Cummings reported to the board that

1. The teachers were following the "higher criticism," . . . treating the Bible as "a collection of myths, folk-lore, dramas, literary productions, . . . and some inspiration."

2. They rejected the [universality of the] flood, the [sudden or miraculous] confusion of tongues, the miracle of the Red Sea, and the temptation of Christ [by a personal devil] as real phenomena.

3. They said John the Revelator was not translated but died in the year A.D. 96.

4. "The theory of evolution is treated as a demonstrated law and their applications of it to gospel truths give rise to many curious and conflicting explanations of scripture."

5. The teachers carried philosophical ideas too far: (1) They believed "sinners should be pitied and enlightened rather than blamed or punished," (2) and they believed that "we should never agree. God never made two things alike. Only by taking different views of a thing can its real truth be seen."

    .   .   .   .

7. The professors taught that "all truths change as we change. Nothing is fixed or reliable."

8. They also taught that "visions and revelations are mental suggestions. The objective reality of the presence of the Father and the Son, in Joseph Smith's first vision, is questioned."[10]

Superintendent "Cummings concluded his report by saying that the professors 'seem to feel that they have a mission to protect the young from the errors of their parents.'"[11]

President Brimhall himself defended the professors—that is, until some students "'frankly told him they had quit praying because they learned in school there was no real God to hear them.'"[12]

Shortly thereafter President Brimhall had a dream.

"He saw several of the BYU professors standing around a peculiar machine on the campus. When one of them touched a spring a baited fish hook attached to a long thin wire rose rapidly into the air. . . .

"Casting his eyes around the sky [President Brimhall] discovered a flock of snow-white birds circling among the clouds and disporting themselves in the sky, seemingly very happy. Presently one of them, seeing the bait on the hook, darted toward it and grabbed it. Instantly one of the professors on the ground touched a spring in the machine, and the bird was rapidly hauled down to the earth.

"On reaching the ground the bird proved to be a BYU student, clad in an ancient Greek costume, and was directed to join a group of other students who had been brought down in a similar manner. Brother Brimhall walked over to them, and noticing that all of them looked very sad, discouraged and downcast, he asked them:

"'Why, students, what on earth makes you so sad and downhearted?'

"'Alas, we can never fly again!' they replied with a sigh and a sad shake of the head.

"Their Greek philosophy had tied them to the earth. They could believe only what they could demonstrate in the laboratory. Their prayers could go no higher than the ceiling. They could see no heaven—no hereafter."[13]

Now deeply embarrassed by the controversy and caught between opposing factions, President Brimhall at first attempted to be conciliatory. He said, "'I have been hoping for a year or two past that harmony could be secured by waiting, but the delays have been fraught with increased danger.'"[14] When an exercise in *administrative diplomacy* suddenly became an *issue of faith,* President Brimhall acted.

And now to Sunday, January 8, 1956. President David O. McKay came to Brigham City to dedicate a chapel built for students of the Intermountain Indian School. I stood next to him to introduce those who came forward to shake his hand. A very old man, a stranger to me, came forward on the arm of his daughter. He had come some distance to speak to President McKay. It was impossible for me not to hear their conversation. He gave President McKay his name and said that many years ago he had taught at BYU. President McKay said, "Yes, I know who you are." Tears came as the old man spoke sorrowfully about the burden he had carried for years. President McKay was very tender in consoling him. "I know your heart," he said. That old man was one of the three professors who had been hired by President Brimhall in 1910.

Let me share with you another experience or two from which I learned valuable lessons. During our BYU years, we lived in Lindon. Early one Christmas Eve, I received a telephone call. I told Donna that I must run in to Provo to the office. By doing so, one of our teachers could have a much happier Christmas.

I thought I was alone in the Maeser Building. Not so. President Ernest L. Wilkinson, whose office was at the other end of the hall, walked into President Berrett's office, then into Brother Tuttle's office, looked in the storeroom, and then stepped into my office. Without saying a word to me, he looked around my office and walked out. Although I knew him to be absorbed in whatever he did, I shook my head and muttered to myself, "Well, [cuss] you!"

Shortly thereafter, Vice President Harvey L. Taylor came into the office and made the same tour. Startled to find me at my desk, he asked, "What on earth are you doing here on Christmas Eve?" I explained why I was there. He then told me how much I was appreciated and how grateful he was for one who would go the extra mile. He wished me a merry Christmas and left.

After he was gone, I had generous thoughts about President Wilkinson. If he was smart enough to have a man like Harvey Taylor follow him around, I could put up with his exasperating ways.

Some time later, I was summoned to a meeting of the administrative council in President Wilkinson's office. They were discussing the appointment of someone in St. George to recruit the graduates of Dixie Junior College to BYU. I recommended the director of the institute there and said, "To appoint someone else would be misunderstood." The others there agreed. But after discussion, President Wilkinson said someone else would be better. I responded, "That's all right, President, but you are still wrong."

Suddenly there was dead silence. When President Wilkinson was greatly amused or angry, he had a way of running his tongue around the inside of his cheeks. He stood up and walked around his desk two or three times. I suppose he was trying to get control of himself. Finally he sat down, and Joseph T. Bentley said quietly, "President, Brother Packer is right."

At that point, I was excused from the meeting. That night I told Donna that we would be leaving BYU, and I hoped we could return to Brigham City to teach seminary. Two days later, I received a memo from President Wilkinson appointing me to the Administrative Council of Brigham Young University.

During the years I served on that council, I came to appreciate President Wilkinson. He had a profound influence on the university; and the naming of a building, this building, for him is little enough by way of tribute to him.

In 1966, BYU underwent an accrediting evaluation. The evaluation of the College of Religion by two clergymen from differing faiths was thought to offer a fresh insight into the role of religion at BYU. These two "outsiders" expressed concern over the intellectual climate and the "revelational and authoritarian approach to knowledge." They recommended that, for the purpose of intellectual ferment and free inquiry at BYU, the university should have one or two atheists on the faculty. President Wilkinson wrote a response to the accreditation report and asked for corrections. He pointed out that "there were no limitations on teaching about these philosophies, but there were cautions about advocating them!" Although the chairman of the commission invited a response to President Wilkinson's letter, none was ever received.

Perhaps the answer came from the 1976 Accreditation Committee. They explained in the introduction of their report:

> "Institutional evaluation, as practiced by the Commission on Colleges, begins with an institution's definition of *its own nature and purposes;* and a declaration of *its goals and objectives* pursuant upon that definition. The institution is then evaluated, essentially in *its own terms,* from the point

of view of how well it appears to be living up to *its own self-definition;* and how well its goals and objectives fit that definition, as well as the extent to which they appear to be carried out and achieved in practice."[15]

That 1976 accreditation report was highly favorable. They found BYU "'to be a vibrant and vital institution of genuine university calibre.'"[16]

Perhaps young men do speak of the future because they have no past, and old men of the past because they have no future. However, there are fifteen old men whose very lives are focused on the future. They are called, sustained, and ordained as prophets, seers, and revelators. It is their right to see as seers see; it is their obligation to counsel and to warn.

The board has long since charged the administration to refine the hiring process to ensure that those who will come to replace you will be of the same quality of worthiness, spirit, and professional competency as you were at the beginning of your careers.

It is not always possible to give the watch care that you deserve. When things come to us a piece at a time, without an explanation of how they fit together, we may fail to see overall changes that are taking place.

Several years ago, the then president of the Relief Society asked why the name of one of the colleges at BYU was changed. It concerned her. She had watched the establishment of the College of Family Living, a decision that was far ahead of its time. The Joseph F. Smith Family Living Center, one of the largest buildings on campus at the time, was built to house the college. BYU stood unique in all the world in organizing such a college. Why, she asked, did they change the name to the College of Family, Home, and Social Sciences? Her concern was that family would be lost to social and to science. The names of the courses were changed, things were shifted about, and their objectives shifted toward the professional and theoretical. I thought the Relief Society president asked a very insightful question, and I shared her concern. She was told that, since there was no counterpart in other universities to a college that concentrated on the family, there were academic reasons for the changes.

When researchers are too focused on what is, they may lose sight of what ought to be. A kitchen then may be regarded as a research lab, and a family as any group of unrelated people who spend the night under the same roof—defined that way because experts in the world convince the government that it is supposed to be that way.

Has anything like this happened in the other colleges as well? Is the teaching of religion given a preeminent place, and are those who teach religion full-time recognized for the vital contribution they make to every other discipline? Has there been a drift in the College of Education? Has the responsibility to prepare teachers been divided up and parceled out and lost? Have words such as training, instruction, and values been brushed aside in favor of loftier theoretical and intellectual considerations? Consider these lines:

> Today a professor in a garden relaxing
> Like Plato of old in the academe shade
> Spoke out in a manner I never had heard him
> And this is one of the things that he said:
>
> Suppose that we state as a tenet of wisdom
> That knowledge is not for delight of the mind.
> Nor an end in itself but a packet of treasure
> To hold and employ for the good of mankind.
>
> A torch or a candle is barren of meaning
> Except it give light to men as they climb,
> And thesis and tomes are but impotent jumble
> Unless they are tools in the building of time.
>
> We scholars toil on with the zeal of a miner
> For nuggets and nuggets and one nugget more,
> But scholars are needed to study the uses
> Of all the great mass of data and lore.
>
> And truly our tireless and endless researches
> Need yoking with man's daily problems and strife,
> For truth and beauty and virtue have value
> Confirmed by their uses in practical life.
>
> [Anonymous]

If students are going to partake of the fruit that is "desirable to make one happy," yea, "desirable above all other fruit" (1 Ne. 8:10, 12), which Lehi saw in his vision, they had better have their ladder leaning against the right tree. And they had better hold onto the iron rod while they are working their way toward it.

Now, in an absolutely remarkable consensus, leaders in politics, government, law enforcement, medicine, social agencies, and the courts recognize that the breakdown of the family is the most dangerous and frightening development of our time, perhaps in all human history. They are casting around for answers.

There is a desperate need for stable families and teachers who know how to teach values. Were we not better equipped a generation ago to produce them? Have some among us measured themselves against the world and its sophisticated intellectual standard? Have they "cast their eyes about as if they were ashamed" (1 Ne. 8:25) and let go of the iron rod of Lehi's vision?

The prophet Jacob spoke of wasting one's time by following those who "when they are learned they think they are wise." "To be learned is good," he further said, "*if* they hearken unto the counsels of God" (2 Ne. 9:28–29; italics added).

Surely you will remember that the board of trustees has directed that in order to contribute to the central mission of the Church,

> BYU is a Church-related [and I might say parenthetically totally owned], very large, national, academically selective, teaching-oriented, undergraduate university offering both liberal arts and occupational degrees, with sufficiently strong graduate programs and research work to be a major university, but insufficient sponsored research and academic doctoral programs to be a graduate research institution.[17]

Let them honor this direction from the minutes of the board of trustees: "Boards make policy and administrators implement policy. Boards must be informed of *all* proposed changes in basic *programs* and *key personnel* in order to achieve better understanding with the administrators."[18]

All of you would do well to read carefully Jacob's parable of the olive vineyard in the Book of Mormon. You might stand, as the Lord of the vineyard did, and weep when he saw that some branches "grew faster than the strength of the roots, taking strength unto themselves." You might ask with him, as we have asked, "What could I have done more in my vineyard?

Have I slackened mine hand, that I have not nourished it?" (Jacob 5:47, 48). And yet some branches bring forth bitter fruit. And you might do as the lord of the vineyard did and as Brother Brimhall did. They pruned out those branches that brought forth bitter fruit and grafted in cuttings from the nethermost part of the vineyard. And by so doing, "the Lord of the vineyard had preserved unto himself the natural fruit, which was most precious unto him from the beginning" (Jacob 5:74).

Now I must speak of the snow-white birds that Brother Brimhall saw in his dream or vision. I say *vision* because another old man, Lehi, told his son Nephi, "Behold, I have dreamed a dream; or, in other words, I have seen a vision" (1 Ne. 8:2). We have now enrolled in our institutes of religion 198,000 students. We spend approximately $300 a year on each of them. We spend more than $7,500 a year on each student at BYU and over $12,000 per student on the Hawaii campus, all of it from tithing funds. That inequity worries the Brethren. We are trying to reach out to those in public colleges, as well as to the college-age members who arc not, for various reasons, in school. We have invited them to attend classes in the institutes.

General Authorities often speak at firesides in the Marriott Center. Lately we have been broadcasting these messages to the institute students by satellite. Last time I was assigned, I spoke from Seattle. I wanted to show an equal interest in and an equal desire to be close to those who do not attend Church schools. They need our help, these snow-white birds who now must fly in an atmosphere that grows ever darker with pollution. It is harder now for them to keep their wings from being soiled or their flight feathers from being pulled out.

The troubles that beset President Brimhall were hardly new. Paul told Timothy that, even in that day, they were of ancient origin: "As Jannes and Jambres withstood Moses," he told Timothy, "so do these also resist the truth: men of corrupt minds, reprobate concerning the faith" (2 Tim. 3:8). Paul prophesied plainly that those challenges would face us in the last days. They seem to cycle back each generation. They emerged in the early '30s. The Brethren called all of the teachers of religion together for a summer school at Aspen Grove. President J. Reuben Clark Jr., speaking for the First Presidency, delivered the landmark address "The Charted Course of the Church in Education" (1938). That address should be read by every one of you every year. It is insightful; it is profound; it is prophetic; it is scripture.

That opposition emerged again in the institutes of religion in the early '50s, and the Brethren called the summer session of which I spoke earlier, with Elder Harold B. Lee of the Twelve as our teacher.

We need to be alert today. Although there are too many now in our schools for us to call all of you together, here at BYU much is being done to reaffirm standards. You yourselves have helped refine the credentials for one who will influence these snow-white birds of ours. That standard is temple worthiness, with a recommend in hand for members and a respect for our standards by those who are not.

But that is not all. There must be a feeling and a dedication and a recognition and acceptance of the mission of our Church schools. Those standards will and must be upheld. The largest block of the tithing funds spent at BYU goes for teaching salaries. We cannot justify spending the widow's mite on one who will not observe either the letter or the spirit of the contract he or she has signed. Every department chair, every director, every dean and administrator has a sacred obligation to assure that no one under their care will pull the snow-white birds from the sky or cause even one to say, "Alas, we can never fly again!" or to "believe only what could be demonstrated in a laboratory" or to think that "their prayer could go no higher than the ceiling, or to see no heaven—no hereafter."

We expect no more of anyone than that you live up to the contract you have signed. We will accept no less of you. The standards of the accreditation agencies expect no less of us. It is a matter of trust, for we are trustees.

I have said much about teachers. Many of you look after housing and food services or maintain the libraries, the museums, or the sports fields or keep the records, protect law and order and safety, service equipment, keep up the campus, publish materials, manage the finances, and a hundred other things. Without you this institution would come apart in a day. You are absolutely vital to the mission of Brigham Young University.

Your obligation to maintain standards is no less, nor will your spiritual rewards fall one bit below those who are more visible in teaching and in administration.

All of you, together with the priesthood and auxiliary leaders from the community who devote themselves to these snow-white birds of ours, are an example, an ensign to the whole Church and to the world. The quality of your scholarship is unsurpassed, your service and dedication a miracle in itself. There is not now, nor has there ever been, anything that can compare with you. Much in the future of the restored Church depends on you. Your greater mission lies ahead.

The prophet Isaiah said:

> He giveth power to the faint; and to them that have no might he increaseth strength. Even the youths shall faint and be weary, and the young men shall utterly fall: But they that wait upon the Lord shall renew their strength; they shall mount up with wings as eagles; they shall run, and not be weary; and they shall walk, and not faint. (Isa. 40:29–31)

President Brigham Young told Karl G. Maeser: "I want you to remember that you ought not to teach even the alphabet or the multiplication tables without the Spirit of God. That is all. God bless you. Good-bye."[19]

Now I would, as one standing among those who hold the keys, do as President Young did, and that is invoke a blessing. I invoke the blessings of the Lord upon you, as teachers, as administrators, as members of the staff, as husbands and wives, brothers and sisters, parents and grandparents. May you be blessed in all that you do, that the Spirit of the Lord will be in your hearts and that you will have the inspiration combined with knowledge to make you equal to the challenge of teaching the snow-white birds who come to you to learn how to fly.

Part I, "The Edge of the Light," was delivered at a BYU eighteen-stake fireside, March 4, 1990. Part II, "I Say unto You, Be One," was delivered at a BYU devotional, February 12, 1991. Part III, "The Snow-White Birds," was delivered at BYU's Annual University Conference, August 29, 1995. President Boyd K. Packer is Acting President of the Quorum of the Twelve Apostles.

NOTES

[1]David Croft, "Church Divests Self of Hospitals," *Church News,* published by *Deseret News,* Sept. 14, 1974, 3.

[2]J. Reuben Clark Jr., "The Charted Course of the Church in Education," above in this volume.

[3]*Hymns of The Church of Jesus Christ of Latter-day Saints, 1985* (Salt Lake City: The Church of Jesus Christ of Latter-day Saints, 1985), 335, verses 1 and 3.

[4]"The Death of Religious Higher Education," *First Things* (Jan. 1991): 8.

[5]Minutes of the Board of Education, June 7, 1990.

[6]Minutes of Executive Committee, April 27, 1982.

[7]Reinhard Maeser, *Karl G. Maeser: A Biography by His Son* (Provo, Utah: Brigham Young University, 1928), 79.

[8]Ernest L. Wilkinson, ed., *Brigham Young University: The First One Hundred Years,* vol. 1 (Provo, Utah: Brigham Young University Press, 1975), 415.

[9]Wilkinson, *First One Hundred Years,* 1:419. Cummings's report detailed additionally that they taught the following:

> Miracles are mostly fables or accounts of natural events recorded by simple people who injected the miraculous element into them, as most ignorant people do when things, strange to them, occur. . . . Sin is ignorance—education, or knowledge, is salvation. . . . Ordinances may be helpful props to weak mortals, but knowledge is the only essential. . . . Memory gems are immoral, since fixing the words fixes the thought and prevents growth. I was told that one teacher, before his class, thanked God he could not repeat on[e] of the Articles of Faith and another took his children out of Primary Association because they were taught to memorize. . . . As we grow or change our attitude toward any truth, that truth changes. . . . To get the real truth in any vision or revelation, modern as well as ancient, the mental and physical condition of the prophet receiving it must be known. After eliminating the personal equation, the remainder may be recognized as inspiration or divine. (Report of General Superintendent Horace H. Cummings to President Joseph F. Smith and Members of the General Church Board of Education, January 21, 1911, Brigham Young University Archives, Provo, Utah, 1–2)

> Moreover, Cummings reported that

> while these teachers extol the living oracles, it came to me from several sources that if their teachings are to be investigated they will demand that the ones who do the investigating shall be men of the same learning as themselves; none others could understand them and do them justice. . . . *Faith* now seems to be regarded with pity as a superstition and is not a characteristic of the intellectually trained. (Report of Cummings to Smith, 3)

[10]Wilkinson, *First One Hundred Years,* 1:423. Cummings also confirmed that

> these teachers have been warned by the presidency of the school
> and by myself, and even pleaded with, for the sake of
> the school, not to press their views with so much vigor. Even if
> they were right, conditions are not suitable; but their zeal over-
> comes all counsel and they seem even more determined, if not
> defiant, in pushing their beliefs upon the students. Report of
> Cummings to Smith, 4.

[11]Wilkinson, *First One Hundred Years,* 1:423.

[12]Wilkinson, *First One Hundred Years,* 1:421. Cummings's autobiography notes: "Teachers urged the students not to let their parents or the authorities at home know what a change was taking place in their faith. . . . The Apostles were good men, but utterly unfit to judge them. . . . Students ceased to pray, and the teachers did not pay their tithing as before. One or two left off their garments and denounced their faith." Autobiography of Horace Cummings, Brigham Young University Archives, Provo, Utah, lesson 41, page 4.

[13]Wilkinson, *First One Hundred Years,* 1:421–22.

[14]Wilkinson, *First One Hundred Years,* 1:430.

[15]Wilkinson, *First One Hundred Years,* 4:112; italics added.

[16]Wilkinson, *First One Hundred Years,* 4:113.

[17]Adopted by Board of Trustees, June 1990; italics added.

[18]Executive Meeting Minutes, April 27, 1982; italics added.

[19]Maeser, *Karl G. Maeser,* 79.

Discipleship and Scholarship

Neal A. Maxwell

I have come to thank and to offer a few words of encouragement and guidance to scholars, whose work collectively has been used, is being used, and hopefully always will be used to protect and to build up the kingdom.

Do not underestimate the importance of what you do as articulators. In praising C. S. Lewis, Austin Farrer wrote, "Though argument does not create conviction, lack of it destroys belief. What seems to be proved may not be embraced; but what no one shows that ability to defend is quickly abandoned. Rational argument does not create belief, but it maintains a climate in which belief may flourish."[1] I am thankful to those who help to provide the needed "climate."

Several notable examples could be cited. It may be too soon to know all the implications of much scholarly research that has been reported in recent years, but it will likely illustrate, again, something basic about the Prophet Joseph. The Prophet Joseph, a very good though not perfect man, will be vindicated in this statement about his own mission: "I never told you I was perfect, but there is no error in the revelations which I have taught."[2]

In this same illustrative connection, you will remember the Lucy Mack Smith description of the Prophet's experience as a lad with an infected leg. Amputation was considered. His story of "doctors" went unbelieved by some. In the Manuscript History, Joseph's "doctors" were named along with references to a

Elder Neal A. Maxwell at the Annual University Conference, August 1975. Courtesy Mark A. Philbrick/BYU.

"council of surgeons."[3] Being so attended to, medically, seemed so unlikely in rural New England. Only a few years ago, however, Dr. LeRoy S. Wirthlin researched this very interesting episode, which shows some micromanaging by the Lord. The medical doctor in final attendance, it turns out, was Dr. Nathan Smith, founder of the Dartmouth Medical School. He brought two doctors and several medical students with him to attend to young Joseph, who resisted amputation and pain-deadening alcohol. It turns out that Dr. Nathan Smith was highly qualified, and he was using a very advanced technique. Thus "the only man in America who could save [Joseph's] leg was just five miles away."[4] Happily for young Joseph, Dr. Smith's plans to leave the area had been delayed by a typhoid epidemic. Joseph Smith could scarcely have led the long march of Zion's Camp years later without this dramatic medical help.

Joseph will go on being vindicated by further disclosures in all the essential things associated with his prophetic mission. Many of you, both now and in the future, will be part of that on-rolling vindication through your own articulation about the Restoration.

In so doing, you may also help another special group who need a particular strengthening. Lewis's mentor in absentia, George MacDonald, noted how "it is often incapacity for defending the faith they love which turns men into persecutors."[5] Happily, defenders beget defenders. Unhappily, dissenters beget dissenters, and doubters beget doubters. Some of the latter may be able to be helped.

I share the next thoughts with you simply because they are especially on my mind.

One of the striking dimensions of the restored gospel is the democracy of demands. Yet it seeks to build an aristocracy of saints. Certain standards and requirements are laid upon all disciples. The member who is an automobile mechanic does not likely have all the skills of a scholar, and not likely you the mechanic's. But both of you are under the same spiritual obligations to keep the same commandments and the same covenants. Furthermore, the mechanic is under the same obligation to develop the attributes of patience and meekness as are you.

Frankly, the world holds to no such democratic view. If one is a superb scholar in a narrow discipline, such is considered enough. One so gifted can then be as bohemian in behavior as one likes. But it is not so in the kingdom, is it?

Of course, we all enjoy certain of the fruits of the labors of secular geniuses who may be visibly or significantly flawed in some respects. Nor would we desire to detract from their important contributions. A just God will surely credit them. However, God will excuse neither them nor us from keeping his commandments, including the requirement given to us by him and his Son to become more like them (Matt. 5:48; 3 Ne. 12:48; 27:27).

My wife took a friend to hear a presentation by a Latter-day Saint of outstanding talent. The friend, who has borne considerable grief and disappointment in her life, truly appreciated the presentation. Then she said simply, "I hope he is as good a person as he seems." It is a shame, isn't it, that such reserve even needs to be felt. But we "have learned by sad experience" that our spiritual applause is sometimes given to the undeserving (D&C 121:39). I hasten to add, from all I know of the foregoing case, the applause is fully justified.

Whatever our particular fields of scholarship, the real test is individual discipleship, not scholarship. But how good it is when these two can company together, blending meekness with brightness and articulateness with righteousness. Such outcomes occur, however, only when there is commitment bordering on consecration. Therefore, a word about consecration is appropriate.

You will recall the episode in the fifth chapter of the book of Acts about how Ananias and Sapphira "kept back part" of the monetary proceeds from their possessions (Acts 5:3). We usually tend to think of consecration in terms of property and money. Indeed, such was clearly involved in the foregoing episode. But there are so many ways of keeping back part, and so many things we can withhold a portion of besides property. All things really ought to be put on the altar.

This holding back may occur even after one's having given a great deal, as likely had Ananias and Sapphira. Having done much, we may mistakenly think that surely it is all right to hold back a remaining part. Obviously, there can be no total submissiveness when this occurs.

Lately, when considering the atonement of Jesus Christ, I have been helped by a particular scripture. It is about how consecrated and sanctified Jesus allowed his will to be "swallowed up" in the will of the Father: "Yea, even so he shall be led, crucified, and slain, the flesh becoming subject even unto death, the will of the Son being swallowed up in the will of the Father" (Mosiah 15:7).

While pondering that very concept, I came across this unsurprisingly parallel quote from Brigham Young, upon whom the Book of Mormon had made such a deep impression: "When the will, passions, and feelings of a person are perfectly submissive to God and his requirements, that person is sanctified. It is for my will to be swallowed up in the will of God, that will lead me into all good, and crown me ultimately with immortality and eternal lives."[6]

There are so many ways in which one can hold back a portion. For instance, one might be giving as to money and also serving as to time and yet hold back a significant portion of himself or herself. One might share many talents but retain a pet grievance, thereby keeping it from resolution.

Scholars might hold back differently than would a businessman or a politician. A few hold back a portion of themselves merely to please a particular gallery of peers. Another might hold back a spiritual insight from which many could profit, simply wishing to have his or her "ownership" established. Some hold back by not appearing overly committed to the kingdom, lest they incur the disapproval of particular peers who might disdain such consecration. In various ways, some give of themselves, even extensively, but not fully and unreservedly.

While these patterns are a clear form of selfishness, I am inclined to think that holding back can also reflect a mistaken understanding regarding our individuality. Some presume we will lose our identity if we are totally "swallowed up." Of course, our individuality is actually enhanced by submissiveness and by righteousness. It is sin that grinds us down to sameness—to a monotonous, single plane.

In any case, there is no lasting place in the kingdom for unanchored and unconsecrated brilliance. Fortunately, those of you whom I know are both committed and contributive. In any case, ready or not, you serve as mentors and models for the rising generation of Latter-day Saint scholars and students. Let them learn, among many other things, submissiveness and consecration from the eloquence of your examples.

This article comes from a talk given at the annual banquet of the Foundation for Ancient Research and Mormon Studies on the BYU campus, September 27, 1991. Published in *BYU Studies* 32, no. 3 (1992): 5–9. Neal A. Maxwell is a member of the Quorum of the Twelve Apostles.

NOTES

[1]Austin Farrer, "Grete Clerk," in *Light on C. S. Lewis,* comp. Jocelyn Gibb (New York: Harcourt and Brace, 1965), 26.

[2]Joseph Fielding Smith, comp., *Teachings of the Prophet Joseph Smith* (Salt Lake City: Deseret Book, 1972), 368.

[3]LeRoy S. Wirthlin, "Joseph Smith's Boyhood Operation: An 1813 Surgical Success," *BYU Studies* 21, no. 2 (1981): 148.

[4]LeRoy S. Wirthlin, "Joseph Smith's Surgeon," *Ensign* 8 (March 1978): 59.

[5]George MacDonald, *Anthology* (New York: Macmillan, 1941), 121.

[6]Brigham Young, in *Journal of Discourses,* 26 vols. (Liverpool: F. D. Richards, 1855–86), 2:123, April 17, 1853.

Our Sacred Trust: Two Addresses

Gordon B. Hinckley

I. Trust and Accountability

I am here representing the First Presidency of the Church and the Brigham Young University Board of Trustees. President Ezra Taft Benson serves as chair of this board, and his counselors serve as vice chairs. I bring you his love and his blessing. I likewise bring the respect and appreciation of the entire board. I speak to both students and faculty in doing so.

I want to thank both faculty and students for the strength of your desire to teach and learn with inspiration and knowledge and for your commitment to live the standards of the gospel of Jesus Christ, for your integrity and your innate goodness. I am confident that never in the history of this institution has there been a faculty better qualified professionally nor one more loyal and dedicated to the standards of its sponsoring institution. Likewise, I am satisfied that there has never been a student body better equipped to learn at the feet of this excellent faculty, nor one more prayerful and decent in attitude and action. There may be exceptions. There doubtless are. But they are few in number compared with the larger body.

I do not want to imply that this is paradise on earth. You may think it just the opposite as you grind away at your studies. But notwithstanding the rigors of that grind, the unrelenting day-after-day pressure you feel, this is a great time to be alive, and this is a wonderful place to be.

President Gordon B. Hinckley announces the appointment of Rex E. Lee as president of BYU, May 1989. Courtesy Mark A. Philbrick/BYU.

This institution is unique. It is remarkable. It is a continuing experiment on a great premise that a large and complex university can be first-class academically while nurturing an environment of faith in God and the practice of Christian principles. You are testing whether academic excellence and belief in the Divine can walk hand in hand. And the wonderful thing is that you are succeeding in showing that this is possible—not only that it is possible, but that it is desirable and that the products of this effort show in your lives qualities not otherwise attainable.

We announced in the October 1992 general conference that another temple will be built in Utah Valley. The reason is that the Provo Temple is the busiest in the Church, operating beyond its designed capacity. The Jordan River Temple is the second busiest in the Church. One factor in all of this is the devotion to temple work of Brigham Young University faculty and students. Many of you, I am told, attend a session in the temple early in the morning before your classes. Many are there in the evening and on Saturday. This all says something of tremendous significance. It speaks of devotion and loyalty, of unselfishness and faith.

Furthermore, this remarkable faculty carry many responsibilities of great importance in the Church at the general level, at the stake level, and at the ward level. You are men and women of faith as well as of learning. I believe you are the equivalent of your peers anywhere in the world in terms of professional qualifications. Beyond this, you speak with conviction concerning the God of Heaven, the Savior and the Redeemer of the World, and the beauty and power of the restored and eternal gospel. I believe you seek to live these principles. I know of no other university faculty—I think there is none other anywhere on earth—where the members can stand and say with conviction, "We believe in being honest, true, chaste, benevolent, virtuous, and in doing good to all men" (A of F 1:13).

I believe that you seek to exemplify that declaration in your lives. I commend you and thank you and extend to you our appreciation and respect.

I repeat, there may be exceptions. But I think those are few. And if such there be, I am confident that in their hearts they feel ill at ease and uncomfortable, for there can never be peace or comfort in any element of disloyalty. Wherever there is such an attitude there is a nagging within the heart that says, "I am not being honest in accepting the consecrated tithing funds of the humble and faithful of this Church. I am not being honest with myself or others as a member of this faculty while teaching or engaging in anything that weakens the faith and undermines the integrity of those who come to this institution at great sacrifice and with great expectations."

I recently read a book that fascinated me, a dual biography of the two great generals of the American Civil War—Robert E. Lee and Ulysses S. Grant. They were personalities as different as perhaps two men could be. One was the epitome of intellect, rigid self-discipline, culture, and rectitude. The other was somewhat careless in his ways, his career marked by failure, but he possessed a shrewd and calculating mind. Each in his own way was brilliant.

Moreover, each was driven by a great and serious sense of trust imposed by those to whom he was accountable. One had greater resources, and, I believe, perhaps a better cause than the other, and this accounted for his victory. But the other was nonetheless a great and remarkable man. I could spend the hour talking about each of them. I mention them only because the author of this book, after tremendous research, concluded: "Trust is what makes any army work, and trust comes from the top down."[1]

I want all of you to know that you have the trust and confidence of BYU's governing board. This is called the board of trustees. It also carries a very heavy and sacred trust. It has the burden of responsibility for setting policies of governance for this great institution and responsibility for the expenditure of the many millions of dollars of sacred funds used to maintain this university.

We share your exuberant gladness when BYU wins a well-fought athletic contest. We share your pride when BYU and members of its faculty or student body are honored by its peer institutions and people. We share your pain and your hurt when the media exploit, as they are wont to do, any untoward, any unseemly, any ugly or misguided statement or act emanating from faculty or students. You are part of this great family we call The Church of Jesus Christ of Latter-day Saints. When one member experiences a significant accomplishment, the others rejoice with him. But when a member does something that violates the code of that family, the entire family is injured and feels the pain.

Every one of us who is here has accepted a sacred and compelling trust. With that trust, there must be accountability. That trust involves standards of behavior as well as standards of academic excellence. For each of us, it carries with it a larger interest than our own interest. It carries with it the interest of the university and the interest of the Church, which must be the interest of each and all of us.

Some few students resent the fact that the board has approved a code of honor and imposed a code of dress and behavior to which all are expected to subscribe. Bishops and now stake presidents are requested to interview each student and certify his or her acceptance of the standards set forth in these codes.

I think I can hear a student, perhaps a number of them, saying to a bishop, "Why do we have to sign these codes? Don't they trust us?"

I am reminded of what I heard from a man—a great, strong, and wise man—who served in the Presidency of this Church years ago. His daughter was going out on a date, and her father said to her, "Be careful. Be careful of how you act and what you say."

She replied, "Daddy, don't you trust me?"

He responded, "I don't entirely trust myself. One never gets too old nor too high in the Church that the adversary gives up on him."

And so, my friends, we ask you to subscribe to these codes and to have the endorsement of your respective bishops and stake presidents in doing so. It is not that we do not trust you. But we feel that you need reminding of the elements of your contract with those responsible for the institution and that you may be the stronger in observing that trust because of the commitment you have made. With every trust, there must be accountability, and this is a reminder of that accountability.

It is so with the faculty and with all of us. We ask that all members of the faculty who are members of the Church be what we speak of as "temple-recommend worthy." This does not evidence any lack of trust. It simply represents a standard, a benchmark of belief and action. The setting of this standard is not new or unusual. It is not new at BYU or in the Church Educational System, though it has been unevenly applied at times. It is a standard applied widely in the Church.

Our thousands of bishops, who stand as common judges in Israel, annually must renew their own temple recommends, as must stake presidents also. The renewal of that recommend becomes a renewal of commitment. We live in a world and in an environment where we are surrounded by the corrosive and erosive elements of the world. We are all human, even though our callings be high and noble. We all need the constant reminder of commitments we have made and standards to which we have subscribed.

Surely, our Father in Heaven loves his sons and daughters. He trusts us. That very trust becomes as an iron rod to which we may cling as we walk the path of mortality. Some stumble and err and violate the trust. They are accountable for what they do.

I am confident the Savior trusts us, and yet he asks that we renew our covenants with him frequently and before one another by partaking of the sacrament, the emblems of his suffering in our behalf.

We are, of course, properly concerned about you who teach at this great institution. You are the bone and sinew of the university. We are concerned that your academic credentials be the very best and that there be a quality of excellence in all you do. We are also concerned with your faith, your principles. I hope you will not regard us as being unduly cautious or unnecessarily critical. We act in the spirit spoken of by Alma concerning teachers in his day. Said he, "Trust no one to be your teacher, . . . except he be a man of God, walking in his ways and keeping his commandments" (Mosiah 23:14).

Yesterday, much of the world celebrated the five hundredth anniversary of Christopher Columbus's voyage of discovery. Scholars may dispute certain aspects concerning the priority and outcomes of that historic venture, but none can ever sell short the man who kept his trust in God as he sailed the track-less sea and who held himself accountable to the sovereigns of Spain, who were his sponsors.

As a boy, I read Joaquin Miller's poem "Columbus" and was stirred by it. I recall a few of those lines:

> Behind him lay the gray Azores,
> Behind the Gates of Hercules;
> Before him not the ghost of shores;
> Before him only shoreless seas.
> The good mate said, "Now must we pray,
> For lo! the very stars are gone,
> Brave Adm'r'l speak; what shall I say?"
> "Why, say: 'Sail on! sail on! and on!'"
>
> . . . .
>
> Then pale and worn, he paced his deck,
> And peered through darkness. Ah, that night
> Of all dark nights! And then a speck—
> A light! A light! At last a light!
> It grew, a starlit flag unfurled!
> It grew to be Time's burst of dawn.
> He gained a world; he gave that world
> Its grandest lesson: "On! sail on!"

Columbus kept his trust and discovered a hemisphere.

I think of Lord Nelson on the morning of the Battle of Trafalgar, when he said, "England expects every man will do his duty." After that fierce and bloody contest, as he stood on the deck of his ship to extend humanity to his enemy, a ball was fired within fifteen yards of where he stood. He fell to the deck, his spine shattered. He expired three and a quarter hours later, his last articulated words being, "Thank God, I have done my duty."[2] A tall shaft and statue stand in his honor in Trafalgar Square in London.

Wilford Woodruff, in 1835, not long after he had joined the Church, was sent on a mission with a companion who was to accompany him. They traveled through mud and floods, experiencing a great variety of hardships in the pursuit of their duty. He wrote in his journal:

> We walked forty miles in a day through mud and water knee-deep.

On the 24th of March, after traveling some ten miles through mud, I was taken lame with a sharp pain in my knee. I sat down on a log.

My companion, who was anxious to get to his home in Kirtland, left me sitting in an alligator swamp. I did not see him again for two years. I knelt down in the mud and prayed, and the Lord healed me, and I went on my way rejoicing.[3]

Wilford Woodruff kept his trust and lived to become a prophet.

I repeat the quotation I gave earlier: "Trust is what makes any army work, and trust comes from the top down."

Trust is what makes a government work, and maybe a lack of trust is one reason for the serious problems we are experiencing. Trust is what makes the wheels of commerce turn. It is what makes possible the strength and growth of the Church. It is what makes Brigham Young University work.

Trust and accountability are two great words by which we must guide our lives if we are to live beyond ourselves and rise to higher planes of service.

This is, and must ever be, an institution in which the soul is nurtured while the intellect is trained.

The motto of this university came from the pen of a prophet of God who spoke under the power of revelation: "The glory of God is intelligence, or, in other words, light and truth" (D&C 93:36).

The charter of its conduct was spoken by another prophet to its founding president: "You ought not to teach even the alphabet or the multiplication tables without the Spirit of God."[4]

Among the marvelous words of the first section of the Doctrine and Covenants are these:

The weak things of the world shall come forth and break down the mighty and strong ones, that man should not counsel his fellow man, neither trust in the arm of flesh— But that every man might speak in the name of God the Lord, even the Savior of the world. (D&C 1:19–20)

We trust you to do so. We love you. We respect you. We pray for you as faculty and students. We place upon you a great and sacred charge to excel in the imparting and learning of secular knowledge and at the same time nurture the spirit within.

I challenge you to stand always on a high plane of moral integrity, of spiritual strength, of professional excellence.

This is a world-class university, a great temple of learning, where a highly qualified faculty instruct a large and eager body of students. These teachers impart with skill and dedication the accumulated secular knowledge of the centuries while also building faith in the eternal verities that are the foundation of civilization.

Such is our unqualified expectation. Such, I sincerely believe, is the desire of all, save perhaps a few. Such, I sincerely hope, will be the resolve of everyone.

May God bless you, my beloved associates, both young and old, in this great undertaking of teaching and learning, of trust and accountability.

II. What the Church Expects of Each of Us

The Church is the great teacher and builder of values. Its precepts are designed to lead men and women along the way of immortality and eternal life, to make their lives more complete, more rich and happy while moving through this veil of tears, and in preparing them for the beauties and wonders of that which lies ahead. Keep faith with the Church. It is true. It is divine. He who stands at its head is the Lord Jesus Christ, the Redeemer of the World. It is the church of the Almighty which carries the name of his divine Son. Its earthly leaders are those who are called of God under a plan which he put in place.

What does the Church expect of each of us, you and me? "We believe in being honest, true, chaste, benevolent, virtuous, and in doing good to all men" (A of F 1:13). May I add a few words on this statement as I speak of what this Church expects of us.

Simple honesty is so remarkable a quality. It is of the very essence of integrity. It demands that we be straightforward, unequivocal, in walking the straight and narrow line of what is right and true. It is so easy to cheat. At times it is so enticing to do so. Better a poor grade than a dishonest act. There has been told and retold on this campus for generations the words of Karl G. Maeser concerning honor. They need to be repeated here and across the world. I suppose all of you have heard them before, but I give them again:

> I have been asked what I mean by word of honor. I will tell you. Place me behind prison walls—walls of stone ever so high, ever so thick, reaching ever so far into the ground—there is a possibility that in some way or another I may be able to escape; but stand me on the floor and draw a chalk line around me and have me give my word of honor never to cross it. Can I get out of that circle? No, never! I'd die first![5]

My father was a student of Karl G. Maeser at this institution long ago. He heard those words himself from the lips of Brother Maeser. He repeated them to us, again and again. They have become engraved as if they were words of scripture. They set forth with simplicity and eloquence what the Church expects of me and of you.

It expects us to be true—true to ourselves, true to our loved ones, true to the best that is within us, true to the faith, true to the names given us. President George Albert Smith, on a number of occasions, told of meeting his grandfather, whose name he carried, in a dream. In that dream, he was asked by his grandfather, "I would like to know what have you done with my name."[6] President Smith said that he never got over the effects of that experience. It was only a dream, but it was real, and it was important. There burned within his heart throughout the remainder of his life a compelling mandate to be true to the name which he carried.

In the language of the article of our faith which I have given you, the Church expects you to be chaste and virtuous. You know what this means. I am satisfied I need not repeat it here. But I do urge you, with all of the capacity of which I am capable, to avoid the corrosive, destructive forces of evil found in pornography. Remember, "wickedness never was happiness" (Alma 41:10). Sin never brought happiness. Transgression never brought happiness. Disobedience never brought happiness. The Church expects you who have taken upon yourselves the name of the Lord Jesus Christ to walk in the sunlight of virtue and enjoy the strength, the freedom, the lift that comes from so doing.

Drink here from the springs of knowledge which flow in the classrooms of this unique and wonderful institution. Partake of the spirit as well as the knowledge of faithful men and women who constitute the faculty of this school. Learn here the disciplines that will help you as you travel the course of your lives, the most important of which is self-discipline, the power to govern your thoughts, your words, your acts, notwithstanding the temptations that come before you. Learn of things of the heart, the mind, the spirit, and the words and wisdom of the Almighty.

The Church expects you to reach out with benevolence in doing good to all men. In writing to the Hebrews, Paul admonished, "Wherefore lift up the hands which hang down, and strengthen the feeble knees" (JST, Heb. 12:12). That admonition was repeated and magnified in modern revelation: "Wherefore, [said the Lord,] be faithful; stand in the office which I have appointed unto you; succor the weak, lift up the hands which hang down, and strengthen the feeble knees" (D&C 81:5).

I know that you are engrossed with your studies. This is important, but in a sense it is a selfish pursuit. Take a little time, now and again, to reach out beyond yourselves to help others. There are those right around you, students in need of a little kindness, a little attention, a little appreciation. You who are extremely able, you who learn with comparative ease, reach down to those who have greater difficulty in mastering academic material that is relatively easy for you. In so doing, you will bless your own life as you bless the lives of those you help. A little tutoring can do wonders for someone who does not quite comprehend. It will do wonders for you as you give of yourself and your knowledge to bless another.

There are those in nursing homes, hospitals, and those who are shut-ins in their own homes. You can bring sunlight into lives filled with gloom, sadness, and pain. Contradictory as it may sound, the admonition of the Savior is absolutely true as anyone can testify who has put it to the test: "He that findeth his life shall lose it: and he that loseth his life for my sake shall find it" (Matt. 10:39).

My dear young friends, give expression to the noble desires that lie within your hearts to reach out to comfort, sustain, and build others. As you do so, the cankering poison of selfishness will leave you, and it will be replaced by a sweet and wonderful feeling that comes in no other way. Never forget that the Church expects you to be benevolent and to do good to all men.

I add to this the related thought that you will grow as you look for the good in others. This season of your schooling is a time not only to expand your minds, but to enlarge your personalities and strengthen your character as you look for the virtues, the strengths, the goodness, in the lives of those about you.

Finally, the Church expects you to work while you are here. It is making a tremendous investment in you, an investment which comes from the sacred tithing funds of the Church. Work is the miracle by which talent is brought to the surface and dreams become reality.

I think President Rex Lee's life is a compendium of these great virtues and expectations of which I have spoken. I commend them to each of you, even at the expense of embarrassing this modest man.

In conclusion, I speak out of my heart with sincerity with love for each of you. You who are here are so richly blessed with a great and precious opportunity. Do not waste it. Do not regard it lightly. It is sacred and of great consequence. Be thankful every day of your lives while you are here. Pray for guidance. Pray for help. Pray for strength to resist that which is evil. Seek the enlightenment of the spirit of Christ. Cultivate and invite the direction of the Holy Ghost.

Every one of you is precious. You are precious in the sight of God. You are precious in the sight of your parents. You are precious to us who count on you to take advantage of this great season of preparation for the world in which you will live.

President Lee, I salute you and honor you as you serve in these waning months of a great administration. Faculty, students, I compliment each of you on the precious opportunity that is yours to walk with fidelity, devotion, loyalty, hard work, and appreciation for all that is good and uplifting.

I leave my blessing with you and commend to you every good thing, that your lives may be fruitful in those strengths and virtues which distinguish the noble and the great and the good from those who live beneath their possibilities. May you be blessed of the Lord is my humble prayer.

Part I was given at a Brigham Young University devotional on October 13, 1992, when Gordon B. Hinckley was First Counselor in the First Presidency. Part II is the concluding section of a Brigham Young University devotional given October 17, 1995, originally entitled, "To a Man Who Has Done What This Church Expects of Each of Us." The first part of that address was a tribute to BYU President Rex E. Lee. President Hinckley became President of the Church in March 1995.

NOTES

[1]Gene Smith, quoted in "Hitching a Ride to History," in *Reader's Digest Condensed Books*, 4 (Pleasantville, N.Y.: Reader's Digest Association, 1984), 299.

[2]Robert Southey, *Life of Nelson* (Boston: William Wells, 1813), 172, 177–81, October 21, 1805.

[3]Wilford Woodruff, *Leaves from My Journal* (Salt Lake City: Juvenile Instructor Office, 1881), 16.

[4]Alma P. Burton, *Karl G. Maeser: Mormon Educator* (Salt Lake City: Deseret Book, 1953), 26.

[5]Burton, *Karl G. Maeser*, 71.

[6]George Albert Smith, *Sharing the Gospel with Others* (Salt Lake City: Deseret Book, 1948), 111–12.

The Dream Is Ours to Fulfill

Bruce C. Hafen

Alma once described Zarahemla in a way that also describes Brigham Young University: "We are thus highly favored, for we have these glad tidings [the gospel] declared unto us in all parts of our vineyard" (Alma 13:23). That blessing would not be possible for us at BYU or for us as LDS people if it were not for so many who live lives of conscientious devotion to the Lord, to his Church, to his truth, and to the well-being of this community. We don't begin to have the problems other large institutions have with drugs, violence, sexual harassment, dishonesty, and other threats that are often encountered in the world. Yet our high expectations make it doubly tragic when one of us does disappoint our community interests.

Our aspirations include a commitment to the equal worth of every person, male and female, regardless of one's station in life. To that end, men should go out of their way to listen to women, and women to men, to see things through each other's eyes. No one should be more sensitive to the individual concerns and perceptions of others than those who approach their stewardship "by persuasion, by long-suffering, by gentleness and meekness, and by love unfeigned; By kindness, and pure knowledge" (D&C 121:41–42). Regarding mutual support and cooperation between staff and faculty, it impresses me that BYU has not followed the recent pattern of other universities, whose costs in support areas have risen faster than their academic costs. As I consider all the good people who labor together in the

Lord's vineyard, I think of Karl G. Maeser's words: "Labor
with the hand is as honorable as labor with the head, but
labor with the heart, when the heart is pure and true, is the
noblest labor" of all.[1]

BYU's central mission begins with Richard Bushman's attitude: "I am a believer. I believe in God and Christ and want to
know them. My relations with scholarship and scholars have
to begin there."[3] And our relations with student activities, support services, and all else we do must also begin there.

The first theme flowing from this vision is that we nurture
authentic religion. I will return to some thoughts on that subject
as my primary topic today. Second, we offer as many spiritually
and academically mature students as possible the richest possible learning experience. Third, we support faculty and academic
programs that develop our emerging role as a major, national
university, positioned in that fruitful middle ground between
the comprehensive colleges and the graduate research universities. Fourth, we seek a campus work environment full of professional competence, harmony, and personal nurturing.

Against this background, let us consider the integration of
our religious and professional aspirations. When our very able
committee on academic long-range planning met last fall [1991],
one person suggested that we begin by reading the teachings of
the prophets about the university. Another suggested that we come
to our next meeting in an attitude of fasting and prayer. In that
very personal kind of mood, each group member expressed his
or her impressions after reading these foundation documents.
To my surprise, every person around that table expressed a varia-
tion on a single theme: we have been too reticent about the place
of religion in academic life at BYU. In Marilyn Arnold's words,

> The committee could not help wondering why, given the
> Board's makeup and concerns and the religious devotion
> of nearly all members of the campus community, this mat-
> ter had not been widely and vigorously discussed before.
> Perhaps BYU is just now reaching the maturity that allows
> it to move, in its quest for academic legitimacy, beyond
> defensiveness and imitation of established institutions.
> Of course, we must not relax our efforts at academic
> excellence, but it is time for us also to become more fully
> the institution envisioned by the prophets.[4]

Bruce C. Hafen at the Annual University Conference, August 1991. Courtesy Mark A. Philbrick/BYU.

The Jewish author Chaim Potok once distinguished between sacred and secular thought systems. The scholar in a sacred system "assumes there is a design and purpose to nature," because God's spirit "hovers over all creation," giving divine origins to the premises of the sacred system. Thus, even the most sophisticated scholar in a sacred system faithfully transmits "inherited old and acceptable new scholarship" while respecting the established "boundaries of the system" according to a "predetermined choreography." By contrast, the scholar in a secular system always probes and challenges the system's boundaries, believing that all premises originate with human beings, the exclusive focus of secular systems. In secular systems, "it is man who gives, and man who takes away."[5]

Today Potok sees "a boiling cauldron of colliding ideas and world views" that makes cultural confrontation between sacred and secular systems unavoidable. He suggests four possible responses for the religious person who faces such confrontation. First, the lockout approach: one can simply dodge the conflict by erecting impenetrable barriers between the sacred and the secular and then remaining in just one system. Second, compartmentalization: one creates separate categories of thought that coexist in a "tenuous peace." Third, take down all walls and allow complete fusion in which the sacred and secular cultures freely feed each other, perhaps leading to a "radically new seminal culture." And fourth, ambiguity: take down most if not all walls and accept a multitude of questions without intending to resolve them.[6]

BYU's history, purposes, and its very nature reflect from every angle what Potok calls a sacred system of thought. How then do Latter-day Saint scholars at BYU and elsewhere handle the natural confrontations between the sacred and our deep commitment to being part of serious university pursuits? We reject the lockout approach that would shut our eyes to life's conflicts and realities. We are in—even though not of—the world. Yet we also cannot accept the total fusion model. Although the gospel embraces all truth, we must give priority to the truths that lead us to Christ, and we cannot allow our most sacred premises to be altered or even minimized by secularist assumptions. At the same time, we are too open to be rigid compartmentalists.

So how do we view the ambiguity and uncertainty that remain? We don't fear ambiguity's questions, partly because, as John Tanner has said, we approach our questions from an attitude of faith.[7]

The Restoration actually provides a fifth alternative for integrating sacred and secular thought systems—the model of eternal perspective. The restored gospel of Jesus Christ is the most comprehensive explanation of life and of the cosmos available to humankind. This idea is illustrated by Terry Warner's essay on Alma's teachings to Korihor. Terry wrote that the main difference between Alma's map of the universe and Korihor's map is that Alma's map is broader. If Alma's map is represented by a ten-by-ten-foot square, Korihor's map is a four-by-four-foot square within Alma's larger square. Alma doesn't have the answer to every question, but he does see and accept the same scientific evidence that Korihor does. Beyond that, he also recognizes evidence of personal meaning and spiritual reality that Korihor's map by definition excludes.[8] As William James said, "The agnostic [expression] 'thou shalt not believe without coercive, sensible evidence' is simply an expression of a private, personal appetite for evidence of a certain peculiar kind."[9] Not that these limits are all bad: we really don't want science or the government to tell us the ultimate meaning of our lives—we make those choices personally, based on evidence available outside the limited scientific sphere. Thus we can integrate a secular map into the broader sacred map, but our sacred system cannot be made to fit within the smaller secular map.

Similarly, Parker Palmer, who recently conducted a valuable seminar for BYU faculty, believes that Western culture's vision of learning suffers from "one-eyed education," teaching the mind but not the heart.[10] "There is an illness in our culture [arising] from our rigid separation of the visible world from the powers that undergird and animate it. That separation [diminishes] life, capping off its sources of healing, hope, and wholeness."[11] He urges us to teach with "wholesight," a complete vision of the world in which mind and heart unite, as Robert Frost has said, "as my two eyes make one in sight."[12] And "the mind's vision excludes the heart, but the heart's vision can include the mind."[13] The aim of wholesighted education, anchored in a heart that guides the mind, is wholeness. In Alan

Keele's words, "Great theology and great scholarship are not only compatible but are mutually and limitlessly illuminating."[14] Yet, because Alma's vision is the broader one, the gospel should influence our view of our disciplines more than our disciplines influence our view of the gospel.

Many thoughtful LDS people have enjoyed Chaim Potok's novels, often because they identify with the conflicts Potok's characters face between sacred and secular systems. The gospel teaches us to take education seriously, but it also teaches us to put the kingdom of God first in our lives. I am acquainted with the spiritual and intellectual biographies of many in this BYU audience and in the LDS community beyond, and I would like to know them all. Each of us, like characters in a Potok story, could recount our personal confrontations between sacred and secular systems of thought. My struggles were typical. I yearned to know if religious literalism is compatible with a fully breathing, stretching life of the mind. I found that the best resolution of the faith-versus-reason dilemmas, better than any book or argument of abstract reasoning, is the example of faithful and competent teachers in my own discipline—one of whom was Dallin Oaks—who have answered my questions with their lives. For a generation of LDS scientists, that role model was Henry Eyring. For many LDS doctors, it is Russell Nelson. To know teachers such as these is to be set free from the burden—sometimes the agony—of wondering whether serious religious belief and serious professional or academic commitments can fill the same heart at the same time.

One of BYU's highest purposes is to help its students—and to help Church members everywhere—confront such questions in ways that strengthen both their minds and their hearts, that they may be fully engaged as productive citizens of both society and the kingdom of God. President David O. McKay once told the BYU faculty that this is "primarily a religious institution, established for the sole purpose of associating with the facts of science, art, literature, and philosophy the truths of the gospel of Jesus Christ."[15] In this vision of BYU, students of the highest potential in every discipline may model their lives after teachers here who are the Henry Eyrings and Russell Nelsons in their fields. That is far less likely at state institutions, even with an

LDS Institute of Religion, because—obviously with some important exceptions—the teachers there tend to be oriented primarily to either a sacred or a secular system. Thus the best way to teach young people who are struggling to find the place of a sacred system in a profane world is to offer them not just theories, but teachers and classmates who have found their own wholesightedness. This opportunity is BYU's unique gift to the youth of Zion.

Spiritual lives really are at stake in resolving the root questions of faith versus reason. For that reason, the risk of confusing our students on these issues is the ugly mirror image of our unique capacity for good, as searing and destructive as our positive potential is magnificent. A valued BYU colleague who is a gifted teacher and an inspired researcher of impeccable academic achievement recently told me that increasing numbers of his students are "falling into his foxhole," seeking help for their wounded religious faith. I asked why he thought there would be more spiritual casualties now—is the world more wicked? Do brighter students see more dilemmas? He said some of the deepest wounds are inflicted when a thoughtful student senses, even through subtle hints, that an LDS teacher whom the student respects is cynical about the Church. That kind of wound can cut to the quick, because it implies to students that the fundamental integration of faith and reason doesn't work, as if in some objective sense it can't work. An LDS student would never draw that conclusion from the cynicism of an agnostic or atheistic professor in a state university, because the student will assume that such a teacher has long been seeing with only one eye. But when someone whom the student believes has spent years looking through both eyes implies that the view is darker with the sacred eye open, the message can be devastating.

Especially perverse is the teacher who conveys cynicism about the Church as evidence of his commitment to liberal education. That stance can put out both eyes at once, because it may offend believing Church members to the point that they attack liberal education as the cause of cynicism. But liberal education is an essential part of the wholesightedness we seek. Indeed, my own liberal education helps me know that cynicism is as intellectually indefensible as dogmatism. In my own student days, the

BYU students who troubled me most were the shallow, religious dogmatists. Now I am just as troubled by the shallow, irreligious cynics who delight in poking fun at "Molly Mormon." The only thing that has changed is the direction of the thoughtless posturing; the superficiality has stayed the same. Neither group has both eyes open. Why would any of us believe we serve the cause of serious education if our primary goal is nothing more than teaching students to "think otherwise" through simplistic posturing and antiauthoritarianism? As Ted Marchese has said, "Beware the cynic as well as the huckster."[16]

Still, one faculty member has urged that we encourage students and each other to engage in public criticism of the Church because the "courage" involved in saying unsettling things will demonstrate that BYU's commitment to liberal education is "indeed working." This argument mistakenly assumes that secular systems are broader than sacred systems. Moreover, there is no connection at all between a superior education and such criticism. Both the educated and the uneducated may be troubled by some Church issue. But whether one expresses those troubles publicly is a function of personal judgment more than it is an expression of integrity or educational depth. It is also a function of how one understands revealed teachings about publicly challenging those we sustain as prophets. Some defend their public criticism on religious grounds, claiming they must protect the Church from its misguided leaders. The irony in that attitude can't help but convey cynicism about the divine influence in a Church based on prophetic leadership. Conscientious private communication may ultimately be of real help to the Church and its leaders, but public expression by those professing to have both eyes open may simply spray another burst of spiritual shrapnel through the ranks of trusting and vulnerable students.

Of course, the premises of our sacred system—and, obviously, the premises of sound liberal education—make spiritual and intellectual freedom absolutely crucial for the development of wholesighted education. You can lead a child to a book, but you can't make the child read it—much less understand it. In my opinion, Satan's plan to save us without agency could not have worked. Without free inquiry and voluntary action, no understanding, no real testimony, and no personal growth is possible.

For example, after Aaron taught him the gospel, the converted Lamanite king wanted his people to embrace the gospel as he had. But instead of imposing his new convictions on his subjects, as did Constantine in the apostate era of early Christianity, the king simply asked that the missionaries be allowed to preach freely. As a result, the Lamanites who "were converted unto the Lord, never did fall away" (Alma 23:6). This commission did not mean, however, that freedom among the people of Aaron and Alma was unlimited. Korihor was initially free to preach his anti-Christian views because there was "no law against a man's belief" in Zarahemla (Alma 30:11). But when his expression moved from pursuing his own beliefs to the point of "destroy[ing] the children of God" (Alma 30:42), he exceeded the limits of the sacred system.

I know that some BYU students and other members of the Church are too trusting, too reliant on authority figures, and they expect the Holy Ghost to do their thinking for them. We must rouse them from their dogmatic slumbers, teaching them to love the Lord with all their heart, might, mind, and strength. They need education that liberates them from ignorance and superstition, developing the tough-minded independence on which self-reliant people and democratic societies utterly depend. Thus Alma counseled his people to "stand fast in this liberty wherewith ye have been made free," to "trust no man to be a king over you," and to "trust no one to be your teacher" (Mosiah 23:13–14). In other words, of course Hamlet's Ophelia should not expect someone else to "tell her what she should think."[17] And beyond doing her own intellectual homework, Ophelia must also, as did Alma, fast and pray "many days that I might know these things of myself" (Alma 5:46).

But Alma's more complete thought was "trust no man to be your teacher, *except he be a man of God*" (Mosiah 23:14; italics added). It is just as important that Ophelia trust the man or woman of God as it is that she not trust authority figures in general. The advantage of having a liberal education in a free society is that no one will tell us what to do. But the disadvantage is that no one will tell us what to do. The rich young ruler who approached the Savior wanted desperately to know what he should do to inherit eternal life: "Master, what good thing shall I do?" (Matt. 19:16). There are at least two very different meanings to that word, "Master." One is the master of a slave. Another is a teacher in a master-apprentice relationship. The young man approached Christ as an apprentice who fervently needed his master's guidance. As Michael Polanyi wrote, "To learn by example is to submit to authority. You follow your master because you trust his manner of doing things. . . . [The] hidden rules [of his art] can be assimilated only [if the apprentice] surrenders himself to that extent uncritically to [imitating the master]."[18]

But how can Ophelia know what teacher, what master in the best sense, she should trust? The scriptural standard is trust no one to be your teacher except a man or woman of God. Alma "consecrated . . . all their teachers," and "none were consecrated except they were just men [who] did watch over their people, and did nourish them with . . . righteousness" (Mosiah 23:17–18). What an aspiration for all the consecrated people who work at BYU, we who, in and out of the classrooms, teach some of the purest and brightest young men and women in all the world. They fulfill their dreams by coming to this oasis of learning in a spiritually parched world, yearning to ask the young ruler's question, What shall I do? And they come believing that the faculty and staff here will tell them not only what to do to learn to think for themselves, but what to do to inherit eternal life. Wholesighted teaching, with both eyes open. We move them from dogmatism through healthy skepticism toward a balanced maturity that can tolerate ambiguity without losing the capacity for deep commitment. By example as well as precept, we teach how to ask good—even searching—questions, how to trust, how to know of ourselves. This university's vitality is a continuing witness for the proposition that within the broad gospel framework, robust faith and healthy skepticism are not mutually exclusive. The chosen, consecrated men and women of God who teach and work here live lives that make that clear.

The ultimate purpose of our integrated teaching model is to teach our students how to live. As Parker Palmer put it, "Truth is an approach to living, not just an approach to knowing."[19] Or as we have recently described the purpose of the BYU Jerusalem Center, our purpose is not only to orient our students to a holy land, but to orient them to the holy life. How can we do that? Each teacher, faculty or staff, must find his or her own way, and some settings are more natural than others for making connections that help students see how secular interests fit within the larger sacred sphere.

Of course, we can't pursue excessive digressions that waste precious time in classrooms, offices, and work places. But many students, such as Amy Baird Miner, tell us that BYU students hunger for "life talks" as well as "grade talks" from their teachers. Joseph K. Nicholes used to love "teaching moments," those unexpected openings when a teacher, a head resident, a job supervisor, or a leader in a student ward senses an opportunity to step back from the subject at hand and open up the bigger picture of life. For example, one student will always remember how a BYU teacher talked soberly about life's larger purposes after witnessing a serious accident on the way to class. I know a BYU professor who concluded a rigorous course on logic by telling his students that now they know the rules of logical analysis. But if they build their testimonies on these rules alone rather than upon the spirit of God, they are built upon the sand.

Our university courses are not Sunday School classes, but our fears about that legitimate concern can inhibit some of us more than they should. As President Spencer W. Kimball once said, "Every [BYU teacher should] keep his subject matter bathed in the light of the restored gospel."[20] We must be cautious about both sentimental emotionalism at one extreme and stale academic neutrality on the other. And of course, we should teach students to respect rigorous standards of evidence, but let us not neglect all "anecdotal" evidence. Every personal testimony is in a sense anecdotal, but testimonies of personal experience are among the most powerful forms of data.

Another risk of integrating sacred and secular systems, especially in scholarly work, is that integrationists sometimes devalue in some lopsided way either the religious or the professional dimension. I have learned firsthand about this problem through the process of writing and publishing articles on family law in scholarly journals. In all of that work, my reasoning has implicitly proceeded from the teachings of the scriptures about marriage and family life. But my interaction with skeptical reviewers and demanding editors quickly taught me that I should avoid the ineffective approaches of shrill profamily writers who have no idea what it means to observe rigorous research methodologies and to master the available literature. One could give several examples of meaningful scholarly integration; I know of none better than the work of BYU's Allen Bergin, whose work on the place of religious values in psychotherapy recently earned the distinguished service award from the American Psychological Association. He has learned to let his work proceed on a small, empirically based scale that reveals its own conclusions, rather than trumpeting in advance a "moral framework" that implies a preconceived dogmatism. His research speaks for itself when he uses Alma's large map rather than Korihor's small one.

Following Allen's example in selected disciplines, we should, as Clayne Pope has urged, "work within our disciplines with the additional light of the gospel to inform and direct our work."[21] Our audience for this integrated scholarship is not just BYU or the Church, but also the entire scholarly world—if our work is rigorous enough to satisfy the highest professional standards. Adapting a phrase from James Burtchaell, we can contribute to society in unique and greatly needed ways when our integration is skillful enough to critique the academy from the standpoint of religion, rather than only critiquing religion from the standpoint of the academy.[22]

A faculty group in one of our academic areas would like to bring Parker Palmer back to the campus to share further his ideas on the spiritual dimensions of teaching. Having read Professor Palmer's work, I applaud that interest. It is reassuring to see someone of another faith validate our interest in religious and professional integration. But faculty on our own campus are already doing the nation's finest teaching of that kind—they just haven't written about their work as much as Palmer has, and our reward system should encourage them. It isn't enough just to ask that BYU personnel avoid damaging students' religious faith in the ways described by our new academic freedom statement. When we go beyond that minimal threshold to ask whether someone has contributed enough in citizenship, teaching, and scholarship to warrant continuing faculty status or other special recognition, we look for extensive fulfillment of BYU's aspirations, not merely the absence of serious harm. The university's new policy on advancement and continuing status describes this approach.

It also matters how job applicants see these issues. I well remember interviewing two well-trained applicants for the same position one day. When I asked how each one felt about the Church influence here, one said, "Oh, the Church is no problem for me—I've learned not to let it get to me." The other said, "The Church and the gospel are my whole life. That is why coming to work at BYU is my lifelong dream."[23] The vast attitudinal difference between these people was, and should be, a major factor in deciding whom to hire. We aren't looking for people who merely tolerate our environment or who will try not to harm it; we seek believing, thoughtful people for whom this is the freest intellectual and spiritual environment in the world.

Let us consider, finally, the conditions on which our work at BYU may enjoy full access to the revealed truth and prophetic guidance that are the source of our sacred system's life and breath. One of Parker Palmer's favorite stories is about Abba Felix, an early Christian "desert teacher." In this story, "some brothers . . . went to see Abba Felix and they begged him to say a word to them. But the old man kept silence. After they had asked for a long time he said, . . . 'There are no more words nowadays. . . . Since [the brothers now] ask without doing that which they hear, God has withdrawn the grace of the word from the old men and they do not find anything to say, since there are no longer any who carry their words out.' Hearing this, the brothers groaned, saying, 'Pray for us, Abba.'"[24] Felix's point, says Palmer, is that "truth is evoked from the teacher by the obedience of those who listen and learn, and when that quality is lacking in students, the teacher's words are taken away."[25] Felix's students had only been curious. They desired not the words of life—they wanted words that created an illusion of life, while letting them avoid the responsibility of living according to truth.

This was the same condition on which Ammon taught King Lamoni: "Wilt thou hearken unto my words, if I tell thee by what power I do these things?" (Alma 18:22). Likewise, we must "hearken unto the words" of our all-comprehending system if we are to learn its truths and see all else in its bright light. The highest liberal arts tradition teaches a similar concept: hubris. For the ancient Greeks, no sin was greater than the intellectual pride by which the learned thought themselves wiser than divine sources.

For us, obedience to divine sources first requires that we live a gospel-worthy life-style. Further, because ours is a sacred system premised on divinely ordered leadership, each of us must nourish a humble willingness to follow prophetic counsel. The statement by the First Presidency and the Twelve in 1991 counseling against any participation in certain kinds of symposia was most unusual, yet very deliberate.[26] Because the statement is for all Church members, it is not primarily a BYU matter, but it clearly speaks to BYU people. It is written in nondirective, nonpunitive terms, but its expectations are clear to those with both eyes open.

Some Church members and leaders have wondered in recent years if BYU's increasing academic stature would develop at the expense of basic Church loyalties. I don't believe that has happened, and I don't believe it will at today's BYU. I believe with all my heart in Elder Jeffrey Holland's "consuming vision that we [can] be a truly great university [that is] absolutely faithful to the gospel of Jesus Christ."[27] But that proposition will constantly be tested, and how we are perceived on an issue as elementary as "follow the Brethren" means more than we might imagine. Tip O'Neill used to say that you find out who your friends are not by seeing who's with you when they agree with you, but who's with you when they think you might be wrong. And the religious core of a sacred system just might ask its followers to trust the religious imperative even when it does not square with their own opinions.

The BYU dream will forever elude us if, as Abba Felix said, "God withdraws the grace of his words from the elders because the young people no longer carry out the teachings of the elders."[28] And even though I believe our collective religious commitment is stronger now than ever before, if a few among us create enough reason for doubt about the rest of us, that can erode our support among Church members and Church leaders enough to mortally wound our ability to pursue freely the dream of a great university in Zion. Somehow we must sense how much is at stake in how we deal with this issue. "Pray for us, Abba,"[29] because the dream really is ours to fulfill.

Almost exactly one hundred years ago, when the Church already had several stake academies, including Brigham Young Academy in Provo, the First Presidency released James E. Talmage from heading LDS College in Salt Lake City and assigned him to create the plans for what Talmage's biographer called "a genuine Church university."[30] Talmage was stirred to the core at "the prospect of founding an institution that would merit recognition by the established centers of learning throughout the nation and the world. It was a dream he had cherished for many years."[31] The proposed name was Young University.

Think of it: just months after the Manifesto of 1890 had been issued, the Church barely rescued from the jaws of utter destruction, Utah not yet a state, already a network of Church academies in place, and those Saints in their poverty wanted to create "a genuine university." This early plan was shattered by the Panic of 1893, but the dream lived on. In the 1920s and 1930s, the Church withdrew from higher education, creating a system of LDS Institutes of Religion and offering to state governments all of its academies but our very own Brigham Young Academy, which the First Presidency determined to keep in order to develop one genuine university.[32] The dream was still alive.

Sixty years later, the Lord's Church of the twenty-first century is expanding miraculously all across the globe. Never again will we see a Churchwide network of colleges or academies, but there is still one "genuine Church university" that has demonstrated its capacity to bless and be worthy of all the Saints, every person who pays a dollar of tithing. Some voices in today's winds claim that BYU will never achieve intellectual respectability as long as it is controlled by the Church. But in the twenty-one years since I joined the BYU faculty, I have watched the faculty, the staff, and the students of this university take an astonishing leap in the quality of their teaching, learning, and scholarship. I can bear firsthand witness that BYU's recent emergence onto the national and international stage is winning, in many circles, the honest and deserved admiration of a society desperate for educational leadership because of that society's moral decay and intellectual confusion. And this leadership role is being thrust upon the university not in spite of its lifeline to the Church, but precisely because of it.

I pay tribute to the thousands of women and men in the BYU community who match and exceed their rich professional achievements with lives of uncompromising faithfulness to the gospel, "offer[ing] in sacrifice all that [they have] for the truth's sake, not even withholding [their] lives,"[33] because they seek to know the mind and do the will of God.

The dream has become a consuming vision: "a truly great university [that is] absolutely faithful to the gospel of Jesus Christ."[34] Its name is Brigham Young University. Pray for us, Abba, for the dream is ours to fulfill.

This address was given at the 1992 Annual University Conference, when Bruce C. Hafen was Provost of Brigham Young University. It was published in *BYU Studies* 32, no. 3 (1992): 11–25.

NOTES

[1]Reinhard Maeser, *Karl G. Maeser: A Biography by His Son* (Provo, Utah: Brigham Young University, 1928), 78.

[2]Paul Pixton, "History Department Memo," memorandum to Brigham Young University Department of History, April 1992. Memorandum in author's possession.

[3]Richard Bushman, Brigham Young University Commencement Address, August 1991, transcript copy, Brigham Young University Publications.

[4]Marilyn Arnold, Bob Daines, and Dennis Thomson, "Summary of the Discussion of the Religious Mission of Brigham Young University," November 25, 1991. Memorandum in author's possession.

[5]Chaim Potok, "Scholars Real and Imaginary in Culture Confrontation" (paper presented to the Utah Academy of Sciences, Arts, and Letters, Third Annual Tanner Academy Lecture, Utah State University, Logan, May 19, 1989).

[6]Potok, "Scholars."

[7]John S. Tanner, "One Step Enough," devotional address, Brigham Young University, Provo, Utah, June 1992.

[8]C. Terry Warner, "An Open Letter to Students: On Having Faith and Thinking for Yourself," *The New Era* 1 (November 1971): 14–19.

⁹William James, *Essays on Faith and Morals*, ed. and comp. Ralph Barton Perry (Cleveland: Meridian Book, World Publishing, 1967), 25.

¹⁰Parker J. Palmer, *To Know As We Are Known: A Spirituality of Education* (San Francisco: Harper, 1983), 11.

¹¹Palmer, *To Know As We Are Known,* 10.

¹²Robert Frost, "Two Tramps in Mud Time," quoted in Palmer, *To Know as We Are Known,* ix.

¹³Palmer, *To Know As We Are Known,* xii.

¹⁴Alan F. Keele, "All Truth Circumscribed in One Great Whole," *Student Review,* June 24, 1992, 4.

¹⁵David O. McKay, "The Church University," *Messenger* 11 (October 1937): 3; see page 10 in this volume.

¹⁶Ted Marchese, "Regional Accreditation (II)," *Change* (March/April 1992): 4.

¹⁷William Shakespeare, "Hamlet," quoted in Thomas G. Plummer, "Diagnosing and Treating the Ophelia Syndrome" (paper presented to Delta Phi Alpha, Brigham Young University, Provo, Utah, April 5, 1990).

¹⁸Michael Polanyi, *Personal Knowledge: Towards a Post-Critical Philosophy* (Chicago: University of Chicago, 1962), 53.

¹⁹Palmer, *To Know As We Are Known,* 65.

²⁰Spencer W. Kimball, "Education for Eternity" (lecture given at the Annual Preschool Faculty and Staff meeting, Brigham Young University, Provo, Utah, September 12, 1967); see page 54 in this volume.

²¹Clayne Pope to author, August 1992.

²²James Burtchaell, "The Decline and Fall of the Christian College," *First Things: A Monthly Journal of Religion and Public Life* 13 (April/May 1991): 17.

²³Personal interviews conducted during author's tenure as provost of Brigham Young University, Provo, Utah, 1988–92.

²⁴Palmer, *To Know As We Are Known,* 41.

²⁵Palmer, *To Know As We Are Known,* 43.

²⁶Statement, *Church News,* published by *Deseret News,* August 31, 1991, 3.

²⁷Jeffrey R. Holland, Spring Commencement Address, 1991 (Brigham Young University, Provo, Utah).

²⁸Palmer, *To Know As We Are Known,* 45.

²⁹Palmer, *To Know As We Are Known,* 45.

³⁰John R. Talmage, *The Talmage Story: Life of James E. Talmage—Educator, Scientist, Apostle* (Salt Lake City: Bookcraft, 1972), 108.

³¹Talmage, *The Talmage Story,* 108.

³²Harold B. Lee, "Special Committee Report," Church Board of Education, The Church of Jesus Christ of Latter-day Saints, Salt Lake City, 1964.

³³Lectures on Faith 6:7, in *The Lectures on Faith in Historical Perspective,* ed. Larry E. Dahl and Charles D. Tate Jr. (Provo, Utah: Religious Studies Center, 1990), 93.

³⁴Holland, Spring Commencement Address, 1991.

BYU President Merrill J. Bateman at a BYU devotional, January 1996.
Courtesy Mark A. Philbrick/BYU.

Learning in Zion: Two Addresses

Merrill J. Bateman

I. Secular Learning in a Spiritual Environment

Twenty-five years ago, I arrived on the campus of Brigham Young University as a newly recruited economics professor. I had received a Ph.D. from one of the more respected graduate programs in the country, completed my military obligation, and was now embarking on an academic career. A few months later, I received a telephone call from a faculty member in another department. The person introduced himself, welcomed me to campus, and then asked if I would answer some questions from a survey he was taking. Although I was somewhat surprised by the call, I agreed. He then asked, "What brand of economics do you teach? Do you subscribe to increased governmental controls for the United States economy? Do sacred truths have any relevance in economic modeling, and do they influence your teaching in the classroom?"

My graduate training helped me answer the first two questions, but I confess that I had trouble with the third. My graduate training had emphasized that the well-being of a nation depends on freedom to trade, freedom to choose, information flows, the development of technology, and the specialization of the factors of production. I also knew that the most efficient combinations of the above require free markets. When government controls are imposed, market signals are disturbed, and efficiency is reduced, causing a reduction of goods and services.

Consequently, I understood that capitalism was a much more productive system than socialism or communism.

On the other hand, I understood some economists' concerns regarding capitalism. Some economists believe that capitalism leads to a severely skewed distribution of income. Some members in a free market society may be wealthy while others starve. Advocates of socialism and other forms of market control defend governmental interference on the grounds that income will be more equitable. They argue that inequality is too high a price to pay for an efficient system. Many economists consider efficiency and equity to be mutually exclusive goals.

At that time, such equity arguments concerned me, but I felt strongly that the costs of a socialistic system were too high. Evidence is even clearer today that the loss of economic freedom also brings the loss of political and religious freedoms. In such an economic system, skewed incomes continue, only at a much lower level. But the idea that a sacred truth or principle might resolve the conflict between efficiency and equity had never entered my classroom presentations.

Although the caller's questions might have been asked in a friendlier atmosphere, I have been grateful these many years that the questions were asked and that the last one was disconcerting to me. It forced me to think about the relationship between secular and sacred truths. I noticed that I had compartmentalized my search for secular truth apart from my search for spiritual understanding. Until then, the processes seemed separate and distinct. I had asked the Lord to help me master secular material as I approached examinations as a student and as I entered the classroom as a teacher. But I had never thought about receiving new economic insights as a result of combining scientific and spiritual methods of searching. Did the Lord's instructions to Oliver Cowdery to "study it out in your mind, then . . . ask me if it be right" (D&C 9:8) apply to secular as well as spiritual truth? Was it possible to extend Alma's injunction to "cry . . . in your fields, yea, over all your flocks" (Alma 34:20) to include economic knowledge? After all, economics was my field. Could a spiritual environment increase the rate of learning and the probability of discovering new secular truths? Are secular truths related to spiritual truths? What are the laws governing the acquisition of knowledge and intelligence? What constitutes a spiritual environment? Is it within each person? In one's search for secular truth, what happens if one abides the conditions that enhance the search for sacred truths? Could spiritual truth resolve secular paradoxes? These and other questions flooded my mind over the years and provide the basis for my presentation.

What Is Truth—Absolute or Relative?

The Lord told Joseph Smith that "truth is knowledge of things as they are, and as they were, and as they are to come" (D&C 93:24). The Lord further revealed that "truth abideth and hath no end" (D&C 88:66) and "intelligence, or the light of truth, was not created or made, neither indeed can be" (D&C 93:29). If truth is a statement of reality, if truth abides and has no end, and if the manifestation of truth (intelligence) was not created or made, then truth is eternal. There are absolute truths!

As President Spencer W. Kimball taught in a 1977 Brigham Young University devotional:

> There are . . . absolute truths which are the same yesterday, today, and forever—never changing. These absolute truths are not altered by the opinions of men. . . . We learn about these absolute truths by being taught by the Spirit. These truths are "independent" in their spiritual sphere and are to be discovered spiritually, though they may be confirmed by experience and intellect (see D&C 93:30). . . . God our Heavenly Father—Elohim—lives. That is an absolute truth. All . . . of the children of men on the earth might be ignorant of him and his attributes and his powers, but he still lives. All the people on the earth might deny him and disbelieve, but he lives in spite of them. . . . And Jesus Christ is the Son of God, the Almighty, the Creator, the Master of the only true way of life—the gospel of Jesus Christ. . . . That is an absolute truth; there is no gainsaying.[1]

God placed truths in different spheres, as the scriptures indicate. As a consequence, there are the sacred truths of the gospel, but also there are truths of mathematics, physics, chemistry, the social sciences, and so on. These secular laws or principles describe the workings of this world. In the search for absolute truth, science often is not able to observe all data or appreciate all the relationships involved. Consequently, scientific discoveries may approach the threshold of truth but not lay claim on the whole truth. Therefore, discovered "truths" are subject to change. This is relative knowledge. Relative knowledge is an approximation of reality or statements based on incomplete information. When scientists attempt to discover truth in the secular realm, they formulate a hypothesis that relates causes and effects, gather data, and then test the hypothesis. In experiments conducted to determine the accuracy of the hypothesis, scientists invariably add an error term to their models to represent the unknown factors or influences that may have been omitted from the hypothesis. If the test reveals a small error term, scientists will have more confidence in the "truth" they are trying to establish. However, the error term rarely equals zero, which would imply the discovery of an absolute truth. If the error term is large, the hypothesis is normally rejected, and scientists reformulate the hypothesis and begin the testing procedure again.

All absolute truth is consistent. In the Lord's words, "truth embraceth truth," and "light cleaveth unto light" (D&C 88:40). When a scientist uses secular methods to discover law that appears to be inconsistent with gospel truths, I suggest that not all truth about the earthly law is known. What appears to be inconsistent in two or three dimensions as discovered by the scientist will be harmonized eventually by additional knowledge in "n" dimensions. Spiritual truth forms a continuum with gospel truths at the higher end of the scale. Knowledge of and obedience to gospel truths are critical for salvation, but all truth is useful and important for mankind. The application of secular truth produces the benefits of faster transportation, more efficient communication methods, time-saving devices, etc. If wisely used, scientific truth will improve humans' health and well-being and will aid the Lord's servants in spreading the gospel.

But all truth, both relative and absolute, is spiritual. As the Lord explains, "All things unto me are spiritual, and not at any time have I given unto you a law [truth] which was temporal" (D&C 29:34). Since all truth is spiritual, the conditions and process for discovering "secular" truth must be similar to the requirements established by the Lord for understanding revealed truth. What are the Lord's conditions for obtaining knowledge and intelligence, and do they apply to secular learning?

The Lord's Requirements for Discovering Gospel Truths

Two principles govern the acquisition of truth and intelligence. They are *diligence* and *obedience* (compare Alma 12:9). Diligence may be defined as energetic application or mental exertion. The scriptures declare:

> Whatever principle of intelligence we attain unto in this life, it will rise with us in the resurrection. And if a person gains more knowledge and intelligence in this life through his diligence and obedience than another, he will have so much the advantage in the world to come. (D&C 130:18–19)

In the gospel context, faith requires diligence. Joseph Smith expounded, "When a man works by faith he works by mental exertion instead of physical force."[2] Diligence is one of the laws of heaven that determines the knowledge and intelligence that may be acquired by the earnest truth seeker. Will God bless people disproportionately to their mental effort or faith? No! That would violate an eternal principle. Learning by faith is not an easy road or a lazy means to gaining understanding.

Obedience is the second requirement for finding truth. In a gospel context, obedience brings faith. A new investigator of the gospel must act on the desire to believe by planting the seed, repenting, studying, and seeking the Lord in prayer. Because gospel truths are of a high spiritual order, they are confirmed through the Holy Spirit. In order to receive a witness from the Holy Ghost regarding the truthfulness of gospel principles, one must be striving to live in accordance with gospel truths. One must be living up to the light that is within oneself. This is consistent with Paul's teaching:

> Eye hath not seen, nor ear heard, neither have entered into the heart of man, the things which God hath prepared for them that love him. But God hath revealed them unto us by his Spirit: for the Spirit searcheth all things, yea, the deep things of God. For what man knoweth the things of a man, save the spirit of man which is in him? even so the things of God knoweth no man, but the Spirit of God. (1 Cor. 2:9–11)

The Principles of Diligence and Obedience
Apply to the Discovery of Secular Truth

Again, all truth is spiritual in nature, revealed through the light of Christ. This is the light that "lighteth every man that cometh into the world" (John 1:9) and is

> the same light that quickeneth your understandings;
> Which light proceedeth forth from the presence of God
> to fill the immensity of space—The light which is in all
> things, which giveth life to all things, which is the law by
> which all things are governed. (D&C 88:11–13)

As President N. Eldon Tanner taught in general conference, "We learn from the scriptures that all truth is revealed through the light of Christ. . . . Thus, the *truths* discovered by such men as Sir Isaac Newton, Thomas Edison, and Albert Einstein were actually revealed to them through the light of Christ."[3]

Because all truth comes through the light of Christ, seekers of secular truth must follow the Lord's requirements for discovering gospel truths. Diligence or mental exertion is one of the requirements that must be followed by seekers of secular truth. Scientists study the problem, saturate their minds with it, puzzle over it, and dream about it. Albert Sabin and Jonas Salk spent years searching for a vaccine to immunize people from contracting poliomyelitis. A reporter wrote that once Sabin focused on a problem, he was tenacious and would not let go. He had a voracious appetite for work—for mental exertion.[4]

What about obedience? What is the level of obedience required for the discovery of secular truth? Again, the answer is that everyone must live according to the light they have. When one is seeking a witness of gospel truth and is being taught those truths, one must plant the seed of faith and live according to the higher truths. When one is seeking secular truth, the revealer is the light of the "spirit of man" (1 Cor. 2:11). Thus the scientist must be striving to live according to the light within him so that new light will cleave to the old. Generally the obedience required in receiving secular truth is of a terrestrial order.

To illustrate the role of the light of Christ, consider the common description of many secular discoveries. After studying, puzzling, and dreaming about the problem, the scientist often finds progress stopped, blocked by a seemingly impenetrable wall. Then at last and suddenly, as if out of nowhere, comes a flash of light, the answer to his quest. Recall James W. Cannon's explanation regarding his discovery of how to unknot an infinitely knotted object in high dimensional space—a topology problem in mathematics. After pushing the problem around for many difficult weeks, the solution came:

> One night at 2:00 A.M., my eyes suddenly popped open. I sat up in bed. . . . I knew how to extend Štan'ko's techniques [a solution to the infinitely knotted object]. I do not know how the answer came to me. I couldn't sleep. I dressed quietly and went walking on the dark streets of Madison. . . . I checked the ideas for all of their consequences. I checked for absurdities. I couldn't find any. The picture was wonderful.[5]

Parley P. Pratt, one of the original twelve Apostles in this dispensation, explained the spiritual reasons for such inspiration:

> When the outward organs of thought and perception are released from their activity, the nerves unstrung, and the whole of mortal humanity lies hushed in quiet slumbers, in order to renew its strength and vigor, it is then that the spiritual organs are at liberty, in a certain degree, to assume their wonted functions, to recall some faint outlines, some confused and half-defined recollections, of that heavenly world, and those endearing scenes of their former estate, from which they have descended in order to obtain and mature a tabernacle of flesh. . . . Spirit communes with spirit, thought meets thought, soul blends with soul, in all the raptures of mutual, pure, and eternal love.[6]

In addition to flashes of insight and the usual procedures of study, observation, and experimentation, truth even comes by accident. Aspartame, the nonnutritive sweetener known as Nutrasweet, was discovered by a chemist in a lab when he accidentally allowed a kettle of amino acids mixed with an enzyme to boil over. In cleaning up the mess, the solution got on his hands and fingers. A short time later, he rubbed his lips with his fingers and noticed a sweet taste.[7] Today, Nutrasweet is a multibillion dollar product.

Given that learning can take place both through study and faith, is Brigham Young University destined to be a leader among the world's institutions of higher learning in discovering secular truth as well as disseminating sacred truth? To the extent that this institution lives up to its mandate of providing a spiritual environment in which learning can take place, the answer is yes.

Spiritual Environment and Secular Learning

I define a spiritual environment as a place inhabited by people committed to living gospel truths. The community members are peculiar in that they are sensitive to spiritual things. They have access to the Holy Spirit because of their faith and works. Their faith is based on a spiritual witness that Jesus Christ is the Savior of the world and that he restored the Father's plan of salvation through the prophet Joseph Smith. Their faith is more than a testimony of belief; it is a force that propels them to action and provides them with power.

The members of this community are a consecrated people in that they bend their will to that of the Father's. Little disputation exists among them, and unity abounds. They understand that contention is not of Christ, but of Satan, who uses it to stir people to anger one with another. A spiritual environment is a place where respect for others is dominant, where people are honest, supportive, and slow to criticize, and where scholars need not fear the motives of their colleagues. Because of faith, scholars do not fear the world. They want to learn from others—both inside and outside of their institution. However, their faith and knowledge of higher truths allow them to sift through secular ideas searching for consistency—for truth which embraces truth. Their faith also provides them with the patience to wait for additional knowledge when secular truth conflicts with eternal truth. The atmosphere which pervades the campus originates within each person. It reflects the quality of life lived by each inhabitant.

In this environment, the words of President Marion G. Romney will be proven:

> I believe in study. I believe that men learn much through study. As a matter of fact, it has been my observation that

they learn little concerning things as they are, as they were, or as they are to come without study. I also believe, however, and know, that learning by study is greatly accelerated by faith.[8]

If faith dominates the environment of this university, then secular learning will be enhanced. One should remember, however, that learning by faith depends on the principles of diligence and obedience. These principles are especially important in a spiritual environment because of the higher knowledge given. But when the principles are applied, scholars will link their mental searching with faith, and discoveries will increase in frequency. I believe this process is well underway at Brigham Young University and will grow at a geometric rate. Both faculty and students are participating in this process, as reflected in the major innovations and knowledge that have come from the University in the last two decades. Surely, Brigham Young University will be one of the means by which the Lord uses Abraham's seed to bless the nations of the earth.

Integration of Truth

Let me provide two examples of how the Lord's principles for gaining spiritual truth can enhance the search for secular truth. The first is an example of a spiritual truth which solves the economic paradox of efficiency and equity. The second is an insight I received a few weeks ago that integrated one spiritual truth with another and allows me to bear witness of him whom we all serve.

For the first insight, I am indebted to Lindon J. Robison, who has published an article entitled "Economic Insights from the Book of Mormon."[9] Robison points out that righteousness, including caring for others, is the solution to the conflict between economic equity and efficiency. He draws on the lessons taught in the Book of Mormon to illustrate that economic development occurs in a society when people are righteous and care about each other. Economic decline occurs when a nation falls into iniquity and the people become hardhearted and full of pride. When there is righteousness and caring, there is also unity and cooperation. Good feelings among people and nations allow for and increase trading activities. Trading allows workers to specialize and to share new technology.[10] Moreover, when righteous people control the government (for example, King Benjamin and his son Mosiah), there is more freedom of choice and taxes are less burdensome. When the less caring take control (like King Noah), the tax burden increases.[11]

Contrast the trading and specialization that occurred among the righteous people of Lib with the life-style of the wicked Jaredites. First, the story of Lib's people:

> And they were exceedingly industrious, and *they did buy and sell and traffic one with another, that they might get gain.* And they did work in all manner of ore, and they did make gold, and silver, and iron, and brass, and all manner of metals; . . . and they did have silks, and fine-twined linen; and they did work all manner of cloth. (Ether 10:22–24; italics added)

Now compare Lib's people with the Jaredites, whose wicked-ness caused their society to disintegrate:

> Wherefore every man did cleave unto that which was his own, with his hands, and *would not borrow neither would he lend;* and every man kept the hilt of his sword in his right hand, in the defence of his property and his own life and of his wives and children. (Ether 14:2; italics added)

Professor Robison concludes that the supposed equity and efficiency paradox of modern economic theory is not sup-ported. In fact, economic prosperity appears to be a companion of equity. He notes:

> The Book of Mormon message is that the distribution of income is based on the level of caring and unity among the people. Among the righteous, income is evenly distributed as are opportunities to progress. The distribution of income is simply a reflection of their unity. . . . By volun-tarily redistributing their income to the poor, they were able to maintain an economic system that included incen-tives to work hard because of individual responsibility and rewards for efforts. Moreover, one of the reasons the car-ing work hard is that they desire to use the product of their work to bless the lives of others.[12]

By applying diligence and obedience to a sacred text revealed by the Lord, Professor Robison has gained truth that solves an important secular problem.

Finally, may I share an experience that occurred at a stake conference I attended as a visiting authority. This experience illustrates the integration of one spiritual truth with another. It was the Saturday evening session (they are almost always the best). The theme was "Keeping the Sabbath Day Holy." As I waited to give my talk, I felt prompted to tell a story my wife had recently shared with me. But I was uneasy because the story did not seem to connect with the theme. Because of the seeming inconsistency, I decided to ignore the prompting. But the prompting came again with more intensity. I asked myself, "How can the story of a little handicapped girl relate to keeping the Sabbath day holy?" And then a thought came, "Why do we celebrate the Sabbath?"

I wrestled with the last question and eventually discovered two answers. The first is that we keep the Sabbath day to celebrate the creation of this earth. The Lord set aside the seventh day to honor the fulfillment of a promise he made to his children that he would create an earth or second estate where they could come and progress. And then another thought pressed upon my mind. The Sabbath day was changed from Saturday to Sunday following the crucifixion, death, and resurrection of Christ. The change was effected to honor God's fulfillment of a second covenant—providing a Savior to open the door for us to return to his presence. Moreover, a meal was instituted and scheduled for each Sabbath day to remind us of those events. As I used my mental faculties to reflect on the Savior's atonement, I then understood my initial prompting and how Heather's story is consistent with honoring the Sabbath day.

Heather was born into an LDS family sometime in the late 1970s. A short time after the birth, her parents learned that she was physically handicapped and that her spirit would be housed in a body with great restrictions. As she grew, she was confined to a wheelchair, was unable to speak, and could send messages only with her eyes. A direct gaze with a widening of her eyes and a smile meant *yes*. A blink meant *no*. In spite of her handicaps, however, one could feel her vibrant spirit inside.

When old enough, Heather began to attend school, where her teacher was a therapist. One morning as Heather and the teacher visited about the prior weekend, the teacher learned that Heather had attended Primary on Sunday. The teacher then sang for Heather the Primary song "I Wonder When He Comes Again." The expression on Heather's face revealed the delight within her. When the song was finished, the teacher could tell that Heather wanted her to continue. After a few songs, the teacher asked Heather if she had a favorite song. Heather's direct gaze provided the answer and offered a challenge. Through a series of questions, the teacher learned that Heather's song was one she had heard in Primary. She wasn't sure which songbook it was in, but it was about Jesus. The teacher then sang every possible song she could think of. Unfortunately Heather's favorite did not appear, and Heather was not about to quit. For some reason, she needed to share her favorite song.

At the end of the day, the two were still unsuccessful, and the teacher agreed to bring a Primary songbook to school the next day. On the following day, the teacher and student went through all of the songs in the book, but to no avail. Finally, the teacher suggested that Heather's mother might help her figure out which song it was. Heather came to school the next day with the new Church hymnbook tucked in her wheelchair. The teacher positioned herself next to Heather and, page by page, began making their way through the book, singing the first phrase of each song. Page after page, Heather's eyes would close in a definite no. Finally, halfway through the book, the teacher began to sing: "There is sunshine in my soul today . . ." Immediately, the little girl brightened and smiled. She looked directly at the teacher, and both began to laugh and rejoice. Success had finally come after a three-day search. As the teacher sang the first verse and began the chorus, Heather mustered all her effort and joined in with occasional sigh-like sounds. After finishing the first verse and chorus, the teacher asked if she wanted to hear the rest of the verses. Heather's eyes opened wide with a firm *yes*. Again the teacher began:

> There is music in my soul today,
> A carol to my King,
> And Jesus listening can hear
> The songs I cannot sing . . .[13]

The little girl's reaction to the third and fourth lines was so strong that the teacher stopped. As the reality and significance of the words pressed on the teacher's mind, she asked Heather if those lines were what she liked about the song. Could Jesus, listening, hear the songs she could not sing? Heather looked the teacher directly in the eyes, and testimony was borne.

Feeling guided by the Spirit, the teacher asked, "Heather, does Jesus talk to you in your mind and in your heart?" The child's look was penetrating. The teacher then asked, "Heather, what does he say?" The teacher's heart pounded as she saw the clear look in Heather's eyes as the little girl awaited the questions which would allow her to share her insights. The teacher then asked, "Does he say, 'Heather, I love you'?" Her radiant eyes widened. The teacher paused and then said, "Does he say, 'Heather, you're special'?" Again, *yes*. Finally, after a pause, the teacher asked, "Does he say, 'Heather, be patient; I have great things in store for you'?" Heather's head became erect; every fiber of her being seemed electrified as her eyes penetrated the teacher's soul. She knew she was loved; she knew she was special; she knew she only needed to be patient because great things were in store for her.[14]

Heather's story helped me to understand why we are asked to keep the Sabbath day holy. Through the Atonement, Jesus can hear the songs we cannot sing and has great things in store for us if we are patient. The Sabbath is a special day to remember his great gift to us.

May the Lord bless you in your search for both sacred and secular truth. May all of us honor him by being diligent and obedient in our efforts to learn and to serve him.

II. A Zion University

For many years, I have been observing the great miracle the Lord is performing on this earth as he builds a Zion people in country after country. In July 1956, I traveled by train and ship from Salt Lake City to London, England, to begin a mission for the Church. Upon arrival I learned that approximately 15,000 members lived in Great Britain in fifteen districts. There were no stakes. In fact, the number of stakes in the entire Church totaled only 239, and all but twelve were in the western United States and Canada. Upon completion of the mission two years later, there were sixteen districts in Great Britain but still no concentration of Saints large enough to organize a stake. In 1971, I returned as an employee of an American company. A few stakes existed in the British Isles by then, but the bulk of the Saints were still scattered and met in small congregations. My family lived in a tiny branch thirty-five miles west of London. The attendance at our first sacrament meeting was fourteen, including my family of seven. We met in a small schoolhouse with many members driving fifteen or more miles to attend. Twenty-three years have passed since our family returned from England, and the small seeds planted by missionaries and others after World War II have turned into a miracle. Two years ago, I returned to Britain on Church business and learned that more than forty stakes now exist in the British Isles. Membership exceeds 166,000.

Since my call as a General Authority in 1992, I have learned that the British experience is not unique. As late as 1966, there was only one stake in Brazil. On a recent trip to São Paulo, the Area Presidency informed us that the 150th stake would be created by the end of 1995, with Brazilian membership exceeding one-half million. The growth in Chile, Argentina, Peru, Mexico, and the Philippines is similar to that of Brazil. In early 1970, there were no stakes in Japan. Today there are twenty-five. Korea's first stake was created in 1973. Today there are sixteen. In 1978, following the priesthood revelation, I was called by President James E. Faust, then president of the Church's International Mission, to accompany Elder Ted Cannon on a fact-finding mission through West Africa. Although numerous groups of people in Ghana and Nigeria expressed interest in the Church at the time, total membership was less than one hundred. West African membership today totals more than 70,000, and stakes exist throughout the region.

The prophets Daniel and Isaiah saw this phenomenon happening in the last days. Daniel stated:

> And in the days of these kings shall the God of heaven set up a kingdom, which shall never be destroyed: and the kingdom shall not be left to other people, but it shall break in pieces and consume all these kingdoms, and it shall stand for ever. (Dan. 2:44)

Isaiah likened the Church to a tent and said that in the last days it would stretch forth across the earth by lengthening its cords and strengthening its stakes (see Isa. 54:2).

How is this done? How are people's hearts and minds changed so that conviction and commitment exist in their souls? What role does Brigham Young University play in this marvelous venture? With regard to the transformation occurring in the hearts of men and women, I have learned that the great miracle of the Church is based on thousands and thousands of small, quiet miracles. May I illustrate with two examples.

Four weeks prior to Elder Cannon's and my trip to West Africa in July 1978, fifty letters were sent to members and non-members in the various countries apprising them of our visit and asking them to meet us at the airport upon arrival. During a four-week period, we visited eight cities in four countries. With the exception of one city, no one received a letter in time to meet us. Toward the end of the trip, we arrived in Calabar, Nigeria, on a Friday afternoon, needing the services of a previously identified member to help us find approximately fifteen congregations in the southeastern part of the country. Each congregation had adopted the name of our Church, and the leaders had written asking for information and missionaries.

The member, Ime Eduok, was not at the airport or at the hotel. Brother Cannon and I checked in and went to our room not knowing where or how to find Brother Eduok in a city of one million. The next two days were a critical part of the trip, and Brother Eduok was the only one who could help us. We knelt in prayer and asked the Lord to guide us to him. We returned to the lobby and asked the desk clerk if she knew Mr. Eduok. She did not. Within a few minutes, a large number of Nigerians had gathered around us discussing our plight but lacking the information needed. Suddenly, I felt a hand on my shoulder. I turned to see a large man standing next to me who said, "Did I hear you say Ime Eduok? He is my employee. I just entered the hotel to buy a newspaper on my way home from work. Ime will be leaving the firm in fifteen minutes. I do not know where he lives. If he leaves the office before you arrive, it is unlikely that you will find him before Monday." The man hurriedly put us in a taxi and gave the driver directions. We arrived at the business just as Ime Eduok was locking the door. Brother Eduok guided us to each congregation during the Saturday and Sunday that followed. Many people in those congregations are now members of the Church, and information gleaned from them formed an important part of the report given to the First Presidency upon our return.

The second incident comes from a story told by Elder Russell M. Nelson of the Quorum of the Twelve.

> [A] beautiful young mother named Svetlana [living in Leningrad, Russia] had importuned the Lord in prayer to make it possible for her to obtain a Bible written in the Russian language. Such a Bible [was] rare, precious, and very expensive. In the fall of 1989, she and her [family] went to Helsinki in quest [of] a Bible. While walking through a park in Helsinki, she stepped upon an object hidden beneath the ground cover of autumn leaves. She picked it up and found it to be the answer to her prayers. It was a Bible written in the Russian language. So excited was she that she joyfully recounted the story of this great discovery to another mother who was also in the park with her youngster. The second mother then [asked] Svetlana, "Would you like to have *another* book about Jesus Christ, also written in the Russian language?" Svetlana . . . answered in the affirmative.

The Finnish woman, wife of a district president, provided Svetlana with a copy of the Book of Mormon and invited her to church. Svetlana took the missionary lessons, joined the Church, and returned to Leningrad with her family. She then invited friends into her home, and many of them responded to the message of the missionaries and were baptized.[15] Svetlana, her friends, and others like them are the pioneer foundation upon which the Church has been built in that part of the world.

Why was a Nigerian with vital information prompted to deviate from his normal course and stop at a hotel to buy a newspaper? How did a rare, expensive Russian Bible find its way into a Finnish park, coincident with the passage of a Russian woman who had been praying for such a book? How did the wife of a Finnish district president just happen to be in the park to share in the joy of the rare prize? Brothers and sisters, who is guiding the Church? We live in a day when hundreds of thousands of small miracles are quietly occurring as the Lord prepares the honest in heart for entrance into his kingdom and the earth for his return. What role does Brigham Young University play in this process? The answer depends on our testimonies and how we view the university in its relationship to the Church.

Apart From or a Part of the Church

Is the university apart from or a part of the Church? Following the announcement of my appointment as president of Brigham Young University, the *Salt Lake Tribune* carried an article on what it means to have a General Authority as the school's leader. The major point of the article concerned the University's relationship to the Church. The news reporter suggested that although some might have assumed prior to the announcement that the university was a secular institution distinct from but reporting to the Church, the call clearly indicates that the University is an integral part of the kingdom. The article surprised me in that I had never thought of Brigham Young University separate from the Church. Prophet after prophet has stated clearly that Brigham Young University is a religious institution with a divine mission, even though secular education is a key part of its purpose. Given the organizational structure by which the University is governed, it seems paradoxical that some might think that Brigham Young University is not an integral part of The Church of Jesus Christ of Latter-day Saints. The Church itself is an educational institution, and Brigham Young University is one of its key components. Thus, one might say that this institution is not only a university in Zion, but is in the process of becoming a "Zion university."

From the very beginning, education has been one of the central missions of the Church. The School of the Prophets established in Kirtland, Ohio, in 1833 foreshadowed the creation of the University of the City of Nauvoo in 1841. The purpose of the Nauvoo school, as stated by the Prophet Joseph Smith and his counselors, was

> to teach our children wisdom, to instruct them in all the knowledge and learning, in the arts, sciences, and learned professions. We hope to make this institution one of the great lights of the world, and by and through it to diffuse that kind of knowledge which will be . . . for the public good, and also for private and individual happiness.[16]

The Prophet Joseph's dream to build a university that would become a light to the world was cut short by a mob's bullet on June 27, 1844. But the dream burned deeply inside another prophet. Brigham Young taught, "Ours is a religion of improvement,"[17] and "every art and science known and studied by the children of men is comprised within the Gospel."[18]

In February 1850, only two and one-half years after the first wagon train entered the Salt Lake Valley, the Latter-day Saints created the University of Deseret, the first institution of higher learning west of the Mississippi and a testimony to the value placed on education by the Saints. Brigham Young University was founded in 1875 by the prophet whose name it bears. It has become the flagship of the Church's educational system. It is becoming the light to the world that Joseph foresaw and through which knowledge is and will be diffused for public good and personal happiness. Let us now explore what it means for Brigham Young University to be a Church entity, a Zion university.

A Zion University

As almost everyone here knows, the word *Zion* in Latter-day Saint literature refers to the "pure in heart" or the "place where the pure in heart dwell" (D&C 97:21; Moses 7:18–19). A Zion people are of one heart and one mind—they dwell in righteousness and have no poor among them. "The word *university* originally meant a community," but it also is used to mean "cosmos" or "totality."[19] In our context, a Zion university is a community of righteous scholars and students searching for truth for the purpose of educating the whole person. They understand that God's children are more than intellect and body. The intellect is housed in a spirit that must also be educated. Sacred or higher truths relating to the spirit are the foundational truths in a Zion community and center on Jesus Christ as the Son of God, the Only Begotten of the Father in the flesh, the sacrificial Lamb who gave his life for the sins of the world, the First Fruits of the Resurrection. Community members also have full faith in the appearance of the Father and the Son to the Prophet Joseph in a vision in a grove of trees, believe that other angelic visitors also appeared to him, and believe that the gospel and the holy priesthood were restored to earth following a long period of apostasy. They know that the Book of Mormon is what it professes to be and that revelation from God to his prophets is the guiding instrument for the Church.

But we must also remember that as a university there is a prime obligation to teach secular truth. Our goal is to achieve excellence in this sphere. There must be no alibi for failure to achieve a first-class rank within the parameters set by the board of trustees. Continual improvement of faculty qualifications and performance is the key to this objective. Faculty turnover in the next few years will be high, but I am convinced that prospective faculty with the proper credentials have been and are being prepared.

Because the gospel is the common denominator at this university and since all truth is part of the gospel, every subject must be taught with testimony. Testimony is not to be encased in particular institutions on campus.[20] Brigham Young University is not a Harvard of the West or a Stanford of the Rocky Mountains with an institute of religion on the periphery. We have the opportunity to be better at discovering and teaching truth, all truth, because testimony can be everywhere and permeate everything.[21] Testimony and the Holy Spirit have as much to do with English and mathematics as with religion if we are diligent in scholarship and obedient to gospel principles. Teachers and students in this community should understand that all truth is spiritual and thus the so-called secular truths may be discovered by revelation as well as by reason.

Arthur Henry King was a great Shakespearean scholar at this university. He understood the process of revelation in the discovery of secular truth. In a BYU forum speech in 1972, he related the following:

> Niels Bohr, [the] Danish physicist Nobel-Prize winner . . . is reported to have said that he owed his discoveries more than anything else to the reading of Shakespeare. That may seem odd unless we have read that apparently frivolous book called *The Double Helix* about the discovery of the form of a genetic molecule by a young American in Cambridge: he tells exactly what happened during the days when he progressed towards that discovery. It is worth reading to realize that great discoveries in science like great

writing come ultimately from—call it what you like—intuition; I would call it inspiration. The wind apparently "bloweth where it listeth"; but can anything worth-while happen on any university campus with which the Holy Ghost is not involved?[22]

My favorite story illustrating the role of the Holy Ghost and the Light of Christ in the discovery of truth comes from James W. Cannon, a member of our mathematics department, regarding his discovery of how to unknot an infinitely knotted object in high-dimensional space. (He was a professor at the University of Wisconsin at the time.) After pushing the problem around for many months with no success, the solution came in an unexpected manner. He records:

> One night at 2:00 a.m., my eyes suddenly popped open. I sat up in bed. . . . I knew how to extend Stan'ko's techniques. I do not know how the answer came to me. I couldn't sleep. I dressed quietly and went walking on the dark streets of Madison. . . . I checked the ideas for all of their consequences. I checked for absurdities. I couldn't find any. The picture was wonderful.[23]

Brother Cannon's experience is not unusual. After studying, puzzling, and dreaming about a problem, scientists often find progress stopped. Then, suddenly, as if out of nowhere, a flash of light comes. Secular truth is revealed by the Spirit as well as sacred truth.

Faculty Responsibility and Academic Freedom

May I now say a few words to the faculty, staff, and administration, although I expect the students to listen as well because it has application in their lives. A Brigham Young University appointment is a sacred trust. More than 27,000 youth of the Church selected on the basis of gospel commitment and scholarship potential are under our stewardship. Consequently, we have a responsibility to nurture their faith and improve their academic skills. The great majority of us are members of the LDS Church, and the prime requisite for employment is a personal testimony of and behavior consistent with the restored gospel. Nonmember faculty and staff are expected to live according to the light within them and standards agreed upon at the time of employment.

Placing commitment to gospel truths first in the life of a faculty member does not demean the second requirement of academic excellence. If testimony and high personal standards are the foundation, outstanding scholarship that includes teaching ability is the capstone. Both testimony and scholarship are essential for this university to achieve its destiny. They are not competitive, but complementary. The new administration is committed to academic excellence. The desire for excellence covers graduate studies and research in selected areas as well as continued improvement of undergraduate teaching. In particular, we believe that teaching quality must be improved in some key areas, and we will be working with the faculty to accomplish this.

A personal commitment to gospel standards by faculty members will increase, not decrease, academic freedom. If applied, the gospel framework will keep us from gathering like flies hovering over the dead carcasses of secular error. As a close faculty friend pointed out to me recently, the greatest limitation on academic freedom comes when faculty take for granted the assumptions of colleagues at other institutions while developing secular theories. We will be more productive and enjoy more freedom if we examine and test secular assumptions under the lamp of gospel truth. We must not blindly accept the choices made by others. These statements obviously apply more to the social sciences and humanities than to the physical sciences, engineering, and the professions. However, even scholars in these areas would do well to measure the worth of their scholarship in the gospel light.

A brief illustration is in order. In speaking of the last days, Isaiah and Nephi indicate that people will "call evil good, and good evil; [will] put darkness for light, and light for darkness; [will] put bitter for sweet, and sweet for bitter!" (See Isaiah 5:20, 2 Nephi 15:20.) Recently, I learned about a movie that was described by a newspaper critic as "wonderful, joyous." It was rated PG-13. The film features seven illicit relationships, including open marriage, fornication, and adultery. The main messages of the film are first, open marriages are acceptable;

second, it is appropriate for men to abandon their wives and families if they become stressed; third, illicit relationships relieve grief and do no harm if secrecy is maintained; and fourth, premarital sex is normal. To a committed Latter-day Saint, the film is not wonderful or joyous, but depressing and sad as evil is called good again and again. There is a stark contrast between the messages of the film and the recently issued "Proclamation on the Family by the First Presidency and the Quorum of the Twelve."

There are scholars in this university who study the family. There are classes taught in several disciplines that relate to the family. If scholarship and teaching at this university are based on the proclamation's standards rather than on the world's standards, academic freedom will increase, and students will be spiritually strengthened to withstand the onslaught of evil— theories and practices that the world calls good. A society that is in moral decline is also in intellectual decline, for the one surely follows the other and follows fast.[24]

The grass is not greener on the other side of the fence. What may appear to be limits on academic freedom derived from the religious nature of the institution actually provide additional freedoms. It is imperative that we not mimic the research and teaching choices of our colleagues at other universities without first using the measuring rod of the gospel.

I believe, using the Lord's measuring stick, that we have the finest faculty and staff in the world. It is clearly the strongest faculty and staff ever assembled at Brigham Young University. I firmly believe that the Lord will strengthen the faculty in the process of time.

A Message to the Students

Finally, I now speak to the students. May I paraphrase an earlier president of Brigham Young University: "Our reason for *being* is to be a university. But our reason for *being a university* is the students." (President Dallin H. Oaks in his inaugural response stated: "Our reason for *being* is to be a university. But our reason for *being a university* is to encourage and prepare young men and women to rise to their full spiritual potential as sons and daughters of God."[25]) For more than 120 years, this campus has had a distinctive character. Strangers who visit are struck by the cleanliness and orderliness of the buildings, the grounds, and especially the people. Although the dress and grooming standards may not seem as important as other parts of the Honor Code, they help us be a distinctive people. I remember visiting other college campuses during the early 1970s while serving as a faculty member at this university. It was the height of the "hippie" period, when long hair, drugs, sloppy clothes, and rebellion were the order of the day. It was so refreshing to return to this campus, to see the clean young people, and to feel the peace that prevails here. This administration is committed to preserving that atmosphere. We ask you to live by your word of honor regarding the dress and grooming standards. A few may be uncomfortable and may not want to abide by them. For those few, please have the intellectual courage and integrity to live the standards or depart peacefully and try another institution.

Last Sunday evening, as I watched many of you at the CES fireside with President Faust, I could tell you have testimonies. You are not doubters but seekers after truth. You recognize the Spirit. Many of you have experienced an epiphany as described by President Faust in that flashes of insight and testimony have come to you at critical times. Many of you have seen the manifestations of divine power. You have made covenants. You have been able to call heavenly power forth in your own lives. You understand that age is not a prerequisite in communing with the Lord and his Spirit.

May I share with you a flash of insight given me by the Spirit twenty years ago in which I learned about this university's major role in building the kingdom. It concerns you, the students. The Bateman family had just returned to Provo from the East Coast following my appointment as dean of the School of Management. We had been away for four years with a multinational corporation and had enjoyed ourselves immensely. Although we knew the decision to return to Brigham Young University was correct because prayers had been answered, I was still struggling emotionally with the new assignment.

In September 1975, we attended the first multistake fireside of the school year, similar to the one held last Sunday evening. We were sitting high up in the Marriott Center near portal C. As the speaker began his sermon for the evening, I looked out across a congregation that must have totaled 18,000, including all of the missionaries from the MTC. They were easy to spot because they were allowed to take off their suit coats! Approximately 2,500 white-shirted missionaries filled the section under portal M, and it was a sea of white. I looked at them and realized that within weeks they would be scattered to the four corners of the globe. It was exciting to contemplate the people they would serve, the change that would occur in the missionaries as they matured spiritually, and the miracles that would bring new members into the Church.

Then a flash of inspiration opened my mind as to the purpose of Brigham Young University. I realized that 27,000 students were being prepared to enter the world. Every year approximately 6,000 would leave Provo, scattering across North America with some going on to Europe, others to Asia, some to Africa, and a number to South America. Some might even go Down Under. If the university performed its roles well, deepening spiritual roots and providing a first-class education, in the course of time strong Church families would grow up in hundreds and thousands of communities all over the world. These BYU families would be waiting when later missionaries arrived. My earlier experiences in London, Boston, Colorado Springs, High Wycombe, Lancaster, Bedminster, Accra, and Lagos had pointed to the importance of just one or two strong families to form a core around which the Lord could build a branch, then a district, and finally a stake. The BYU families would be good neighbors, have strong relationships with business associates, and, if well-trained, be leaders in their communities. These strong families by example and invitation would open doors for missionaries to enter.

I then knew why we had returned to Brigham Young University. It provided a satisfying feeling on the journey home that evening. Students leaving the university with a first-rate education combined with spiritual strength based on faith in Christ and his restored gospel have a tremendous advantage in the world. They know who they are. They need not be afraid. Faculty members should know that their teaching and research are building something of great worth. Brigham Young University is a major contributor to the central mission of Christ's kingdom on earth.

I testify, brothers and sisters, that this institution will not fail. As Daniel prophesied, the kingdom will not be left to other people. Joseph's and Brigham's vision that the spiritual can be combined with the secular without the latter overcoming the former will prove true because of faith and priesthood power. Brigham Young University will be a light to the world, dispensing truth for the public good and for individual happiness. I say this in the name of Jesus Christ. Amen.

Part I, "Secular Learning in a Spiritual Environment," was delivered on March 8, 1993, at the third annual Laying the Foundations Symposium at BYU and appeared in the written proceedings of that conference. It was also published in *BYU Studies* 35, no. 2 (1995): 43–55. At that time, Merrill J. Bateman was a member of the Second Quorum of the Seventy. Elder Bateman began serving as president of Brigham Young University in January 1996. Part II, "A Zion University," was given January 9, 1996, as President Bateman's first devotional as president of Brigham Young University.

NOTES

[1]Spencer W. Kimball, "Absolute Truth," in *Devotional Speeches of the Year 1977* (Provo, Utah: Brigham Young University, 1978), 137–38.

[2]*Lectures on Faith*, 7:3, comp. N. B. Lundwall (Salt Lake City: Bookcraft, n. d.), 61.

[3]N. Eldon Tanner, "Ye Shall Know the Truth," *Ensign* 8 (May 1978), 15; italics in original.

[4]"What the World Owes Dr. Sabin," *Deseret News,* March 15, 1993, A6.

[5]"Mathematical Parables," *BYU Studies* 34, no. 4 (1994–95): 94. James W. Cannon is Professor of Mathematics at Brigham Young University.

[6]Parley P. Pratt, *Key to the Science of Theology,* 10th ed. (Salt Lake City: Deseret Book, 1973), 120–21.

[7]Evelyn Roehl, *Whole Food Facts* (Rochester, Vt.: Healing Arts Press, 1988), 115.

[8]Marion G. Romney, "Learn by Faith," in *BYU Speeches of the Year 1968* (Provo, Utah: Brigham Young University, 1969), 4.

⁹Lindon J. Robison, "Economic Insights from the Book of Mormon," *Journal of Book of Mormon Studies* 1 (fall 1992): 35–53.

¹⁰Robison, "Economic Insights," 45.

¹¹Robison, "Economic Insights," 47.

¹²Robison, "Economic Insights," 49.

¹³"There Is Sunshine in My Soul Today," *Hymns of The Church of Jesus Christ of Latter-day Saints* (Salt Lake City: The Church of Jesus Christ of Latter-day Saints, 1985), 227.

¹⁴Jean Ernstrom, "Jesus, Listening, Can Hear," *Ensign* 18 (June 1988): 46–47.

¹⁵Russell M. Nelson, "Drama on the European Stage," *Ensign* 21 (December 1991): 15; italics in original.

¹⁶Joseph Smith Jr., *History of The Church of Jesus Christ of Latter-day Saints,* ed. B. H. Roberts, 2d ed., rev., 7 vols. (Salt Lake City: Deseret Book, 1971), 4:269.

¹⁷Brigham Young, in *Journal of Discourses* (London: Latter-day Saints' Book Depot, 1854–86), 10:290.

¹⁸Young, in *Journal of Discourses,* 12:257.

¹⁹Arthur Henry King, "The Idea of a Mormon University," *BYU Studies* 13, no. 2 (1973): 115.

²⁰See King, "The Idea," 117.

²¹See King, "The Idea," 117.

²²King, "The Idea," 117–18.

²³Cannon, "Mathematical Parables," 94.

²⁴See King, "The Idea," 119; also 2 Nephi 9:28–40 and Moroni 9:18–20.

²⁵Dallin H. Oaks, Inaugural Response, November 12, 1971, 18; italics in original.

Scripture Index

AUTHORS

Merrill J. Bateman Brigham Young University president, 1996–present

Hugh B. Brown Second Counselor in the First Presidency; member of the BYU Board of Trustees, 1958–75

J. Reuben Clark Jr. Counselor in the First Presidency and spokesman on educational matters for the Church Educational System; member of the BYU Board of Trustees, 1939–61

Bruce C. Hafen Provost of BYU, 1989–96

Franklin S. Harris BYU president, 1921–45

Gordon B. Hinckley President of The Church of Jesus Christ of Latter-day Saints, 1995–present; member of the BYU Board of Trustees, 1961–present

Jeffrey R. Holland BYU president, 1980–89

Spencer W. Kimball President of The Church of Jesus Christ of Latter-day Saints, 1973–85; member of the BYU Board of Trustees, 1951–85

Harold B. Lee President of The Church of Jesus Christ of Latter-day Saints, 1972–73; member of the BYU Board of Trustees, 1951–73

Rex E. Lee BYU president, 1989–95

Karl G. Maeser BYU president, 1876–92

Neal A. Maxwell Church Commissioner of Education, 1970–76; member of the BYU Board of Trustees, 1981–present

David O. McKay President of The Church of Jesus Christ of Latter-day Saints, 1951–70; member of the BYU Board of Trustees, 1939–70

Dallin H. Oaks BYU president, 1971–80

Boyd K. Packer Member of the BYU Board of Trustees 1962–present; member of the Church Board of Education

Robert K. Thomas BYU academic vice-president, 1968–83

Ernest L. Wilkinson BYU president, 1949–71